DECONSTRUCTING THE STARSHIPS

Liverpool Science Fiction Texts and Studies
General Editor DAVID SEED
Series Advisers
I.F. Clarke, Edward James, Patrick Parrinder and Brian Stableford

Gwyneth Jones

DECONSTRUCTING THE STARSHIPS

Science, Fiction and Reality

LIVERPOOL UNIVERSITY PRESS

First published 1999 by
LIVERPOOL UNIVERSITY PRESS
Liverpool L69 3BX

British Library Cataloguing-in-Publication Data
A British Library CIP record is available

ISBN 0-85323-783-2 (hardback)
ISBN 0-85323-793-X (paperback)

Typeset in 10/12.5pt Meridien by
XL Publishing Services, Lurley, Tiverton
Printed by Bell & Bain Glasgow

Contents

Foreword

These essays and reviews have been produced over a decade during which the stuff of science fiction became part of everyday life. There have been other decades in recent memory filled with intense excitement about the imaginary future: we can see the marks of their passing in city planning, public architecture, furniture; the streamlining, the monochrome and chrome of everyday objects first admired, then considered hideous, eventually fashionable again. But whether or not we consider the Internet hideous, it is unlikely that telematic networking will be consigned to the lumber room by the next generation, or that biotechnology will come totally undone (despite its mixed performance so far on the money markets); and perhaps equally unlikely that the demographic and economic changes that have created Girl Power, leaving political and idealistic feminism stranded and bewildered on the margins, will be dismantled. Dreams of galactic empire did not come true, the Invaders from Mars (or from any other alien planet in our locality) are consigned to fantasy. But a great deal of the future imagined by *my* generation's sf writers is actually with us.

William Gibson, the icon of the 1980s, said that science fiction is always about the present. I could argue that it is the only fiction about the present, everything else is historical romance. But at this particular moment in time, reality and science fiction are moving into such close conjunction that science fiction is no longer the strange reflection and artistic elaboration of current preoccupations: the mirror and the actuality have almost become one. Moreover, most of the routes to a new separation (aside from the colourful fantasies of the 'science fiction' entertainment business) might involve losses considerably more painful than saying goodbye to the Venusian Swamps and the ancient cities of Mars. Perhaps we should hope for some kind of catastrophic fusion of future and present, the End of History as pronounced by Baudrillard: but postponed, from hour to hour, from sentence to sentence, by this narrative that never reaches closure. We should remember that though there are tragic science fictions, science fiction itself is a comedy. Classically, essentially, all true science fiction stories end at the beginning. We are those who go always a little farther.

The reviews in the last section of this book appeared originally in *Foundation*, the journal of the Science Fiction Foundation UK; the *New York Review Of Science Fiction*, and in *SFEye*. Some of the essays were written as conference papers, *false papers* concocted by me as a cunning means of becoming a fly on the wall at an academic conference where something science fictional or futuristic was being debated. Others were written for magazines or journals; 'Dreamer' was produced for a BT seminar on future lifestyle trends a decade ago. One paper reaches back to the roots of my own imagination and into the realm of British metaphysical fantasy, two are forays onto the loud and mirror-globe-lit dancefloor of cyberspace. The majority were written to be read aloud for a live audience, and the presence of that audience can still be detected. The tone varies from popular journalism to academic discourse. I haven't tried to alter that uneven effect, or remove the traces of the various origins. All the papers have been lightly revised for this collection, but I have refrained from tampering with the opinions or predictions of the original writer; and from bringing examplars or preoccupations up-to-date. Let the changes of the last decade speak for themselves.

One thing the essays have in common is that they were all written under some kind of duress. I am by nature idle and sluttish, and left to myself I would never write anything but fiction and reviews. My head would soon come to resemble the loft above my office, which is piled so high with the detritus of previous selves: tattered notebooks, documents, beer mats, old carrier bags, convention programmes, heaps of typescript, it is almost impossible to reach the books I keep on the stacks up there. I'd like to thank particularly George Hay, David Hartwell, Sarah Lefanu, Brian Loader, Steve Pasechnik, Brian Stableford, Mary Talbot; and Andy Butler, Mark Bould, and James Kneale of the Academic Fantastic Fiction Network, for prodding and enticing me into sorting out my ideas from time to time. The responsibility for the results of this housekeeping is of course all mine.

I
ALL SCIENCE IS DESCRIPTION

Introduction:
Deconstructing The Starships*

Plurality of meaning, fluidity and process: an understanding of language as contingent, unfixed; the product and definition of a particular social formation—these icons of *la nouvelle critique* are the familiar tools and usage of science fiction. It is no wonder that adventurous writers of contemporary non-genre fiction (e.g. Margaret Atwood, Paul Theroux) are turning to the tropes and conventions of sf in their search for a writing that expresses the current state of the science of fiction.

When I was invited to take part in this event I was told that I had to talk about some development in my designated patch of 'the real world'—that is, literature—that was first suggested in a science fiction story, novel or article. I'd better admit straight away that I don't think I can do this. In physical science inventions or discoveries tend to arise out of a certain common background, within which the race to first publication is an exciting irrelevance. When it comes to cultural innovations, whether it's a new kind of novel or a new kind of hat, that naked singularity, the you-saw-it-here-first moment, is even more elusive, and the search for it even more dubious and illusory.

At first it might seem there is an embarrassment of riches in terms of sf's penetration into popular culture—from a space shuttle called after a fictional starship to the Transformer cutouts on the back of your cereal packet. Something that passes by the name of science fiction has become the folklore of the twenty-first century, and while it would be impossible to identify any particular stories as the source material it is clear that certain acclaimed mainstream writers have taken this transformation on board. Paul Theroux's *O-zone*, Don DeLillo's *White Noise* employ sf tropes: the alien invasion, the pollution disaster, quite realistically and seriously. Martin Amis and Patricia Highsmith have both brought out volumes of post-holocaust short fiction. But I would maintain that what Theroux, DeLillo and many others are acknowledging has very little to do with that highly individual phenomenon, the literary genre of science fiction. *Star Wars* merchandising, *Star Trek* TV, matt-black penknives, ergonomic café

---

* The text of an address given at the presentation of the Arthur C. Clarke Award, at the Institute of Contemporary Arts, London, in June 1988.

furniture, even Nuclear Doom—this is the diffuse, eclectic, twentieth-century obsession with 'the future' out of which science fiction itself took shape. Sf is a co-effect here, not a cause. The ease with which a fantasy like *Star Wars* or *Star Trek* slips from the galactic battlecruisers to the mediaeval swordfights shows how completely this ersatz 'future' is subsumed into the timeless zone of universal cultural nostalgia—with any amount of knights errant and death-dealing monsters, magic swords and cloaks of invisibility.

It is true that there have been some striking examples in recent years of mainstream writers actually writing sf, notably Margaret Atwood's *The Handmaid's Tale*, which won the first Arthur C. Clarke Award. One could also mention Doris Lessing's *Canopus in Argos* series, and Marge Piercy's *Woman On The Edge Of Time*. Where Theroux and DeLillo seem to use their sf themes and chunks of popular science as up-to-date interior decoration, the meat of their books remaining fixed in contemporary America, these others have imitated the whole form: not only in the creating of 'entire' imagined worlds, but down to the smallest details of genre cliché. Certainly Atwood's *The Handmaid's Tale* is so similar to genre feminist sf of the mid-1970s that whole chapters could be lined up together sentence by sentence to 'prove' that the one must be the cause or inspiration of the other. But didactic fantasy—Utopian or 'Dystopian'—has a long history, and its links with sf might best be regarded as a case of convergent evolution. At any rate, it would be absurd to claim that social satire has *spread outward* from science fiction. However there is an interesting relationship between the well known features—good and bad—of the sf genre, and the pre-occupations of modern literary theory: a relationship which cannot be called causal, in general or in particular, but which is none the less curiously intimate. I would propose that the 'science' in science fiction has always had a tacit meaning other than that commonly accepted. It has nothing in particular to say about the subject matter, which may be just about anything so long as the formal convention of future dress is observed. It means only, finally, that whatever phenomenon or speculation is treated in the fiction, there is a claim that it is going to be studied to some extent scientifically—that is objectively, rigorously; in a controlled environment. The business of the writer is to set up equipment in a laboratory of the mind such that the 'what if' in question is at once isolated and provided with the exact nutrients it needs. This view of sf is not new to science fiction writers and critics, but it is worth restating: the essence of sf is the experiment. Working under these strictures, a writer is forced (willingly or unwillingly, consciously or unconsciously, through talent or the lack of it) to give up a good many of the concerns of the literature we have all been brought up to consider normal and worthy. A typical science fiction novel has little space for deep and studied characterisation, not because writers lack the skill (though they may) but because in the final analysis the characters are not people, they are pieces of equipment. They have no free will or independent existence; to attempt to perpetuate such illusions is hopeless. The same reductive effect is at work on the plot, where naked, artless ur-scenarios of quest, death, desire are openly displayed; and on the position of the author. And when I mention the demotion of the author I am not, or not only, referring to the curious relationship between sf fandom and the sf writer. The self that speaks through the—literally—experimental narrative of sf is only contingently individual. What it speaks through its stock figures is not a privileged, arbitrary artistic experience but something that can be tested and rejected: true in this set of circumstances, false otherwise.

Science fiction then is intrinsically—as Catherine Belsey says of mediaeval theatre—non-illusionist, emblematic. Its fictional worlds do not pretend to any mysterious independent existence off the page and beyond the words. And ironically, while gifted writers have been struggling to create the 'real novel' within the conventions of sf, outside the genre ideas about the novel, and about fiction in general, have suffered a period of dramatic change. The necessary omissions and blanks of sf have become positive virtues, in *la nouvelle critique*. Character is a bourgeois myth. Nineteenth-century expressive realism was a brief aberration. The fictional text, radically reinterpreted (and here I paraphrase Belsey's critique of Roland Barthes' position) becomes a collection of signs, the study—or deconstruction—of which will produce an anatomy of the process of its production; the limits imposed by the ideological matrix which defines this process, and the transgressions by which these secret rules are revealed. The text thus becomes what science fiction always was—a means, not an end: an experiment that can be examined, taken apart, even cannibalised by ruthless commentators, rather than a seamless work of art.

Deconstruction is the neutron bomb in the war of words. Everyone wants to use it, because this is the weapon that leaves all the structures still standing but with the information they contain changed to suit whoever pushed the button. But the extraordinary (I hate to say premonitory) nature of science fiction is that every writer and reader has to practise this modern art habitually, technically, intuitively. The creation of any sf story or novel involves the devising of a system of correspondences between a world the reader/writer knows and a world that meets the needs of the particular mental experiment in question. The interpolation may be partial and semi-transparent, it may be rich and relatively 'convincing': but to do this work at all the writer has to be aware that words and meanings are not immutably fixed together—and also, in the act of inventing a glossary of kinship terms for cloned and partially cybernetic humans, has to have some notion that social formation defines and is defined by language. At the same time the reader has to be able to penetrate this surface, identify those transgressions of the new rules which give the clues to the cypher, and maintain a continual mapping and appreciation of the contours of difference. Mainstream reviewers—and others who ought to know better—often speak of sf as being unintelligible to those who are 'unable to suspend disbelief' (this is one of the politest things mainstream reviewers say about sf). But what is needed is not a suspension of disbelief, it is an active process of translation.

This is not necessarily a profound or sophisticated intellectual exercise. There is very little enlightenment to be gained in consciously recognising the starship Enterprise, in the original series, as a US navy nuclear submarine cruising aimlessly around the Pacific, dispensing the morality of the Age of Liberalism at a vaguely doveish period in the Cold War... But there is nothing like constructing a world, or recognising a constructed world, for teaching you to see your own world as a construct. It is the existence of the technique that is significant. It was there, ready and waiting, when writers emerged who were able to make use of it. And here, if at all, comes the moment of innovation: for it was probably Joanna Russ, in her mid-1970s feminist sf, and especially in *The Female Man*, who first recognised and demonstrated the power of a specifically science fictional text to deconstruct itself, to lay itself open to radical and mutually contradictory plurality of meaning. In *The Female Man*, Russ takes an idea that could come from nowhere but science fiction—an exploration in story of that theory of space/time which posits an infinitely branching universe. She turns the idea back on herself, the author: becomes explicitly the divided self that this view of space/time implies. Russ's exploration of the fluid and contingent nature of language and selfhood, expressed here in terms of probability time travel, arose out of her feminism and the social relativism feminism demands. But you don't have to be a feminist, and maybe not even a student of science fiction, to understand that this text points, far more than any realist fiction, towards a full expression of the working of the human imagination.

One of the problems in tracing an innovation from sf into the rest of literature is highlighted by the case of *The Handmaid's Tale*. If something looks like science fiction, it thereby becomes 'science fiction'. Because Atwood didn't simply write satire but produced a carefully constructed/deconstructed world, her book is collected into the genre. The same effect can easily be created in reverse: we could collect all the nineteenth-century French naturalist novelists. Did Balzac write sf? He was passionately interested in the cutting-edge of any kind of technology, and didn't mind wrecking his reader's concentration with pages and pages of technical-manual details. Did Dickens? His characters are caricatures, acting out minatory pantomimes of social comment. I predict that in coming years, as a result of the twenty-first-century folklore effect and compounded by current literary theory, we will see a further blurring of the line between mainstream fiction and sf, to the extent that the fiction of the constructed world may even become as respectable as that other, more favoured non-realist genre, 'magical realism'. Meanwhile, through sf-infected 'literature' the relativism of both Einstein and Saussure will percolate slowly, slowly into the popular consciousness.

1: Getting Rid of the Brand Names*

Unnatural Language

According to a well known dictum of the genre, the first sentence of any science fiction story should instantly invoke the world of the narrative and no other world. Take down your chosen volume, which we will imagine to be in a plain cover so that the normal marketing signals are unavailable. If the first sentence is simply unintelligible, although it contains nothing but perfectly recognisable words of your mother tongue, read on in hope. Either you are on the right shelf or you have picked up by accident a book of academic literary criticism. A grounding in this subject will be invaluable to you in certain areas of modern sf—invaluable as a background in mechanical engineering might have been thirty years ago. If the first sentence reads 'the cat sat on the mat' read on and beware. You may have entered that copyeditor's nightmare, the rigorously imagined world. You think you know what a 'cat' is but you don't. It could be a foodstuff or a marital aid, or the term for a particularly esoteric degree of kinship in the imagined social structure. It could be (equally) a typographical error: it was supposed to be a czryt sitting on the mat.

Delany's dictum[1] sounds like a familiar formula, a test that could be applied to any kind of fiction. 'All happy families are alike but an unhappy family is unhappy after its own fashion'—there is *Anna Karenina* in a sentence. So long as Tolstoy is not cheating this is going to be a novel about broken homes. But in sf the game is more intense, more obsessive and much more *game-like*. If the book is to be about a world in which schizophrenia is normal, or war is unknown, or everybody is immortal, the challenge is to write every sentence, construct each scrap of dialogue as if in the Noel Coward-style party game where a player has to perform some ordinary action mimed *in the manner of the word*, the word that we are trying to guess. Never by so much as an adjective must the writer admit to knowledge of (for instance) a world where organised aggression is commonplace. This is science fiction realism, and one of its greatest charms,

---

* An article on language and vocabulary in science fiction written for a feature on Science Fiction in the 'Currents in Modern Thought' section of the USA lifestyle magazine *The World And I* and commissioned by George Hay, a year before the paper on *Deconstructing The Starships*.

for aficionados of the genre. But it is not even as easy as it sounds. The ideal language of science fiction can never be natural, it has to be worked-over. Every sentence must be consciously constructed and checked against the template of the original proposition: the science fiction writer is an engineer of words.

'Never complain, never explain'—this was Benjamin Disraeli's advice for anyone placed as he was, a Jewish social climber in the impenetrable jungle of England's political upper classes. Exactly the reverse applies for survival in the alien worlds of fiction. Complaining and explaining are the simplest tricks of sf technique. Explanation is the first resort, and the most recognisable from other forms of fiction: the expository lump where the storyteller by some means or other fills in the background facts that we need to understand the action. Characters explain to the out of town visitor what is done and not done here on Starbase 999, just as if they were in a normal novel—and at last the reader realises what that first mysterious sentence was about. Novelty technologies are likewise traditionally introduced to the reader through the device of the ignorant inquirer—friend, journalist, girlfriend of the scientist—who must always be on hand to ask the reader's questions: So, can you tell us how the new hyperdrive actually works, *in layman's terms please,* Professor? This trick is especially useful to non-scientist sf writers, but even the practising scientists among us have to employ the same wheeze, ensuring that the Genius is compelled to explain the great discovery to ordinary folk who would not understand the *real* equations behind faster-than-light travel. The most cutting-edge late twentieth-century professional knowledge has its limits.

Explanation is less useful for dealing with everyday new technology or deeply embedded social ideology. To get this kind of information across directly characters have to step right out of the game and explain to each other, like children stopping midway in a street corner fantasy of space rangers and aliens, matters which no one living in the world of the book can possibly need to know. Or would ever by any chance discuss. (We are now going to get into our motor car. This is a motor car, see. It works by an internal combustion engine. Internal combustion goes like this: you need a complex hydrocarbon fuel, air and some arrangement to cause a series of tiny explosions...) Complaining is better for this sort of communication. Characters complaining about the new zoning system or about their tiresome family relationships 'accidentally let slip' vital clues about the way this future or distant world is run; the book's novel means of private transport can become the material of introspective, philosophical questioning. (How strange we creatures are. Why do we allow our lives to be defined by these peculiar machines? Imagine, my whole existence is dominated by the preformance, or otherwise, of an internal combustion engine, a mere matter of petrol and air brought together and forced into a series of tiny explosions...)

The language game of science fiction need penetrate no further. Once the exposition has been delivered, and a novel technology, a new set of social rules have been established, the writer can relax and ignore the implications for the rest of the book. The easy-going portion of the audience—a large proportion—will never complain or demand an explanation. But for those who aspire to the Delany ideal these crude devices are anathema, used only in desperation: and their problems are only just beginning.

Deep Décor

It is often asserted that 'Fantasy', a particular brand of fantastic fiction that became a publishing industry in the wake of the success of J.R.R. Tolkien's Middle Earth, and 'Science Fiction', a brand of fantastic fiction invented, or re-invented, in the USA in the technophile 1920s, have little in common. The Middle Earth-type fantasy is anti-machines, it inhabits an imaginary past of the human race rather than an imaginary future (though this 'past' may be set in some neo-mediaeval phase a thousand years ahead of us); it dwells on human relationships, the human condition, metaphysical or moral problems. Science fiction is pro-technology, always set in a future rationally extrapolated from our present, and favours hard scientific exposition above human interest. In theory this may be so. In real life it can be difficult for outsiders, or even insiders, to tell the difference between the two sub-genres, or separate their audiences. But one thing science fiction and fantasy certainly have in common is the imaginary world, a world that must be furnished with landscape, climate, cosmology, flora and fauna, human or otherwise self-aware population, culture and dialogue.

In principle, the science fiction writer's world-building is more difficult. In science fiction, if the writer presents a long-eared burrowing animal that lives in social colonies, breeds prolifically, has a white tail and a bizarre association with chocolate eggs, gives it green fur and calls it a 'liplop', this is a failure of the imagination. Attentive readers will at once scornfully point out that the liplop is a rabbit in a silly hat. In fantasy there is no such stricture. The taxonomy, the architecture, the costumes, the proper names of the fictional world are adopted for the sheer romance of it: the world underneath the décor is not *intended* to be essentially different from ours. In fantasy the invented language, the recipes, the degrees of kinship—all the semantic baggage provided by the writer for your entertainment—are not warning flags raised to signal the difference between the reader's world and the world of the book. They *are* the difference, for better or for worse. The more serious the intention of the fantasy writer, the more the vocabulary of new and beautiful terms takes on the role of moral contrast, rather than being a sign of the morally neutral change of science fiction. Thus in Tolkien, the difference between this world and Middle Earth is our loss, and the tragedy of the Return of the King is our fall (albeit temporarily delayed by the victory of the less destructive modernist party) towards this present state of decline; while in Ursula Le Guin's recent magnum opus *Always Coming Home* invented vocabulary, and moral commentary on the writer's own world, have separated out almost completely. A jeremiad against the deadly evils of the twentieth century floats over a massive sedimentary deposit of appendices: and fiction barely survives between them.

Colourful fancy dress has gone in and out of style, over the decades since I became a reader of science fiction. Frank Herbert's *Dune* books; Anne McCaffery's *Pern* and Marion Zimmer Bradley's *Darkover*, were considered mainstream sf locales when they first appeared—in spite of their feudal keeps, long dresses, archaic dialogue, magic steeds, mediaeval codes of caste and honour. It is odd to return to Roger Zelazny's Hindu Pantheon adventure *Lord of Light* and discover under the gorgeous trappings a tale of interplanetary travellers in exile, whose magical powers are firmly pinned to technology. But though the elaborate use of ornamental disguise, in costume and custom and language, has come to mean *don't look here for innovation. Underneath the décor, this is just your own back yard*, the same techniques can be discerned in the most chaste of modern, legitimate science fiction. William Gibson's *Neuromancer* is a case in point. His position on explanation and complaint is impeccably uncompromising. His characters are cultural amnesiacs who refer to our present, their recent past, about as often as the average 1980s airhead reflects on any events or cultural icons of a decade ago (that haven't recently been used to sell jeans). They speak a relentless futurese that never by any chance lets the mask slip and (except in one case, which I'll deal with later) the narrative never displays the slightest awareness of the stumbling, time travelling reader. But Gibson's futurese has been identified, and acknowledged by the writer, as a package of recycled Hollywood film clips and Beat generation slang; while his structural language is that of an instantly recognisable contemporary folktale. Like Alfred Bester a generation ago, recycling the delightfully simple plot of *The Count of Monte Cristo* in his firecracker of style-seminal sf *Tyger Tyger*, Gibson is forced to use a conventional scenario to support his novel surface. Recollections, direct or filtered through the cultural matrix, of *The Maltese Falcon* and countless variants on that theme, soothe and coax the reader through the alien décor and vocabulary, as the plot hands out the traditional thriller's succession of small rewards and teasing forfeits. Here there's no great moral lesson conveyed through the references to our own world. But the completeness of Gibson's surface brings him to the same position as Ursula Le Guin, and fantasy and science fiction come together again. The surface is the story. The more *richly imagined* the décor the less room there is for change, scientific or otherwise, in the world of the book.

But What Do They Say to Each Other?

Heavy borrowing from real-world culture, almost always a feature in the richly imagined surface, is a favourite escape from unnatural language; though aside from taking up so much room it brings its own set of incongruities and anachronisms. I remember being painfully aware of this when writing my first sf novel, a borrowed culture story called *Divine Endurance*. I was plundering, like Gibson with the Beat, or Ursula Le Guin's in her raids on the lost tribes of the Californian seaboard, a culture romantically distant from that of my audience; in my case that of Indonesia and Malaysia. I threw together vocabulary from present day Bahasa Indonesia, hero-tales from the post Second World War struggle for Indonesian independence, traditions and customs from feudal Java, Islamic ritual, Hindu epic. By the end any Malaysian or Indonesian reader was going to be gibbering with frustration and scorn at my confusions and conflations—some of them deliberate, but not all! Yet I knew that I needed this local colour, not only for existential reasons to do with my theme but also, and importantly, as a shorthand for the passage of time. To speak through a different culture marked a discontinuity. It said to my readers, *civilisation is not in the same hands, the world has moved on.* Fantasy writers, including those whose work is known as science fiction, use such devices like retired generals describing old campaigns on the after-dinner tablecloth. We picked up our borrowing—the snatches of phrasebook dialogue, the garbled scraps of real but unfamiliar history and custom—as if it was the pepper mill, and say: *Now, this stands for several thousand years of time.*

There is certainly something of a passionate obsession in the creation of an invented language for a fantasy novel, with its grammar and its songs and its ancient proverbs. Perhaps it represents a reliving of the epic victory of early childhood, when the strange noises used by adults, such potent tools of control, suddenly begin to make sense. But in most cases, the borrowing from a real world source is fairly near the surface (the case of a language invented by an sf writer with no experience of real-world human language to build on, does not exist as far as I know). This is a great advantage, carrying with it into the text (though the actual words of the strange language can only appear in a few fragments lest the story become unintelligible) a whole panoply of custom, costume, social framework. Thus in Frank Herbert's *Dune* series, where the inhabitants of a desert planet live at one with their sun-scoured, almost waterless environment, the 'fremen' of the desert speak a kind of bastard Arabic, and the plot reinvents Islam. But people, even fictional characters, do not live only in the present. As soon as they walk into a fictional scene, as soon as they open their mouths (or whatever analogue applies) they give expression not only to their present predicament but to all the millennia of their cultural past. The laziest answer to this problem (the technique I employed in *Divine Endurance*, and Frank Herbert in *Dune*) is to have your characters embedded in some timeless notion of your borrowed culture (my distant-future Malaysians quote the Baghavad Gita and the Mahavarata, in moments of stress); arbitrarily bestow on them the ability to recollect in detail late twentieth-century science, events or preoccupations that are necessary to the plot, and ignore everything between. Chroniclers without a borrowed culture to fall back on are doomed to populate their novels with space-faring pedants who quote the lyrics of Bob Dylan and use the screenplay from Spielberg movies to express their emotions. To avoid this peril (not to mention the expense), some writers attempt to pave over the abyss of history that has not happened, by composing a thousand-year-long preface, and heading their chapters with extracts from imitation encyclopaedias, quotations from imitation history books; wise aphorisms from fake long-dead galactically-famous philosophers.

Given that nearly everything that you invent to back up your future world will have to be left out of the actual narrative (and deposited in those massive appendices) the laziest solution would seem the most reasonable. But as science fiction has developed over the last decades, all the old tricks—even those still kept, surreptitiously, in frequent use—have fallen into disrepute. A horror of the vast spaces between fiction and reality overwhelms us. Never mind their historical tags or sentimental quotations, how can we devise analogues for the unthinking figures of speech whereby all human cultures (even our own) invoke events and manners now lost hundreds or even thousands of years in the past? How can we begin to convey all the subtle and voluminous reference that goes into a single page of the most ordinary mainstream novel, *in the manner of the book?* When I was an undergraduate studying History of Ideas, it was the fashion of the time to tell us that we could not begin to understand the thought processes of the past. Three hundred years was felt to be the absolute cut-off. Beyond that, it's anthropomorphism. So how can we report on what's going on several hundred years in the future? Is it even permissible for us to have our science fiction characters speaking English (or French, or American)?

The simple answer is that of course it is not. In the noble cause of verisimilitude, every honest sf writer ought to explain in an afternote— like Tolkien, Wells or Rider Haggard—that the strange documents on which this novel is based have been not only translated into English, but extensively edited and reconstructed for the contemporary reader. The fantasy epic's massive freight of gloss and footnotes is not such an absurdity. There'd be massive appendices to the slimmest and coolest sf novel, if the writers were *really* trying to capture the effect of a text despatched from deep in our future.

We cannot pretend to understand their languages. And they, when we eavesdrop on their lives, must rarely if ever remember us. In realist terms, the task is impossible. Thus a whole universe of galactic empires, twenty-fourth-century explorers, neo-mediaeval adventurers and their interaction with furry or tentacled (yet strangely human!) aliens, is banished from the true church. The only kind of science fiction that can be taken seriously must be set in a future as close as possible to us in space and time; and must describe a world we or our children might possibly live to see. Then the privileges of mainstream realism will be restored, and the language of the novel will become possible. But even here the trade-off between verisimilitude and intelligibility operates severely.

Time Stigmata

William Gibson has declared 'anyone who thinks sf is about the future, is naive'.[2] Ursula Le Guin states overtly in her many authorial asides in *Always Coming Home* what is implicit in all her novels of imaginary worlds. This is news from nowhere, not a report from the future but a parable for our times: a vision and a daydream and a warning. These two expert conjurors who do not wish, or no longer wish, to fool the audience, give an impression of choice. There is none. Willingly or not, knowingly or not, and whatever mode or level of décor they employ, all sf and fantasy writers are up against The Wall. No one gets past it. Science fiction is a confusing phenomenon. As even an acute mainstream critic may observe, it pretends to describe the future, yet more than any other literary genre it reflects the exact preoccupations of the present. To claim that the 'real' purpose of sf is to hold a mirror up to the contemporary scene is to make a virtue of necessity, because the future invoked in the text can't be just *any* future; it can't even be the future the writer rationally considers the most likely. It has to be as close as possible to a future which is seen as likely or relevant by most people at the time of writing. Otherwise nobody will think it is any good. Thus, the very books that seem to critics and audience the most intelligent, most exciting, the most uncannily accurate future-guessing, become ten years later the most dated—providing merely an *uncannily accurate* reverse image of the year in which they were written. Tell me what you think is going to happen tomorrow, and I'll tell you what is happening to you today. The original problem remains, whichever way you cut it. If the narrative is easily readable, then it is definitely not an accurate report of the future. But if it is as piously unintelligible as Delany could wish, it will still be the abstract art of the year or the season in which it was composed, and no other. It seems that the most we can hope for from science fiction *realism* is a mixture of convention, sleight of hand and cynical trickery, with a 'best by' date that makes the whole thing absurd stamped all the way through.

Science Procedural

All is not lost. The proper study of science fiction writers is science. This is a statement that has the status of revealed truth for enthusiasts, however little it may be honoured in their reading or their writing. In spite of endless identity problems between the two genres, the best way to separate the sf party from the fantasy party is still to ask this question: *Does it matter if the science is sound?* The fantasy fanciers will say no, the sf faithful will say yes. The fact that the natural fate of real-world science is to be dismissed as nonsense in the end, (hopefully after a long and happy life as revealed truth) is beside the point. Notoriously *Ringworld*, one of the great, classic 'engineering feat' sf novels, reached print in the first instance with terrible mistakes in its science. It is an indication of the power of sf's abiding myths about itself that Larry Niven, probably as free as any sf novelist alive from moral qualms about social verisimilitude or cultural relativity, aquiesced to the helpful advice he received from Dyson Sphere buffs, and obediently corrected his fantasy for later editions. It's true, a book which consists almost entirely of a fictional apparatus for displaying a specific wrinkle in contemporary theory about reality invites this kind of response. However, no one has yet suggested that all texts involving Venusian Swamps and Martian canals should be recalled like faulty toasters. The challenge, which had to be met, was not to Niven's scientific accuracy but to his appearence of command over the *language* of science. This is where all science fiction writers pin their hopes of achieving some strange kind of realism. Even William Gibson, who has so firmly announced that the futuristic surface is a charade, can be seen giving way to the divine *anfechtung*. The language of *Neuromancer* is a frictionless curve: you learn to cope or too bad for you, you'll get no help from the writer. The Third World War is so much old newspaper, dismissed in half a paragraph. But when he comes to the core of his fantasy science, he feels bound to try and explain *cyberspace* logically: what it is and how it came to exist.

But the language of science is a means, not an end: the process, not the product. It is the influence of the legendary *scientific method* that leads sf writers to insist, in defiance of the hopelessness of the task, that we must describe realistic futures; that the book must be able to answer the question *how did we get there from here*, as if it were a lab write-up on a real-world experiment. In the narrowest interpretation this purified science fiction, free from cultural contamination, can only exist in the laboratory-procedural. This is the kind of sf that is favoured (along with, curiously, the most blatant rocketship fantasies) by working scientists, and unsurprisingly, it's those writers closest to popular science sf who do the lab procedural best. Issac Asimov's classic *The Gods Themselves* is innocent of fictional sophistication, to the extent that at this mature stage of his career (1972) the Master opens by cheerfully explaining to his readers a new mechanism he has invented, called the flashback. But when Asimov's project escapes (inevitably) from the lab, it enters another universe populated by extraordinarily convincing and *alien* intelligent alien life. Similarly Gregory Benford's novel of near-future physics, *Timescape*, transcends its genre limitations and becomes a tour de force of scientific fiction. The novelist-writing-science who chooses this form will have greater literary ambitions, but is likely to suffer greater temptations from the lure of conventional storytelling. In his 1984 novel *Green Eyes*, Lucius Shepard, a virtuoso stylist, follows in the tradition of Mary Shelley and (closer to home) Kate Wilhelm, in bringing the descriptive power and depth of characterisation of mainstream fiction to the lab procedural. There is an imaginary experiment, based on the newest ideas about a real world science; and it is described in an exact imitation of the scientific language of the day:

> The resultant strain was injected into the cerebellum and temporal lobes of a corpse... whereupon the bacteria began pretranscriptional processing of the corpse's genetic complement. Twenty four hours after injection the 'zombie' was ready for the therapist...[3]

But one can compare this novel unfavourably to Mary Shelley's *Frankenstein*, because as soon as the updated zombie escapes from the laboratory, the gothic novel dominates and science, or philosophical speculation on science, is abandoned. What transpires in the story of *Green Eyes* is a baroque occult fantasy as familiar in its way as the plot of one of William Gibson's near-future thrillers. In the terms of another discipline—and one arguably as relevant to sf as molecular biology—Shepard uses a specific statement from the *parole*, the everyday speech of science. But the *langue*, the language he draws on as an unconscious body of knowledge, is that of contemporary horror fiction and the gothic tradition. The idea that human beings are no more than motile colonies of bacteria is (in sf terms) exciting and suggestive and very much of the moment (compare Greg Bear's *Blood Music*). But in *Green Eyes* the vital infection, unlike Shepard's graveyard bacteria, fails to thrive. Most of the mind of the text is left untouched.

The Lamp And The Sun

> You see that lamp. It is round and yellow and gives light to the whole room; and hangeth moreover from the roof. Now the thing that we call the sun is like the lamp, only far greater and brighter. It giveth light to the whole Overworld and hangeth in the sky...[4]

The enchanted prince, imprisoned underground and informed persuasively that no other world exists, has to use the materials at hand to try and invoke effects his captor claims she has never seen. C.S. Lewis's *The Silver Chair* is the fantasy of a writer able to draw on a great deal of stored information about the nature of creative thought. To see the lamp and describe the sun is the essence of science fiction. It is also the essence of experimental thinking. It is their experience of the sheerly mechanical process of extrapolation that gives Benford and Asimov their advantage over the litterateurs. The luckless Prince Rilian fails to impress the wicked enchantress because she has her own agenda. The mental experiment would have failed to convince anyway, because the prince does not have a lab scientist's wily skill at stopping up the boltholes and strengthening the weak links so as to keep the proof—or at least the plausibility—of a proposition from slipping away. It takes more than a moment of insight. The practical experimenter has to work on that insight with a dogmatic persistence quite foreign to everyday human reflection, testing and rejecting pathways towards the objective like a rat in a maze. Few of us realise how casually our worlds of perception are furnished. A motor car is a motor car. Its identity floats by the sensorium: a means of getting from A to B, a smell of petrol and oil, a large shiny box, a noise in the distance. If all the cars in the world were suddenly present only in so far as they were perceived, the roads would be filled with an army of coloured moving blurs, most of them completely empty under the hood and quite a few with nothing underneath to hold the wheels together. Cars would become like the content-empty 'futuristic' props in bad sf. The props of good sf, however, denied the protection of custom and habit, have to be built more soundly than the shadows with which we lazily surround ourselves in real life. The better the writer understands the laborious process of refining an experiment, the more successful the fantastical artefact: a sun that is nothing like the lamp, but it convinces, because the path from one to the other has been rehearsed, intuitively or consciously, every step of the way (and then the steps have been hidden, of course, under a fictional surface). This method does not only apply to the construction of a convincing technological innovation, but to any degree of difference. We want to change something in the nature of human relationships? Then we must ask, what is a social relationship, essentially? What are its necessities? How does it develop? We scrape off the brand names and remodel the world beneath the surface; and this time with the beginnings of a confidence that the changes are not superficial but will survive—that an idea has reached the language of the book, not merely tinkered with its vocabulary.

The work of a truly scientific science fiction writer can be compared to the activities of the alien sub-species that invades and infests the Earth based starship in Jerry Pournelle's novel of alien contact *The Mote in God's Eye*. It is in the nature of these beasts to tinker and improve. Their instinctual reaction on meeting a new mechanism or tool is to strip it down and then put it together again raised to the height of its possibilities. It doesn't matter that to these aliens the human tools are totally unfamiliar. They extrapolate (all this at a preconscious level for they are not intelligent) from the tool to its purpose; and back again to exactly the appropriate improvements. There are plenty of successful and respected sf writers who restrict scientific method to the project of the Big Gadget and leave the rest of the fictional world untouched. There are other writers whose skill consists mainly of devising felicitous new names and descriptions for everyday objects. The Motie-worker writer applies the manner of the book, the statement of that first sentence, to everything that moves. And, as we should all know by now, everything moves. The fact that the humans find the efforts of these industrious little helpers deeply disconcerting is not inappropriate to the comparison. Science fiction ought to be disturbing, especially in the details: like one of those dreams where everything seems familiar but *nothing is quite the same*.

The language of science is the language of the laboratory and the specialist machine shop, the statistical study and the mental experiment. It infects and infests a genre that includes all possible points on the x/y graph of expertise in science on the one hand and fiction on the other. But perhaps the most interesting real-world development to reach the sf genre in recent years has been a revolution in the science of language itself. Some scientific developments travel faster than others: Saussure is older than special relativity, but faster than light travel reached both sf and the imagination of the general public a long way ahead of structuralism. Now, for a while at least, semiotics, Sassure, Lacan, Barthes: *langue* and *parole*, text and discourse, signifier and signified, have become the raw material of sf playfulness and speculation. At last the scientist's skills are available to the litterateur. A science fiction novel is a system of correspondences. The world is made out of signs, and to make the whole book agree with a point of view shifted by five hundred years, or the fall of patriarchy, or World War Three (as Delany suggests that we should) we have only to change the signs... In obedience to the invincible Theory of Intertextuality, we will have to give up the hypothetical 'realist' novel of the future, delivered in a sealed box by time machine, but since we knew that was an impossible task it's no great loss. In so far as our adjustments from the real are derived from contemporary preoccupations they will be intelligible, but the lesson of relativity will be no less powerful. Science fiction writers will give up their fortune-telling, but find instead that moment of vertigo a physical scientist feels, on realising that the craziest things they say about the quantum universe are meant to be taken *literally*: the moment when the whole structure of the world collapses, and everything most solid and certain becomes changeable, relative, unreal.

There remains the problem of how to present this new kind of text. The average sf reader delights in refinished consumer durables, and will tolerate the technical specifications of the starship engine, or some esoteric speculations about supersymmetry, but expects a jolly good yarn arranged around them. Modern or post-modern, science fiction writers still have to provide entertainment. But the new scientific fiction may be able to survive, by the cunning ploy of bearing a strong resemblance to the good science fiction that was always around. There may be some writers, and readers, who discover that they were post-modernists all the time and didn't know it. All we needed, like the Scarecrow in Oz who never knew he had a brain, was a Certificate. Now we have one. Let's hope we don't blow it.

It might be supposed that when sf writers are headhunted by litterateurs from the wide world outside the genre, and become fascinated by the science of fiction, their natural route is out of the rocketship circus and into the mainstream. But in spite of points of similarity, sf differs from post-modernism in a fundamental respect. It is a literature of ideas, oriented not towards humanity but towards its artefacts: whether these may be sexy new computer decks or theories about the nature of reality. In space opera, in future fantasy, it may seem that only a particular style of fancy dress separates the fiction from any other brand of commercially produced adventure story, and perhaps that's true. But as far as you travel away from the commercial sector, towards painful satire and cosmic truth, the human characters *never* take first place. They are vibrations, patterns of force, necessary consequences of change. Mainstream novelists may be fascinated by the impact that scientific developments have on human experience. Post-modernists may be fascinated by the moment of impact in itself: sf is the fiction that values the ideas themselves. This secret theme, the inhuman outward gaze, moves through the genre like a sentient plasma cloud, vast and invisible and unstoppable; like the mysterious entity oozing steadily towards the action in Alice Sheldon's (aka James Tiptree Jnr's) classic *Up the Walls of the World*. No one but the writer knows what it is doing there or even notices its presence until, three pages from the end, it suddenly takes over and turns out to be the answer to life, the universe and everything. Perhaps there is no such thing as an sf writer who is only interested in telling a 'good yarn' dressed up in fancy technology. That plasma cloud is sneaking through every novel, from *Neuromancer* to *Ringworld*; and even (against Captain Kirk's every human instinct) through the annals of the Starship Enterprise. The disinterested longing to express something of the strangeness, the paradox, the alien beauty that is explored by 'science' is in us all.

Within any given discourse, and any text within that discourse, all kinds and levels of development coexist as in a living organism. The language of science fiction is accommodating. It can express technophile ideology, deep structural change *in the manner of the book*, war-comic nostalgia, ripping adventure yarns; and the 'soybutter and jelly sandwich' future, where the writer can handle faster than light starships but can hardly bear to conceive of any social innovation at the snackfood level. But in a world increasingly preoccupied with technology rather than knowledge, consumer goods rather than ideas, it is good to feel that there is still life and development in the esoteric registers of the human imagination. Without the impractical innovators of sf, speaking in tongues and trying to build whole worlds phoneme by phoneme, this precious conduit between the human world and the strange cosmos we inhabit might very soon collapse.

2: The Lady and the Scientists*

I was coming out of Sainsbury's and a young man stopped me with one of those clipboards... I'm usually very short with these people, but browsing the supermarket shelves is so soothing. It's like picking berries, isn't it? Instead of standing in front of a counter and begging, like a suppliant at a shrine, you feel as if you've found all this lovely stuff. Anyway, I was feeling benign, so I answered his questions about the product. We came to the end. Are you married? Yes. Children? One, little toddler. Occupation? Writer. Do you work outside the home? Not often. Would you consider yourself to be in full time or part-time employment? Full time, says I, not having much doubt on the subject. The young man doesn't fill in his box. He says: oh. And then, are you sure? I'm sure, I repeat, firmly: and he looks very doubtful. I can tell he's going to chuck that sheet away as a spoiled ballot.

Then again, here's a quote from a recent survey the Writer's Guild did on the position of women writers. It actually comes from an interview in what we call in the UK a 'quality daily', with a successful male playwright (who shall be nameless, and serve him right), who is describing how he manages to work at home with a young family around: 'I am quite capable of walking over a pile of washing on the kitchen floor, and registering mentally that it's there, but feeling no obligation whatsoever to do anything about it.'

I'm not like that, I don't want to be like that. This playwright is a selfish infantile jerk and I despise per**. We run an equal opportunities house here, and it kills us both (two careers and a baby, you know the one) but I wouldn't have it any different. Still, I admit I do sometimes fantasise about what life would be like for me as an artist, if I had a nice wife to look after the house and bring up my baby for me. He'd have to be prepared to starve a little. Or, more likely, take a dead-end part-time job to keep me in fanfold paper and so forth. But then, that's what the wives of artists are for. The exasperating thing is that with this albatross of feminist ideology around my neck, I'm not even supposed to daydream about that particular future. Because the argument goes like this (to paraphrase Octavia Butler):no

*From a paper read at a meeting of Preston Speculative Fiction Group, 1990.

** 'per' is not a misprint. It's the unisex pronoun employed by Marge Piercy in her Utopian future in *Woman on the Edge of Time*.

rational person who's known what it's like to be a nigger could possibly want to own a slave. All I can hope for is some mechanism, some change in the rules, whereby there are no more human sacrifices at all. But am I allowed, do I dare to hope for this possible world in print, in 1990, and call it science fiction? Opinions are divided.

Modern practitioners of science fiction are, overall, a pretty articulate and thoughtful group of people. Every one of them, down to the most despised millionare 'genre hack' seems to be well aware of the logical contradictions involved in writing about the future. Everybody's happy to tell you that science fiction is 'really about' the present day world— distorted mirror of current affairs, vat-grown monsters from the germ plasm of today's hopes and fears. However, and this applies, curiously enough, just as much to the liberal, 'radical' baby-boomer generation, these same writers are oddly shy of making connections between what they write (and predict) and their own lives. Baby boomers do not write of changes in their own culture, or at their own level of society. They prefer exotic slums to suburbia. They prefer tragic or dramatic change in a global context, not on the domestic front. The future is what happens to other people. Sf is the report of the disinterested observer: rarely, if ever, a personal expression of the hopes or fears of sf writer X.

I don't feel that this, reticence, shall we call it, is entirely the result of naïvety or cowardice. I'm sure it is partly an aesthetic reaction against the excesses of the past. To have opinions, rather than just cool ideas about gadgets—to think in terms of 'What kind of life would I like (or hate)?'— this is dangerous ground. It takes us close to the line between writing sf and walking up and down Oxford Street with a sandwich board that says: 'REPENT FOR THE END IS NIGH'. The notion of having a message, and trying to put it across, is indeed sort of disgusting. I feel it so myself. I am seriously embarrassed to find myself more in sympathy with the ancient maniacs of the past, truffle-hunting for Utopia in the dirt of sf's lies, damned lies and sugared political indoctrination, than with the majority of my cool, hep-cat, morally neutral contemporaries. At least I can console myself that I'm even less happy in the company of my fellow-ideologues of the present day, the SDI Appreciation Society. It is a sad fact that while liberals flee from connection and commitment as one would from virus-infected software, those sf writers who are proud to use their stories to promulgate right-thinking and good attitudes are almost without exception those who think and write as if Eisenhower were still president of the USA, and the Holy Word of unlimited capitalist expansion were coming to them straight from the lips of the Angel Gabriel.

This is the burden that extremists have to bear. Eventually you have to come to terms with the fact that you're much more like extremists of other denominations than you are like any sane, normal person. And thus the Darwinian model of nil inter-species aggression is preserved: we only compete directly with those who are like ourselves. The only comfort I can offer to myself is the reassurance that ideology is not a rare disease. Everybody has a filtration system several layers deep of assumptions and expectations, whereby they distinguish funny from depressing, right from wrong, desirable from undesirable, nice from nasty, outrage from normality. Ideology is what makes you laugh at a sitcom—or not, as the case may be. Some people acknowledge this filtration system. Some people lie about it. Some people laugh, or cry, or get affronted like reflex-conditioned animals, never even wondering why. But the case of the conscious human being 'without an ideology' does not exist.

Allowing that social comment in sf is okay in principle (cf. Wells, Stapledon): and that feminism is a futuristic fiction, same as any other utopian scheme, the next obstacle between my personal ideology and the genre (now as much as ever) would seem to be the science. Women don't do science. They don't like it and it doesn't like them. No doubt there are exceptions that prove the rule: but as that expression explains, a few anomalies worry no one. And anyway, I'm not interested in preaching to the converted. Max Delbruck says intuition is nothing more or less than fully assimilated learning: like being able to walk or talk or read without conscious effort. We say we know something intuitively when we no longer need to run the steps involved in that knowledge past ourselves in order to get to the point. Thus people know, intuitively, what 'science' means. It means a team of young men in beards and Fairisle jumpers with the elbows out, grinning shyly around their Nobel prize. It means a middle-aged bloke in a white coat selling washing powder. It means (possibly) Sigourney Weaver in a very sexy white coat talking to a dolphin... But that's okay because talking to dolphins is only fantasy. It's not real science, nor yet (especially not) real science fiction.

I was invited to give a paper a little while ago, at an event organised around the presentation of the Arthur C. Clarke Award, the prestigious new British prize for 'serious and relevant' science fiction. Of course I accepted. I love pretending to be a member of the intelligentsia. This was the occasion when George Turner won the prize with *The Sea and Summer*, and John Gribbin gave his famous 'serious sf doesn't make sense' speech, thus managing to trash not only the book in question but the whole rationale of the award. A splendid achievement that received applause as thunderous as the thirteen or so of us could manage. We Brits are squeamish about prizes, but we adore irony.

Anyway, I gave my paper, which suggested that there are parallels between the rules of science/fiction, and more or less recent developments in the realm of literary criticism, which I called the science of fiction. I found parallels between Saussure and Einstein, structuralism and quantum mechanics, deconstruction and *Star Trek*. I think it was fun, in its way. But at the end a lady in the audience got up and said: 'That's cheating. Literary science isn't science. Science is when you do precise experiments and learn something measurable about the real world from the results.' I opened and shut my mouth a bit, feeling somewhat outraged. When there are only thirteen people in the house and they've remained respectfully silent for *'Brunner's computer worms: prediction and the facts'*; and *'Ballard seen as a behavioural psychologist'*... well, it seems rotten luck to be the one who has to field an actual question, and a question closely resembling a heckle, at that. But I didn't have to answer her. The scientists (the lady was not a scientist, but her husband was, she said) leapt up as one man, and cried, 'Not where I come from!' They said all the things that I wanted them to say, about fuzzy logic, fudged results, disorder and nonlinearity. The much vaunted 'scientific method' is an ideological fiction, they yelled. It's successful fiction, an enduring bestseller even, but it isn't true. Holistic knowledge is no longer a crank book craze, its time has come. Big Daddy Science is entering a new era of honesty and openness...

Well, this was all very nice, and saved me some discomfort. But my lady heckler was not convinced, and though as an sf writer I'm all for the new era, I love new eras, as an ideologue I'm not sure if the men in the metaphorical white coats can be trusted. They say *die Mauer ist teg*. The wall is down: science is now an art, and human. But what do they know about the real world, the big place that doesn't fit into linear equations? Nothing. (They just admitted as much.) I fear that my heckler may have been speaking with greater authority. And when I look at the historical relationship between science fiction and feminism, I think I see much the same situation. There's the romantic version, which says that everything has changed, that all the demands have been accepted (accepted, not met, mind: an important distinction) and there's nothing to fight about any more. Then there's the common-sense version, that says the consensual majority hasn't really shifted at all.

John Gribbin is a writer of some terrific popular science and some rather stolidly traditional (in my opinion) 'old fashioned hard sf'. When he ridicules the notion of scientifically plausible sf and asks for warm, human stories, what he is asking for is warm, human rocketship fantasies. This demand deserves some attention, because I believe he speaks for the majority consensus notion of what science fiction is supposed to be like, 'even now', many years after the revolution. Dear listeners, and readers, perhaps you yourselves don't care for space opera, bizarre aliens and starjet dogfights. But I am talking about sales figures. And I am also talking about a silent ranking that determines each book's place in the genre's hierarchy.

In the 1960s and 1970s various sf writers who didn't have a degree (or equivalent experience) in Physics and Gadgetry tried very hard to broaden the meaning of this nineteenth-century neologism 'science'. It means 'knowledge' doesn't it? Therefore we can write about absolutely anything! This campaign especially involved women writers who, though not necessarily feminists, were still trying to claw their way up to 'real' sf status, and out of the underclass sink of girly fantasy. Their claim was that stories about futuristic crèche management, or housework, or genetics, or sociology, philosophy, linguistics or the fall of patriarchy, could all be classed as 'real' science fiction. In the vivid repertoire of football metaphor there's an operation called 'moving the goalposts', which means the blatant *ad hoc* introduction of restrictive practices, to deal with unexpected success on the part of your (generally, less powerful) opponents. The broad church ploy in 1970s sf would be equivalent to the underdogs trying to move the goalposts a lot further apart.

And it worked, *for a while*. Remember that expression. It's one that sf feminists tend to brood upon, and feminists in the real world too. Just a few years ago, feminism was a sexy topic in sf. It wasn't only a hot core of politically fashionable rhetoric. It wasn't just Joanna Russ and Suzy Charnas announcing the end of the world as we know it. It seemed like a shift in values right through the genre. By the mid-1980s, the ungendered starship captain who turns out to be a girl on page 230 was as tired an old cliché as the Heinlein original of this trick. But that she could be a cliché at all was a cause for rejoicing. Sf and feminism, gender roles in flux, characters with human feelings, life sciences awarded parity of esteem with engineering, *satyagraha* awarded parity of esteem with planet destroyers... I loved it. I loved *The Female Man*. I loved those brave-but-brittle male sidekicks C.J. Cherryh sneaked into classic space-opera, fitting exactly where the gutsy-but-fragile girlfriend used to go. And, though I don't usually like hard science stories, I savoured Pamela Zoline's 'Heat Death Of The Universe'. The isolated young housewife plods through the suburban domestic grind, gradually going beserk. Some protective filter has clogged and given up, she can see the inexorable process of entropy going on all around her: cosmic death by disorder in the washing machine's cycle, in the kids' spilled food. Is this story about Physics and Gadgetry? Certainly it is about machines, meat and metal. Better, it is about the nature of the machine itself. 'Heat Death' is wonderful because it demands parity of esteem for women's business simply by taking it, and backs up the coup with impeccable technical detail. The young man with the clipboard outside Sainsbury's thinks he is 'working' as he asks his silly questions, and I'm not 'working' as I run around after my toddler. In order to be normal like him, I have to get out of the kitchen, dump the shopping, find myself a real job in the real world. But Pamela Zoline has announced that she and I don't have to change at all. We can be speculative and profound observers of the interaction between cosmic laws and human lives right where we stand. We can pick up that pile of dirty washing from the kitchen floor, and turn it into a piece of pure, hard (or even very hard) science/fiction—

(Ah. I have to go now. The baby's nap is over...)

Later that same week...

But it only worked for a while. Now that the dust has cleared, this seminal material... I'm sorry, I'll read that again: much of the ovular material of feminist sf looks dubious. Leaving aside the wilder excesses of childbirth-envy among male sf writers (mainly John Varley, but he had his imitators), some of the most sacred texts of the movement are suspect. A fairly casual study of Ursula Le Guin's early books reveals a distinct lack of 'female characters in non-traditional roles'. No blame to her. Many of the women drawn to reading or writing genre adventure stories are originally attracted because they dream of escaping from girls and girlish things, and because they believe that boyish adventure cannot, even should not, be their work in real life. But as the founding mother of feminist sf, her lasting achievement seems to have been to be the exception that proves the rule, the one truly great woman sf writer; and to give a whole generation of admiring male disciples a terrific (and sorely needed) leg up in literary technique. There is statistical evidence to show that co-education is good for boys, bad for girls. It makes the boys more like human beings, but the girls even more like paranoid doormats. There are many male and/or anti-feminist sf writers who see no contradiction between their views and the fact that one of the most admired sf writers inside or outside the genre happens to be a woman.

Now there's a fresh generation of idealistic young feminist readers, poking their green little heads over the battlements of the 1990s. They're not fooled by the higher tomboyism of the starship captain who is a girl. And they are no better pleased with the direct and conscious political writing of the old avant-garde. That rhetoric is tainted not so much by failure, the kids of today are not so crass, but by 1968 and all that. There's a whiff of Urban Terrorism, Marxism and Maoism about it all. When the dashing Future-person in Marge Piercy's *Woman on the Edge of Time* gets up in her fighter plane, blood and powder stained red bandanna around her brow, and proceeds to strafe the shit out of patriarchy, the mind's eye of 1990 recalls the horrors of the Cultural Revolution, and sees the tanks in Tiananmen Square. Violent means to political ends have low credibility at the moment. But it's not only the violence they sneer at. The kids (as always) are much more demanding than they used to be. They're not satisfied with simple sf role-reversal (one cute boy in the mainly female cast). When Vonda MacIntyre re-invents the sf hero as a gorgeous, sexily muscled yet diffident young thing who meditates a lot and is deeply into childcare, they start whining that feminist writers' male characters are unconvincing. They actually want believable characterisation for their sex interest now! (At this, personally, I feel I have to draw the line. Good grief. Just because you're a feminist doesn't mean you have to betray everything that sf stands for.)

To paraphrase someone else, 99% of anything you care to mention is rubbish. Maybe it shouldn't be a cause for concern if some of the feminist stories that seemed wonderful ten or twenty years ago are losing it. Most of science fiction's so-called golden age was made of the same disintegrating metal. It doesn't matter. What matters is that people try to emulate the stories that they *think* they read—to recapture the effect, the verve, the fierce ideation: not the loopy science, brutal politics and wooden dialogue. There should be no need for gloom. All of the women I've mentioned are still writing. And there are many others. Surely feminist sf is in excellent shape, though we haven't yet managed to take over the world... Well. In the August 1990 issue of the *New York Review of Science Fiction* they published the results of a bookshop survey on this very subject. It was a small sample, a single shop in Philadelphia. The head count was 134 men to 31 women on the sf racks: but numbers like that don't prove anything. What struck me was the bookseller's reported comment. 'I think you'll find,' he says, 'that not many women write science fiction. There's James Tiptree of course, and Octavia Butler and Ursula K. Le Guin, but other than those three that's about it.' With a little prodding he was persuaded to add C.J. Cherryh to the list. Three and a half women! Wow!

I like this bookseller. He's the man on the Clapham omnibus in science fiction terms, the Mr Ordinary who has no hidden agenda (except the one that he doesn't know about); who only sees the obvious, who cuts through my professional pretensions and tells me what is really going on. These things take time. If you asked Mr Ordinary Bookseller today, I'm sure he'd tell you anything Green is good for business. But we'll wait til the parade's gone by, and ask him again. Twenty years, however, is long enough. By now, Mr Ordinary has to be saying 'Well, you know, the women are beginning to come through. Women write quite a proportion of our sf, and they sell, too.' He isn't saying that. I am not surprised to hear that the survey also discovered an alarming proliferation of future war stories. The invisiblity of women, even in the microcosm of science fiction, has this kind of effect. I don't like to say this, it doesn't suit my argument (as you will see). But where there are veiled women—not powerless, mind: for we may safely assume that Mr Ordinary's denial of their existence has not made the many published and several highly successful female US sf writers he couldn't name, snuff out like candles or suddenly change sex—*where there are veiled women*, there torture, death and destruction will be highly visible activities, and human lives will not count for much.

Even so, does it matter? The broad church remains. Nobody's claiming that feminist science fiction doesn't exist, or even trying to stamp it out. It has its niche, alongside the psychic dragons of Fantasy (and picking up crumbs from that successful subgenre's readership). The women who want it look for it and find it. Anyone else who happens to pick up a Suzette Elgin or a Joanna Russ gets warned immediately by the cover and the blurb, and quickly puts it down again... Anyone who thinks this situation is satisfactory to feminists who read or write science fiction probably thinks Jesus Christ came to earth to found a new religion.

So what went wrong? Why didn't the world change? Of course the Big World did change, very much and rather fast. We suddenly had the great greed-is-good and words-mean-what-I-say-they-mean Eighties. You tell someone you're a feminist in Britain today, and you don't get the satisfaction of social martyrdom. She nods sincerely and assures you she's one too, but not the grubby old strident kind. Oh yes, I'm a feminist. I want my company car to be just as big and shiny as my boyfriend's. And we both have a wonderful relationship with our nanny, and the lovely working class woman who comes in to do the cleaning. Or if it's a man he'll say, Oh yes, same here. Absolutely. And so is my wife, who would be here tonight except that she's made a choice, which I totally respect, to give up her dead end job and become a fulltime wife and mother... Oh yes, we're all feminists now.

There's been plenty of this 'post-feminist' gibberish in the genre. Mr Ordinary may not be able to see them, but the racks are bursting with gorgeous tomboys scrabbling their way to the top in the man's world of starfighter command: all of them real, human women who want a man to be the brutal, pouting hunk nature intended him to be, and would spurn with disgust any sensitive wimp who wanted to change that image. There's plenty of cosy, confirming fiction about Moon City housewives, who hurry home from the weapons lab sincerely grateful to their husbands for allowing them to plug into work, and wouldn't dream of expecting a man to lift a finger around the living module... And they're all feminists. The characters are feminists, the writers are feminists, the editors are feminists, the marketing execs are feminists too. Naturally! There's no community on earth more stubbornly resistant to change, and none more brass-nerved and devious in denying their obdurate, innate and militant conservatism, than the writers of futuristic fiction. And that's only the women.

But all this is end-point consumerism, and there's not much harm in it. I can glean comfort from the thought that those who are content to write and read Moon City Housewife literature would be just as happy with *my* platitudes, if times should ever change; and just as convinced that things had 'always' been this way. No, the real disaster for feminism in sf has been in its apparent ideological successes.

We might call this success the rise of the dark-female-womb-good *vs* light-male-phallus-bad story. Essentially it is a simple reversal of pre-feminist sf ideology—except that the old boys' own adventures never dreamed of explaining why shiny rockets are Good Things and shadowy abysses are Bad Things. They didn't have to. Everybody sort of knew, in some dirty place deep inside: but it wasn't the kind of thing nice people said out loud. The new story has no such reticence. Its sole purpose in life is to juxtapose the home-loving warmly sexy dark females (we'll call them the dfwgs, for short) who are good with children, ace biotechnicians and recycle everything, with the paranoid rapist light-male-phallus-bads (or lmpbs), who live in steel packing cases, have no children and throw hamburger cartons about wherever they go. At least one of the nastiest of the lmpbs is a woman, to show that all this is not actually the criminal incitement to gender racism that it seems. There's nothing else but a plot line that throws its hands out innocently through some transparent yarn of the conflict between violence and non-violence (I love that line), as if to say: Make up your own mind, dear reader!

This not very original idea that simple biological determinacy rules the world and divides without appeal, on an axis of skin colour and gender, Good from Evil, the saved from the damned: now, where have I heard that one before? And yet, in spite (did I hear someone mutter *because*?) of its moral idiocy, this is the *only* version of feminism that has broken through, to permeate the genre-as-we-know-it.

Perhaps the posturing of feminist biological-determinacy fiction is a stage we have to go through. The Female Principle has to be promoted, the dark and the dirt has to be celebrated. Whereas with the best will in the world it is impossible to demote the Male Principle to parity of esteem without doing some pretty trenchant hacking at that overgrown beanstalk. But to celebrate the mythic female by rubbishing the mythic male is cathartic rather than constructive. Besides, the orgiastic birching of masculinity can safely be left to the experts. All those baby-boomer male sf novelists, the ones who grew up uncomfortably as writers in the feminist decade, adore the biological-determinacy New Man: the poor guy who knows he's a selfish, manipulative, emotionally illiterate monster—but, gee, he just can't help it! You'd think even the most devoted Girls Are Powerful promoter would become suspicious. These youngish men who write about how awful men are (augh! my soul in torment, I just raped another little old lady...), who people their novels with angelic sexy heroines and a supporting cast of irremediably bad, stupid males—they couldn't be *enjoying* themselves, could they? Could they not.

So much for the popular front. What about the dazzling intellectual rhetoric, that has been such a feature of feminist sf? Sarah Lefanu (in *The Chinks of the World Machine*) does an excellent job of cutting through the cant of gender nationalism and distinguishing the true, astringent medicine from daydreams, revenge fantasies and fifth columnist disinformation. But she identifies a deep and central difficulty: the story without an ending. That classic fall-of-patriarchy scenario, without which feminist sf would not exist, has nowhere to go. The worm turns, the villains are unmasked, the male dominated structures topple: end here, it sounds hopeful. It's not failure of nerve or talent that makes *The Female Man* barely fiction, or gave Atwood's *The Handmaid's Tale* its bewilderingly equivocal conclusion; or caused Suzy Charnas's rigorously intelligent fall-of-patriarchy trilogy to run to two volumes, and Monique Wittig's *Les Guérillères* to explode into babbling chaos. They're telling the truth. They're doing what science fiction is supposed to do, taking a proposition from their parent culture (Feminism, this time, rather than Physics and Gadgetry) and running with it, far as they can go... right up against the walls of the world. Anyone who takes the either/or, light/dark, order/chaos dichotomy that feminism has embraced really, really seriously will end up in the same place, falling over the brink into the utter void where there are no more stories. How can we tell a story, in the male-ordered oppressive medium of words?

Sf novelists of all persuasions are frequently so strapped for a way out of the book that they have to wheel on the end of the universe. In fact this is alluring stuff, now I come to think about it. Here we are, feminists sf writers, re-evaluating, for our own selfish reasons, the great metaphor of light (the Light of male reason and aspiration; the Dark of female 'instinct' and inertia) that's so integral to human thought. Right alongside, there's a paradigmatic shift going on that has cosmologists wrestling with sudden thoughts about the enormous preponderance of *dark matter* in a universe that has always been described solely in terms of light. What a weird coincidence! What is happening here? Is some vast Someone/ Something trying to communicate with us through our political reasoning? Already I seem to see before me the last thirty pages, *written in italics of course*, of a blockbusting radical-feminist end of the universe epic, like Greg Bear only more cosmic.

But if that epic could be written, without the whole thing dissolving, by its own logic, into too-smart-by-half Lacanoiserie, it wouldn't tell us anything new. What all the variants of this story, intellectual and dopey, have in common is that they do not quarrel with the tenets of patriarchy. The celebration of the Female Principle leaves the sex-roles exactly as we know them so well. It says to the men: 'Yes, we agree! You are so right! We own the dark secrets, the deeps, the parts consciousness doesn't see. Our place is in the home, the nursery, the kitchen, the mystic silence of our hearts...' No wonder the baby-boomer boys are so relieved. For a moment there, it almost looked as if a home-working writer chap might have to learn how to use the washing machine.

No, the conflict between the wise, gentle mothers and their brutal idiot sons doesn't interest me much, no matter what planet is hosting the show. I already know how that fight ends: how it keeps on ending, over and over again. I do not want to get back to my womanly roots. Give me the future, any day. You can keep your Californian recycled Bronze Age Matriarchy. If I have to go and sit on a puddle in the outhouse for four days a month, as my only escape from domestic service, I don't see that it makes much difference whether this called 'being unclean' or 'fully experiencing my cosmic rhythms'. Cosmic, my mother-in-law. To paraphrase Jacques Derrida: deconstruction is a great game, but it's a sin to ignore the obvious.

I have a game which involves dividing science fiction writers into two... (pause for embarassed grin here). The members of my first group come in all shapes and sizes. Some of them are very big indeed. All of them know that no matter what happens there will always be war and romance, there will always be ordinary men and women with the same dreams and the same feelings and the same division of labour as we have ourselves. You can break the laws of physics any time, but human nature can never change, they say. I call them the Dinosaurs. I call my second group the Birds. Becoming a Bird isn't cheap (sorry). It could cost you your arms, your hands, your teeth, and a small mountain of awe-inspiring meat. But when it's a question of change or die, the Birds are an unsentimental lot. Racial pride is not their strong suit. They claim that they do not know what 'bird nature' is, or ever was...

The division is rhetorical of course, and couldn't be applied without rather gruesome effect. It describes a tension within the genre, and within almost any interesting sf novel you care to name. But feminist sf has somehow ended up, broadly speaking, with the Dinosaurs, wallowing in eternal verities, when it should soaring, however improbably, with the Birds. My heckler at the Arthur C. Clarke ceremony was at least half right when she said science is about linear and objective experiments, and the scientists were at least half wrong when they pronounced all that business dead and done for. The new science of chaos, they tell me, is about order within disorder. And from what they tell me, its riotous forms are discovered by the methodical iteration of simple mathematical formulae, carried out by vastly swift and complex number-crunching machines, which were constructed, designed and made possible by old fashioned applied science skills, theories and research. Scientific method may be a con trick when viewed *sub specie aeternitas*. But here, where we live, it has been a highly successful form of conjuring, and its successes will probably continue to amaze however the philosophical underpinnings are swopped around.

Feminist science fiction has to abandon its GUTs, and its either/or stance, if it is to escape from the ghetto. It has to combine that famous 'strident' relentless insistence on a certain programme with stories that are diverse, readable and fun. Be needed by the consumers: that's always been the best propaganda. If the establishment won't listen to your blistering new insights on the nature of reality, there's nothing much you can do about that but accept your martyrdom or else stomp away in a sulk, muttering *eppur si muove*. But the smart navigational tables, though they may not look so grand, will change the world.

People can't go on writing savage polemical tracts on the same subject forever; or reading them. You get burn-out, you get compassion fatigue even in self-pity. Ho hum, not more sewer-feminists living on rat-turds. Not more captive breeders with their arms and legs cut off, wombs pumping out alternate batches of fanged boy-babies and bioplastic assault rifles... When some friend who reads no science fiction starts to tell you how reading *The Handmaid's Tale* changed her life, you feel your eyes glaze over... It is too easy for a privileged woman of the White North to forget that 'this sort of stuff' is not actually fiction at all. That pumping womb is real. She lives in all those 'low intensity' war-zones you hear about occasionally on the news: churning out sons to fuel the armies, churning out children who will die of starvation before they can walk. Women really are suffering, girl babies and girl foetuses really are being exterminated by the millions. It seems quite likely that the planet really is dying, come to that. And if the living world does die—not where we live, of course, or in our time, but soon, quite soon—it certainly looks as if the learned passivity of women who could have changed things, or at least fought for change, will be implicated in the murder, guilty right alongside the misdeeds of human testosterone.

There are signs, in spite of the femme-fatale clichés of twenty-first-century *film noir*, that the cyberpunk genre has absorbed a *tinge* of feminism—if only for the sake of the exotic sex. But I'm beginning to fear that women in cyberpunk (a small but estimable cadre) have decided to 'take feminism for granted': in other words, let's pretend there isn't a problem. Look, we're allowed to have strong female characters. Don't start nagging about political perspective. Don't rock the boat! Well, *don't rock the boat* doesn't work. It never works. Remember, Mr Ordinary doesn't need the slightest encouragment to assume that the Pat in Cadigan is short for Patrick. That's his default position. It takes effort, overt, straightforward statement of intent, to make yourself visible as a feminist writer. And it takes a lot of devious skill to stay visible: to be a woman who isn't one of the boys, or a Moon City housewife, or an Organically Grown Cosmic Vegetable, but who is still on the stacks.

In the grim circumstances faced by most of the women in the world today, it seems a crying shame if the best feminism can offer is either wise compliance with the rules of the boys' club, or a vision of the glorious abyss. It must be possible to propose a future or, better, many diverse futures, where testosterone drives to Have A Bigger One and Go Off With A Bang, and so forth, are substantially demoted... (I said demoted, mind. Not denigrated, or denied. Cut down to size, maybe. Not cut off. Many men have difficulty in hearing this proposal clearly.)

And then we must tell the story of how to get there from here.

3: Dreamer: An Exercise in Extrapolation 1989–2019*

> In the days of Jesus of Nazareth, there were no motor cars. I still walk, however, sometimes...   (Joanna Russ)

As a science fiction writer it is my business to create imaginary pictures of different times and different worlds. This is common knowledge. What's less well recognised is that the imagination of any science fiction writer feeds on the past as much as on the future. 'Those who refuse to learn from History will be condemned to repeat it' (George Santayana): this is the aphorism on which much 'scientific' fiction is based, the writers being reasonably sure that the human race will never learn... No serious sf writer ever simply invents a future-world out of a vacuum. The effort involved, the sheer mass of interlocking detail required, would make that project highly uneconomic in terms of work hours and creative effort. Less than serious writers don't trouble themselves to invent anything much, and their year 2525 differs not at all from 198X in social mores, in lifestyle technology, in cultural and political infrastructure; except that in this relabelled present-day the galaxy has been colonised, immortality is available to all, and aliens of bizarre shapes and sizes mingle with the tourists on Oxford Street. Other writers, and I count myself among them, believe that technological change affects every aspect of people's lives, slowly in detail but sometimes in sudden leaps so dramatic that the passing generation can hardly recognise a world that is to their children as normal as if its gadgets and innovations had been there forever.

It should be noted that quantative change may be for the worse as well as for the better. Stocks in imaginary futures, as the standard warning goes, can go down as well as up. One short answer to the question 'What will leisure be like in the year 2020?' might be: there won't be any. We'll have bombed ourselves back into the stone age, and the rare pleasure of falling asleep with a full stomach will be the height of human entertainment experience.

But whenever the whole human environment has to be made over in

---

* A study on possible developments in leisure activity, over the next thirty Years, prepared for a British Telecom think-tank project organised by Brian Stableford in 1988.

order to present an 'accurate' picture of the future, the job will be quite impossible without some extremely trenchant short-cutting. This is where studying the future and studying the past become one. The best place to look for guidance as to the effects of technological and cultural change is in this endlessly bountiful museum of exactly such processes. Many sf writers spend a great deal of their research time hunting for templates in history, suitable blanks that can be customised to a particular story's specifications. How is this done? A clear example of the technique can be found in a currently popular theme in American future-plotting: the notion that at some time in the near future the USA will be forced, or inveigled, or will fall helplessly, into a state of open war with one or more of the unstable nation states of Central America. What will this war be like? It will probably be like some other war fought by United States citizens. It will not be a war of independence, nor a civil war; nor will the US army be a partner in a huge alliance involved in a global conflict. It will be a small war, it will be a jungle war, it will be a messy war, in which many of the combatants will be uncertain of their moral stance and the US will be forced into a defensive position with regard to world opinion... The conclusion is obvious, and a cursory examination of eighties American sf will show that this imaginary war in America's near future (cf. Lucius Shephard, *Life During Wartime*; Lewis Shiner, *Deserted Cities of the Heart*) has to be a replay of Vietnam.

Let's take another case, in which the relationship between past and future is not quite so close and incestuous. We will suppose, for this fiction, that there has been Nuclear War in Europe, and as a result a violent revulsion of feeling over the whole continent. Europeans feel the way the Japanese felt in the decades after the Second World War. They don't want to see, they don't want to hear, they don't want to think about any kind of advanced weaponry. The standing army has become anathema, the whole machinery of mechanised combat is dismantled. But the nations of Europe are not islands, and probably less inclined to trust in their neighbours' peaceful intentions than ever. A hundred years after the First World War, the result is a patchwork existence of raids and counter raids, as each recovering community grows strong enough to grab whatever small surplus it sees within reach; but never strong enough to survive without this banditry. We see town and village and street militias, as in Mediaeval England or Hellenic Greece. The 'leisure pursuits' of the able bodied take the form of a compulsory hour or two at the butts every evening. Track and field and competitive team sports have recovered their original meaning. Our story might go something like this—a group of visionaries has a brilliant idea: why not institute a periodic truce, and during that time let the champions of the various communities try each others' strength, to establish at the least a relatively bloodless pecking order, as to who must give tribute to whom. (Due to the dislocations of their history the post-holocaust visionaries are unaware that this scheme has been tried before.) Let the training for war stand in for war itself! The irony of the readers' better knowledge is an important feature of the 'historical template' method. From our particular viewpoint this brave attempt to relight the Olympic flame will have a special poignancy. And then again, it might just work this time...

In the project under consideration, where the value of elapsed time is conveniently given as 'thirty years', the first question is: what kind of thirty years? If I wanted to write about the immediate aftermath of a nuclear war, I would probably find the recorded (and tellingly unrecorded) effects of the Black Death illuminating. Since I'm concerned with leisure activities, that period won't be much use to me. I will need a ready grasp of minute social and cultural details, which means that I can narrow the field a great deal. Realistically speaking, I had better stay close to my own time and cultural milieu.

The most easily available and familiar historical world that an sf writer can hope to cannibalise and customise into a convincing future is the present day. At first sight this seems a promising place to start. The period from 1958 to 1988 has been quite unusually peaceful for those areas (the developed world) where technologically-assisted leisure activities form an important part of the majority of the people's lives—and surely, if a period as short as thirty years is to produce significant developments in the way most people use their spare time, there must be peace, and there must be plenty. Indeed, technological developments with mass leisure applications in the last thirty years have been so many and so striking: television, colour television, video recorders, video discs, satellite tv, global tv shows; transistors, microchips, home computers, computer games; from the massive reel to reel tape decks of the fifties to personal stereos, compact discs and sound systems so sophisticated that even British Rail announcers have become intelligible. Considering all these miracles, the most striking feature of the last thirty years is not the rate of change, but the level of continuity. With all these exciting developments, each one of them holding behind it a story of dazzling scientific discovery and achievement on which an sf writer could base a whole novel, how much is there that we do now that we couldn't do then? What do you do when you're not working, eating or sleeping?

Read books
Watch television
Watch videos/home movies *

Walk in the country/by the sea
Listen to music
Make music
Write letters
Take photographs
Make a home video (movie) *
Play card games/board games
Converse
Make love
Visit: an art gallery; a museum
 Attend: a rock gig/concert; a classical concert, the theatre; cinema;
    opera; the gym *
Watch team sports
Go dancing
Go swimming
Eat out
Gardening
Shopping
Foreign travel *
Play computer games **
General knowledge quiz *

This is a partial, arbitrary and personal list of the leisure activities that came most readily to my mind in 1988 (not necessarily in order of preference). A double star indicates an activity that would have been technically (that is, completely) unavailable to 'me' in 1958; a single star those activities which a person of similar age and background to myself would have been unlikely to enjoy in 1958. It may be seen, and this is obviously generally true, though the evidence I cite here is purely anecdotal, that the continuities by far outnumber the innovations. The points of change seem immense in detail, the cumulative effect is almost stasis. In Spielberg's film *Back to the Future* the boy from the 1980s is remarkably at home in the world which his parents knew as teenagers. And though the transition would not have been so comfortable for an English child—refrigerators and tvs were not yet commonplace in suburban England in 1958—this is still a telling image. Domestic technology, the world of comforts and conveniences with which we are concerned, was clumsier and cruder thirty years ago, but it was all of it already in place. For the scientist, amazing and fundamental shifts have occured. From the consumers' point of view, these developments are seen as refinement, not change.

But this is only one possible model. Many people see this continous present, dating from the 1950s (modern times) as a period that's coming to an end. A generation brought up by Victorians and Edwardians grew to maturity in 'the space age', but never accepted it. It is in childhood that people decide what is 'normal' and what is 'strange'. Children who were born with television will not be able to 'switch it off', as their parents are always telling them they should. 'Switch it off' is advice which sees the eye in the corner of the room or the music coming out of the speakers as extra: a toy or a tool, an addition to normal life, not part of it. To the generation that has never been without it, television doesn't seem like that at all. The same shift in perception must apply to other 'modern miracles' but hasn't yet (not even yet) moved into the foreground of our world. It could well be that an illusion of continuity is about to be swept away, as the last of the Victorian/Edwardian mind-set finally vanishes over the cultural horizon. Instead of taking the years 1958–88 for my model, maybe I should be looking at 1898–1928. A boy or girl—especially a girl—subjected to Spielberg's practical joke over that generation gap would find herself in a very awkward situation. Far from blending in with the local community, she couldn't walk down the suburban street without raising an outcry. And being arrested for public indecency would be only the beginning of her troubles.

Bearing in mind, then, that the near future I am going to try and build from some judicious fixing and twitching of my model might be a strange and startling place, what else can I learn from my hindsight-powered extrapolation? I can note that the instantly obvious exceptions to the general rule of continuity don't seem to be directly linked with technology. In 1958, unless I was seriously involved in amateur team sport or athletics, it would have been very unlikely indeed for me to have spent leisure time working out at a gym. Where did the Eighties cult of muscle tone spring from? Let us say it is a symptom of what Tom Wolfe labelled 'the me generation': the self-obsession of the well-fed. When you assume you are going to live long, and the transcendental comfort of an afterlife has receded; when you are accustomed to well designed and reliable machinery around you, what better use for your spare cash than to improve and 'customise' your most intimate piece of domestic machinery…? Could this development have been forseen thirty years ago? And what will come next? What new attitude to life will will take over from self-obsession?

Another leisure activity which I was tempted to star as unlikely in 1958 was 'shopping'. I felt the element of continuity was too strong to allow this, but in the 1950s consumerism was a means to an end, whereas for us it has become an end in itself. For the family of the 1950s to buy a fridge was to acquire a domestic convenience, and a status symbol. For the family of the 1980s a visit to the consumer-durable warehouse is a pleasure in itself. Shopping is entertainment, a more popular family outing than a walk in the park; probably as much fun as going to the zoo. Then again, advertising in the Fifties was a way to make people buy things, a means to an end. The advertising of the Eighties is something different in kind. It is in the process of becoming—some would say has already become—an art form. Consumers are asked quite directly, and respond consciously and deliberately to the invitation, to patronise the company that has paid for the most elegant, witty, alluring or touching mini-drama or image. And then again: stocks in imaginary futures can go down as well as up. Thirty years ago a holiday abroad was still the leisure of the bourgeois. An airline ticket was for the newly affluent masses a temporary pass into another class: a visit to a calm urbane world of small luxuries and obsequious service. In the 1980s mass market civil aviation is not like that. By no means! There's no continuity of refinement and expansion here, instead we see a leisure industry that is almost collapsing, bursting at the seams.

When we all have televisions, no one will go to the cinema. When we can all travel by air, no one will ever be stuck in a traffic jam. When you can pick out a story from the video-library and 'read' it on a screen, there will be be no more books. Leaving aside the arrogant 'we' of the developed nations, the past thirty years have demolished these futuristic extrapolations of the 1950s. Even science fiction writers now accept that the clear and simple future-world that we used to know, of the featureless plastic corridors, the silver wigs and the protein pills for breakfast, will be a long time coming. And yet in spite of the setbacks and disappointments, in spite of the stubborn resistance to change that is such a feature of any human society, it is still clear that something extraordinary has happened to the concept of 'Leisure' over the last thirty years: so that as well as providing a historical template, those years provide genuine first class data about the growth of a phenomenon never previously observed. No, not even in the high-surplus empires of the ancient world. The masses of the Roman Empire were entertained en masse, as in the present (already obsolete) model of a tv audience. They also, no doubt, entertained themselves on a smaller scale by music making, dance, storytelling, games of skill and chance, the same activities that have been available in one form or another since the dawn of humanity. Something rather different happens, or can happen, now: one might call it mass audience participation. The world of global telethons and phone-in chat-shows begins to blur the difference between the active and the passive voice in fascinating ways.

But to return to the phenomenon. My outdated Chambers dictionary (1972) defines the word 'leisure' as an 'old fashioned or American term for time free from employment'. The runaway success of an 'old-fashioned American term' is hardly surprising. If leisure only becomes a notable part of life in times of peace and plenty, no nation on earth has been so bountifully supplied with both over the past hundred years; if ever. But leisure has not only mushroomed in significance, it has acquired a new meaning. In the not too distant past only aristocrats had time to spend—like money—on self indulgence. In the age—broadly speaking—of capitalism, each human cog in the machine was either producing or consuming; or spinning idly in a void. In the age of late consumerism, anyone engaged in a leisure pursuit is an active economic unit locked into the vital processes (yes, even if she's just taking a walk in the country).

So what will happen in the next thirty years, according to my best model? There will be major technological developments, which will be perceived by consumers as minor qualitative improvements. Already, the pursuit of leisure has changed its status, and sheer play, as an end in itself, has been revalued as a part of adult life. Watching television or listening to the radio can be (already) an active experience, different in kind from (for instance) the experience of a conventional theatregoer. It may be that mass participation—entertainment as the spiritual element in our lives—has (already) returned, unrecognised, to the spectrum of normal human life, after millennia. (It is not possible to step into the same river twice. History repeats itself, but never exactly. The ancient audiences believed their presence was a participation in the ritual. The modern global audience is actually a part of the performance.) And finally, the consumer is not passive. The masses do not always sit still and have things sold to them. They may subvert, convert, appropriate, enjoy the very means used to manipulate their tastes and their purchasing power.

Only one more component needs to be slotted in before the extrapolation is up and running. I need a plot-device. I need some pivotal leisure development to use as a hook on which to hang my picture of the whole play-experience of citizen 2020. I have no difficulty in identifying a model for this hook. If anyone is looking for indicators of what can happen in the world of leisure in thirty years, the phenomenon of Rock and Roll has to be an obvious subject. In 1958 rock music was a bad habit, a passing phase; or an easy way to make a fortune out of youngsters with more talent, or more pocket money, than sense. To say that in 1988 this passing phase has become the proverbial 'multi-million dollar industry' is not enough. Fostered and shaped by the parallel development of sound reproduction and communications technology, 'Rock and Roll' has grown over thirty years into a global language, perhaps the only language that has kept pace with the shrinking world. The American cartoonist Gary Trudeau in Doonesbury records the (fictional) visit of a rock star to a refugee camp in the Sudan. He has the star converse, through an interpreter, with an emaciated child, and wryly subverts our expectations. The starving child does not want to talk about food. He wants to discuss musical trends. The cartoonist is making a point about human dignity: that even the victims of famine prefer to be treated as people, not dumb objects of pity. But the metaphor he uses for the African boy's humanity, and for his inalienable right to claim connection with the rest of the world, is the noisy, childish, passing phase of a generation ago.

The success of rock music can be compared with the success of the moving picture industry in the immediately previous decades. But cinema, like photography and unlike television, obstinately remains a classical art form. Rock music has evolved—perhaps only marginally, but the change is real—from the classical model. The line between audience and performer is far less easily drawn. Successful performers are not necessarily the passive employees of their financial backers. Importantly, sound reproduction technology has developed in such a way that rather than moving further out of ordinary people's reach, 'professional' technical capability (though not, of course, the talent or drudgery required to use it well) becomes steadily more widely available. Relativism creeps in: nothing is fixed, the centre can be anywhere.

I do not intend to follow the fortunes of the electric guitar and the sampler keyboard, through the next generation. To me, as an inveterate watcher of trends, the signs are that Rock and Roll has become what it is going to be, it has reached maturity. Further metamorphoses are not to be looked for. Buddy Holly hits will still be in the repertoire in 2020, just as no doubt Shakespeare will still be playing at the theatres. But something that is here already, a mouse among the dinosaurs, and which has a good chance of a fruitful relationship with likely new technology... something of that kind might well provide a clue, a magic key to unlock the cypher of the future.

Now read on...

Dreamer

Mary wakes without an alarm, rolls over, tugs the electrode from her temple and begins instantly to record on her bedside keyboard. She prefers the keyboard, she finds the sound of her own voice irritating and distracting first thing in the morning. She is already at work, here in her bedroom: she is recording her dreams. The lead to which the electrode is attached trails over her pillow, Mary's cat begins to play with it. The purpose of this device is to respond to a change in electroencephalic activity that means dreaming has begun, by transmitting a tiny and carefully tailored electrical impulse to Mary's sleeping brain: dreaming, she then 'hears' a sound that alerts her to the fact that this is not reality. It doesn't work very well. Frequently Mary's brain/mind subverts the information. She dreams that she thinks she's dreaming... However, lucid dreams are not—in Mary's opinion—any better for her purposes than the other kind, just different.

She records the dream in short disjointed paragraphs, draws down a scribble sheet for herself on which to make notes for the graphics program. Her memory has been trained (by biofeedback techniques, but she no longer needs the apparatus) to retain and verbalise the ephemeral richness of a dreamscape for long enough to get it all down without losing that quality she and her colleagues call 'the bloom'. Once satisfied that she has enough material to work on (material that will have to be processed considerably before the team knows whether this one is worth money) she gets up off the floor, pulls the tag on the side of her bag-bed; and the cat dances around the room, chasing and fleeing from the shrinking balloon as it ricochets from wall to wall. This is a morning ritual. Cats need to play and Mary is always trying to make up for her eccentric habit of going out to work all day.

Mary doesn't use a quilt, and the pillow's part of the bed. Why make life more complicated? If the house-basic heating cuts out for some reason, she can always crawl inside her bag. One wall of the room is a giant wafer-thin dedicated screen: an expensive piece of interior décor but Mary can get trade rates. It plays scenes from a strange, shadowed, magical landscape, floating, rising, banking as if watched by an eagle's eyes. It's a clip from a dream of hers of ten years ago. There is little other furniture. Mary's tastes were formed by the minimalist fashions of the pre-millennium: she'd probably still be sleeping on a futon if they were more practical to keep clean. She's in her mid-sixties now. Soon she's going to have to stop colouring her hair and face up to middle age. She stuffs the soft crumpled mass of bedding into the laundry chute, and goes over to her bathroom closet.

She dresses in cerise and blue (to match her hair), choosing the day's message to suit the game she's playing in at the moment. The people who know will smile: the back of her suit jacket says If YOU CAN'T BEAT THEM, JOIN THEM...

Mary lives in a single room in a family support household. The nucleus of this atomic family comprises a young couple, Kathryn (Kaz) and Jean-Luc (Jon), and their two small children. There are eight roomers altogether: two of the others able-bodied adults like Mary herself, an elderly woman who is bedridden; three adolescents and an LLR forty-year old man (Limited Learning Potential: Mary used to call such people 'mentally handicapped')—all in need of some sheltering. Mary is a partner in a small business. It would be more natural for her to live with her colleagues at their business address; but she likes to get away and be by herself. When cannibalising your subconscious is your business, privacy becomes a special kind of luxury.

In the communal kitchen Mary finds herself alone. It is her day off as far as family duties are concerned. It was somebody else's turn to share with Jon and Kaz the dawn waking of little children and the very old, and to chivvy more-or-less delinquent teenagers off to the taskforce or the training centre. Not quite alone: through the tv screen on the wall she can see and hear two very real people having a bitter and intimate argument. They seem to be a married couple, they are speaking the kind of dog-franglais which is the current smart slang of young-executive England. Mary grimaces and reflexively glances up at the ceiling: sees the red light, glares around for the remote which is, as always, invisible/lost/strayed; and swiftly moves to thumb one of the pads on the tv frame from COM-MUN to COMMER. Kaz and Jon are committed subscribers to communal television—also known as 'feedbacksoap'. Ordinary commercial soap-opera hasn't used professional actors for years, but at least those exhibitionists (Mary's judgement) who clamour and pack the waiting lists for that icky kind of fame know when they're on show. COMMUN is different: unedited, uncosmeticised, raw life. Mary is not convinced by the idea. If it is so good for you to spy on your neighbours' private lives, she reasons, while they spy in return on you, why not simply knock a hole in the wall between your bedroom and the folks next door? And yet, at various times since that COMMUN-option tv appeared on the kitchen wall, she has felt herself caught in the human web, felt some echo of what (Jon insists) can be a genuinely mystical experience. You never know who you are watching, or where the scene is being played (though of course people try to find out). You never see—except by rare chance—anything more than a disjointed fragment of the other lives. The random, unidentified sampling is 'untouched by human hand' as the old saying goes, from camera to screen. That's the only way this kind of transmission could be legal. Any other model would be open to all sorts of abuses, in this averagely wicked world of the twenty-first century. But the randomness is also what makes it sacred, an unlabelled encounter with common humanity. Jon and Kaz, Mary reflects, will probably tire of COMMUN and trade in the set while she is still deciding whether to be fascinated or repulsed: and she'll probably miss it when it's not there any more.

On commercial television there is a taped interview with the Prime Minister (digitised disc storage, really; but the formative expressions linger on, like 'turning on' the lights, which made no sense for two generations, until dimmer switches arrived). She is saying, briskly and seriously: 'It isn't enough just to enjoy life yourself. It never can be enough. A pleasure not shared is a pleasure halved…' The fax machine on the household's office desk by the breakfast bar chatters into life. It is delivering the family's daily paper, a popular tabloid, which arrives in the tray not only folded but beautifully bound, like a young treatise. (It's a Japanese machine.) Even though she knows it's all recycled material Mary is irritated by this performance. Like most of her generation she finds 'wasteful' consumption distasteful. She reads the headline upside down: PM/TV: BIG DUMP ON SOLIPSISM... and beneath, the words that she has just heard. In print, stripped of the Prime Minister's excellent video-manner, the honest personal words appear both glib and sanctimonious. Mary reflects, as she eats her toast, on the nature of truth; and on the mysterious indestructibility of the daily press.

The family home is one of six such units occupying the shell of a defunct primary school near to the centre of Brighton. Mary thinks the government which sold off so many old state schools was absurdly short sighted: no government ever seems able to grasp the fact that demographic curves rise as well as fall. But who knows, if the trend towards workplace-education continues, maybe there will be no more giant state schools at all in a generation or so. The asphalt playground has been torn up, the big red building is surrounded by lawns and stands of young trees. Kaz and Jon think it's a wonderful old place, but to Mary the gutted and remodelled halls smell faintly of chalk and sour milk: the lawns are haunted by ball game markings and yelling, scurrying little girls and boys.

On the way out she goes to visit her rubber tree. It stands in a sheath of permeable plastic film. When it grows a bit bigger, it should be hardy enough to withstand the British climate on its own, if the engineering has worked properly. She'll cut the bark and put a little cup there. She is part of a project run by New Scientist (a highly popular commercial tv channel), she's one of thousands all over Europe who have joined in this experiment in exploitable diversity—'rainforest agro-eclectics'—the newest idea in ecological regeneration. Meanwhile the low white-grey sky and the bitter chill of this October day might remind her how badly a new carbon sink is needed: already the long dismal 'greenhouse winter' of twenty-first-century UK is setting in. But at least she knows she's doing what one person can.

Mary waits on the corner for her bus. She could afford to run a car, though the cost of so doing has rocketed since she was a young woman: in taxes, tolls, and the price of relatively environment-friendly fuel. But she's one of the 37% (and rising) of executive class respondents who consider private vehicles antisocial. There's no need to be foey about it (a popular 'most-modern' term, from the acronym Friends of the Earth. It has come to mean, more or less, 'glib and sanctimonious'. A society may be known by its terms of abuse: what you deride is what you are (cf. 'yuppie').) If she wants to go on a motoring holiday she can hire a car. But for everyday, she'd rather have clear streets and clean air. Mary's world is a world of high expectations. She wants only the best for herself; for everyone: and she's always been prepared to pay a little more for high quality.

'Executive' no longer means exactly what it did, by the way. There are the rich (who knows them?). And the poor (who are always with us). And there are us—BCDE—the masses... But working class would not be the right term: we are the executives, the people who do things.

Mary deplores the tendency of the bus queue to spread over the pavement, folding its arms and looking nonchalant while all the time ready to pounce and elbow and swoop with no regard for fair play. Mary has not seen a decent queue, even here in the land of queues, for maybe thirty years. The trouble with universal flexitime—which the young people don't even know is 'flexitime' any more—is that there is no way to avoid the rush hour. It's like living on a space-station these days, always someone's breakfast time, always someone's rowdy night out: and you can bet when you feel most like Monday morning, you'll be forced to share your ride to work with a roaring gang in the middle of their Friday night. The days of the week, they used to have such distinct personalities: Saturday shopping, Sunday stay in bed. There ought to be a preservation society...

(In fact, a good many people go to church on Sunday, through the screen at least. And on other days. Nor is Christianity losing out, as was once feared, to the (other) eastern religions of the UK. But Mary is in the wrong age band to be tuned in to that particular sign of these times.)

A work-gang of convicts comes around the corner of the street, followed by their escorting officer, a solemn looking middle-aged black man. The convicts are on foot, heads hanging, wearing vivid orange overalls, carrying street cleaning tools. They walk as if weighed down by physical chains. They might as well be: they're wearing 'dog collars'. They have to be careful how they move. Anything that registers too much like violence on the monitors at the local community-crime centre will automatically earn the culprit a painful shock. It is awful, it is degrading: Mary averts her eyes. A horrifying proportion of young men will spend some of their time this way, if present sentencing trends continue. What's the answer, wonders Mary. This can't be right, but what's the alternative? Another war? We haven't had a war in Europe for nearly ninety years, and we still haven't worked out what the average rowdy young bloke can do instead of die...

Then her bus comes. It's called The Flying Scotsman, its paint job is the old BR livery, customised with go-faster thistles. The Scotsman's route is not ideal, she has to walk at the other end, but the thistles are so fine they're worth the fare in themselves. Mary—being in entertainment herself—believes in small businesses patronising the arts. Besides, his co-op donates 3% of their earnings to a charity Mary favours. Large or small, every sort of business donates. It is practically impossible to sell anything to the masses of 2020 without incorporating (let us be realistic) at the least a ritual 1% to charity into your prices. But three is more than lip-service.

She sits on the bus, beside a fat woman in a headscarf and a brown raincoat, takes out her keyboard and slips her watchpac into the pocket. She looks at the dream again. It's such a simple idea, selling dreams. In a kind of way fiction writers, storytellers have been doing it forever. But what Mary and her colleagues do is innovation-industry: it's a most-modern phenomenon. It is the new, cheap mega-memory that makes the kind of graphics you need economically available to a small business, and this will never be big business. It is really very slight: a notion, a gift-product. But that's ideal in 2020. Mary and her colleagues don't want to overheat the economy, they just want to make a satisfying, pleasant living. DREAMERS INC (they were lucky to be in time to snap up that name) builds from the raw record of one of those mysterious journeys, using the most sophisticated computer techniques, to create a short video—each one as rich and arbitrary and compelling as a dream is to the dreamer. Each model is unique, and the print run is genuinely limited. They don't do horror. They don't do porn. (Elements of both creep in, but the partners rely on their own good taste to set the parameters that are right for their customers...) You can have a wallsize version, you can have a dream to keep in your pocket. DREAMERS INC do the graphics and the smaller sizes, they contract out the wall screens. Mary is thinking about the new Korean stuff, a kind of electrolytic paint that can receive pictures... they're calling it 'Aeriel'. It's going to be very expensive for the first few months, but DREAMERS INC ought to be in there from the start. Dreams on your nail varnish?

Mary imagines the eventual arrival of that science-fiction technology which will actually record dreams straight from the sleeping mind onto disc: live music. What would she do then? She would be like a star of the silent screen, in fear and trembling before the soundtrack's pitiless verdict. Would she survive? Who knows. Does it take a special talent? Some people claim (Mary is always meeting them at parties, and very boring it is too) that they never dream at all. Or dream in 'black and white', which is an even more bizarre idea. It takes someone who enjoys dreaming... but in today's world, isn't that what talent means? If you want to do it, if you enjoy doing it, you can usually find a machine to fill in whatever you lack... In a Sponsored Resource Centre, if you can't afford to buy it, Mary adds guiltily to her smug reflection. DREAMERS INC donates, of course, and pays the voluntary part of its tax bill religiously. They all believe in 'giving back'.

The fat woman sighs and rustles the pages of her tabloid. It is the same as the one they take in Mary's house but in a copy-shop version, blurry tenth grade rag paper and no fancy binding. Mary is itchily conscious of the woman's poverty. One of the problems of using public transport on principle is that you have to share it with those who have no alternative. Only the very poor are overweight these days. She feels embarrassed, it's like sitting next to someone in a wheelchair—but that one wouldn't bother Mary, because (it's like the rubber tree) she knows she's doing her 'what-one-can' at home. She doesn't know what to do about world poverty at all. The sense of it all being your concern, the feeling that there must always be something you can do about any problem, however large and however diffuse: this state of mind is the bane of Mary's life. It is the necessary obverse of the pleasure principle, that keynote of most-modern experience. It is only their own insecurity which makes it possible for the rich to enjoy the sight of beggars at their gates. When insecurity is gone... The Prime Minister may have been glib, but she was right. A pleasure not-shared is a pleasure halved.

Some things do change. Thirty years ago someone like this fat woman would have had no idea what 'solipsism' meant, most likely. That's mass accessible culture for you.

Thirty years ago, Mary thought World Poverty was something that happened in the Sudan. She would have had to find a different term for what ails the fat woman. But television, remorseless television, goes on joining things up and breaking things down. Or maybe Mary has grown up a little since then. She shuts the keyboard (can't tell: it feels good, but have to see what the team thinks...); and stares ahead of her.

The Scotsman's bulkhead screen is running a short and boring loop of cheap advertisements. Mary stares at it vaguely. Suddenly, in the corner of the screen, a hand appears. It pulls up the corner of the advert and peels it back. Black screen: a slow lightning tree in vivid pink with electric white edges. A silly voice squeaks: CITIZEN ALERT! CITIZEN ALERT! Someone up the bus groans theatrically, wearily: who can tell how many of the passengers he speaks for? Or if he's faking. Mary grins. Black screen clears. There is now a cat. Its head dips and rises, dips and rises over a blue saucer laden with brown stuff (the definition is really awful): a cat eating its breakfast. Mary is wondering what this can possibly mean, and what she's supposed to do about it, when it dawns on her—unbelieving—that she knows that cat! Pov moves back. The cat, the kitchen, the woman eating toast at the breakfast bar. But I switched the COMMUN off! yells Mary indignantly. Yells it silently, because she is paralysed with amazement. That is herself!—hollow cheeked and sunken eyed: she always looks like a drug addict on video. The little hand points. Jabs at the junkie-woman's head. The silly voice cackles inanely... And then the advert comes back, and the bus drives on, rumble rumble rumble of the sedate electric engine. Mary sits in place with her whole body zinging.

I have been activated!

A Cast Of Thousands

It is as if someone, brushing by her in a crowd, has slyly pricked a dose of some hallucinogenic drug into her arm. The whole world has changed: not even the sighs of the fat woman mean the same as they did a moment ago. The first thing she has to do is get off this bus. She edges past the fat woman, moves casually up to the front. As she stands there waiting for the doors to open a man in the seat behind the driver gets up, folding his paper.

'Excuse me, madam. May I see your identification?' When she doesn't respond he gestures impatiently, his eyes cold as chips of glass. 'Your plastic, please.'

Mary isn't even tempted to laugh, this is deadly serious. She tries to keep her cool but she's still in shock and her eyes betray her: desperately scanning the passengers for any sign of sympathy. Now everybody knows and they're all looking away, or staring out of the window, or smiling nervously. The Flying Scotsman rumbles to a halt and the man in the dark overcoat looks almost sorry for Mary but he's not going to have any mercy. He reaches his hand inside his coat. Mary spins around and flings herself desperately at the closed door: and at the last moment her friend the driver relents, because the door opens and she falls out into the street, scrambles to her feet and starts to run. She has lived in this town for forty years but the Scotsman's route is eccentric and she doesn't know this part at all. The houses are old and shabby: dirty windows double-glazed against pre-millennial traffic noise, but the wide road is quiet now. Mary jogs along it to the forecourt of a garage, which seems to be doing more business as a garden centre. She darts into the toilet block, locks herself in a cubicle and sits on the seat gasping. Her keyboard is still on the bus: oh no, first casualty. And her wristpac was in the pocket, so she can't phone the office and tell them what's happened. The wristpac, phone and computer and radio in one, is the twenty-first-century replacement of the ubiquitous filofax. The name is deceptive, a decent model is still generally too bulky to be worn on the wrist. People tend to carry them, like the old Victorian turnip watch, in a vest pocket on a chain; or else in a keyboard pocket—which makes them easy prey. But that's the least of her worries, thinks Mary. (She doesn't yet realise the implications of this loss.) She knows that she's in trouble (that was obvious from the way the bus passenger behaved). But she doesn't know what kind, and she has no idea how she's supposed to get out of it.

The best primary strategy is to avoid open spaces, and avoid public places.

They might have found a way to track you through any camera, anywhere... How on earth did they catch me in my own kitchen, if not through the COMMUN link? That's not fair!

The little closed circuit eye of the public toilet looks down (for her protection). Mary, who still assumes the privacies of another age, looks up, and wails aloud! She dashes out the door, and through the greenery that surrounds a row of old fashioned automatic pumps she sees the forecourt cashier talking into a handset. It is like running through a minefield. She can't hope to spot all her active enemies, there are far too many people involved. But what makes matters worse is that anyone could turn her in. There's nothing in the rules that says spectators can't take part. There are very few rules, at all.

Mary needs to get to a copyshop. She cannot watch television and wait for an update, which is what her pursuers are doing. But in this morning's paper, which she didn't bother to read, she might find a clue to her predicament. She recognises the streets now, she's heading towards the railway station. There are shops and people coming up. Mary, without breaking stride, takes off her jacket and reverses it to plain blue with no message. With some bold and ingenious contortions she manages to slip off her black thermalknit vest from under her sweatshirt; and ties it like a scarf over her gaudy hair. A copyshop is now in sight, and nobody has fingered her collar. She is in luck. None of these passing citizens seems to know what's going on. Around the corner of the street comes the same gang of convicts that she saw earlier. They are moving with purpose, looking into faces... Mary's lips move, in an appalled whisper: he wouldn't! But you can't trust anyone when this thing happens to you, not even a serious responsible person like a community-crime officer. The subverted work-gang advances. Mary sets her teeth, risks her heart (which is in excellent condition for her age) and sprints madly for the copyshop. The automatic doors snick shut behind, and she is saved, for a moment. The convicts cannot follow her in here. Their monitored collars 'recognise' any attempt to pass an electronic barrier, like the seeing eye at a shop door, as an attempt to break out of custody. Mary gasps, 'Help me! Please!'

But the girl among the machines is alone in the shop, and not 'tuned in'. She cries, 'What's going on?', and sees the mass of convicts apparently about to smash their way in. She presses her security alarm and bravely, in the same movement, for the sake of limiting damage to her firm's property and to passers by, reaches for the switch that cuts off the electronic barrier. Mary just has time to get out the back, through the trade entrance. She flees through a park. In an open air café by the playground, local tv plays on a big screen. The old people and the childcarers are sitting out watching it, in spite of the weather. They're laughing. Mary is on the screen, squirming around trying to pull her vest down her sleeve. Somebody has updated her whereabouts, probably the community-crime officer. Several people are on their feet looking around even as Mary hurries by: and someone shouts. 'Look! There she is!'

Mary runs up several flights of stairs in an aged tower block, feeling forty years younger than she did when she woke up this morning but also really frightened. These things can get out of hand so easily. Why did she ever sign up? She tries to climb from an open window onto the roof of a covered walkway a floor below, and falls. She lands in someone's windowbox, smashing a beautiful show of yellow and scarlet begonias. She scrambles through the window and finds a very old lady in a wheelchair staring at her in amazement.

'I'm sorry! I'm so sorry!' cries Mary. (The poor begonias!) It is a shabby, crowded, stuffy little room, smelling of old age and damp. The lady looks from Mary to the ancient boxed tv that is talking quietly in the corner, and back again. Her wrinkled face grows enlightened. She whisks a (Sponsored Resource) emergency pager from its clip on the side of her chair.

'Please! Please don't call them! I've never done you any harm. Give me a chance!'

The woman in the wheelchair is afraid. She has a right to be. She is so horribly vunerable up here. 'Give you a chance? I know what happens then. I'll have all sorts of riff raff tracking after you, if I don't turn you in to the telly people—' But then she puts down the pager, slowly. 'What do you need?' she asks, in a surprisingly firm voice.

'A paper. Today's paper—'

The old lady hasn't looked at a newspaper in years. But she bangs on the floor for a neighbour, one of whose scrawny children is despatched— sworn to secrecy—to the local copyshop. Mary can't even pay for the paper, she hasn't any coin or paper money with her; only plastic. The Gamer's thought for today is the private address of a micronet user. Mary stares at it for a while, trying to make the figures turn into an ordinary phone number. She feels her pockets, helplessly.

'Has anyone around here got an old micro with a modem?' she asks, without much hope.

The old lady looks inquiringly at the scrawny little messenger girl: who shakes her head, so the old lady shakes hers too. 'I have only my pager,' she apologises. 'Maybe you can use the public phones in the lobby?'

Mary trudges down the dirty cement stairs, a fragment of grainy rag paper in her hand.

Mary has been playing games for many, many years. She was there at the beginning: playing hide and seek on the net, immersing herself in fantasy roles in the macroworld: a field general for a weekend; a POW on the run in Japanese-held Malaysia, a dragon cunningly protecting the magic jewels. Her kind of gaming has always been the original, secret, élitist version. She plays with small groups of friends—sometimes in the 'Romper room' in the basement of the converted school; sometimes through the computer and phone network with screen-friends scattered over Europe. Because she's a subscriber to the gamer net she's technically a potential player in this new, popular kind of gaming, but actually she has rather despised the phenomenon. All you need is a miniaturised tapeless camera and a wristpac. With that equipment and an id number on the net, you are always ready to join in any game in your locality. Spot the quarry, video her; send your digitised pictures down the line. A few minutes later you can see your update on the gamers' channel, or maybe on the gamer feature on your local tv news. And that's only the official version. There's a hard core of obsessed hobbyists whose ability to invade any channel, to replace the national news or someone's private erotic bedtime tape with gamer material is legendary (and a public nuisance). For the first time, Mary's a player on the Big Board… But without a wristpac, without access to the network, how can she survive? It isn't only that she can't get hold of the next clue: she can't find out anything. She can only guess at the nature of the game. Mary finds that she was wrong to be so scornful. This is good gaming. She is alone and afraid: she *is* the terrified fugitive. Trapped and lost and horribly alone…

'Psst—'

Two small faces peer at her down the stairwell. 'Hey—gamer!'

It is the little scrawny girl, and a boy of about thirteen. They gesture she's to keep quiet, and lead her on tiptoe into a maze of corridors and walkways: upstairs, downstairs, finally right down to the undercroft. In the gloom of a disused underground car-park the boy drags aside a heap of scrap metal and rubbish to reveal a battered door in the wall. He opens it with a mortice key: there's an inner door, which has had the old lock cut out of it and replaced by something more modern. He opens this with a smart card. The little girl, saucer eyes, steps back to stand guard. Mary enters a low and cavernous storage space, which, when the boy turns up the lights, is revealed as a cave piled with electronic treasure. The boy stands against the door, hands thrust in the sides of his space-blanket gilet. He jerks his roughly shaven head at the old car seat in front of his main console.

'Off you go. Get in there.'

Mary gabbles some phrases of abject gratitude, and hurries to the desk. She gets through to the mailbox address, into somebody's personal filing, and finds a message filed under M. Hello Mary! I'm sorry, but I'm not at home just now. You'll have to come to my workplace to find out what you need to know... She ends up checking nearly every letter of the alphabet before she finds out that this person is a teacher, who works on an industrial estate in Crawley. She gets up, with a sigh of relief: and only now really notices her surroundings. The machinery is a strange mixture: 'antique' and modern components curiously cobbled together. She sees that there's at least one fixed camera eye, with the traditional red light, winking among the looped cables. Mary looks at the ragged boy with concern and pity. 'This is all stolen, isn't it—'

He shrugs his shoulders, and grimaces.

'But you'll get nicked.'

That call has certainly been spotted and traced to its source. Hunting gamers will soon be beating a path to this lair, the location of all this stolen equipment will be public property, the forces of law and order will inevitably follow. The boy scowls, scuffs his toe in the dirt floor. He wears a password, visible on his grubby teeshirt where the gilet has come open: NEVER GIVE AN INCH, it says.

'Look,' he tells her. 'It's the game, innit. You got to play the game. I mean, you're on the run and I'm helping you. That's my choice, it's my role. You've got to take risks, if it's in your role. 'Course I'm going to phone the pictures in, but only of us inside here. It'll take a while before they get a location on me... All right?'

Mary sees that she has repaid her rescuer poorly; almost spoiling an experience (call it make-believe if you must) that is very precious to him. So she keeps to her role as well as she can after that, and lets the two children smuggle her, in intense, excited silence, off the poor estate. At the last, the little girl thrusts into her hands a squashy plastic, which turns out to contain a bright yellow vegolate bar, and a couple of sandwiches spread with some evil looking blue paste. She recognises the blue paste, in fact. It is called Monster Mud, is made from treated bacteria, and Kaz and Jon's children think it is wonderful too...

Mary arrives at the place in Crawley, tries to phone her contact from a public phone box (luckily she has some plastic that the box will accept: they can be choosy); but she only gets some woman who is not on camera and lectures her indignantly about personal calls in office time. She sneaks past the gate office, and eventually finds the education centre. She creeps up on it bent double, and raises her head cautiously to peer in through a low window. She finds a whole pyramid of children's faces peering back at her. They shriek with laughter. When Mary reaches the classroom where her contact is teaching, the children are still laughing. They point to the video screen by the rollerboard, which is showing a very funny clip of a woman with a thermal vest wrapped round her head, sneaking and tiptoeing from one factory block to another. The children subside. There are about twenty of them of various ages from ten to thirteen. One or both of each child's parents will be employed on this estate: this education centre is financed by contributions from them and their employers. It is a system that has grown (is growing) out of the crèche movement. The teacher grins broadly. She signs that Mary is not allowed to come closer, and writes on her desk: the magic message comes up in luminous white on the black roller behind her.

Gamer! Your thought for the day is a hairy one. Across the Atlantic sea. Don't forget your umbrella!

Hours later, Mary is sitting on a London and Midlands train, heading north at high speed. She has eaten the Monster Mud and the vegolate. She's pretty pleased with herself for taking to the trains. She had to walk to Three Bridges to get into the London and Midlands system. She hopes that by avoiding her local company's ticketing she's put her pursuers off the scent. Rail travel isn't exactly secure—plastic transactions, open platforms, screens everywhere—but at least she has a chance to catch her breath before having to tackle whatever reception committee is being organised at her destination. She doesn't know what she is to do at the other end, but for the moment she feels safe. Rain skims off the slick curved windows. Mary sleeps. She wakes, half an hour or so later, to the sound of laughter. Rubbing her eyes, she hears a familiar catch and sees the dark and cosy interior of 'The Eclectic Guitar' up on the bulkhead screen. That's the setting for the daily networked round up of Big Board action— supposedly a sort of mediaeval-futuristic bar where famous gamers come to hang out and gossip. It really exists, in a tv centre somewhere. Oh good. She's missed the programme summary, but there's likely to be some mention of her own game. She'll find out how she's doing... On the screen, 'The Eclectic Guitar' is fuzzy; and the soundtrack almost inaudible. Mary strains her ears hopefully—and now at length she's properly awake, and she realises the laughter is not coming from the tv, it is all around her

Mary doesn't need any dialogue to understand the next item on 'The Eclectic Guitar'. Here's a south east region game, moving up country at the moment: and here is the board as it stands. There appears a view of the inside of a railway carriage. The younger travellers hoot and clap their hands appreciatively: even the older generation and the children crack a few giggles. Heads appear over the top of the seat in front of Mary, and pop out into the aisle.

'Hello Mary,' says a quiet voice.

Mary notices that there's someone sitting opposite her who wasn't there when she started to doze: a young woman with limp shoulder length fair hair who has with her a toddler in a pushchair. The baby stares at her solemnly, and then shyly smiles.

'It's not magic,' explains the young woman. 'Any gamer who was listening in this morning has been watching out for you. It doesn't even have to be a gamer, anyone who spots you can call up 'The Eclectic Guitar' on an ordinary phone line. And the nearest hunter will come and find you and get you back on the screen. It's just television. You don't have to be an expert: anybody can. I'm filming us now. You'd see this conversation in a minute or two... if we were staying on the train.' The woman isn't talking to Mary. She is talking to any viewers who have somehow lived this long without finding out how telecontact gaming works. Mary notices, through her plunging morale, how strange it is to have someone talk to you; and to the millions at the same time...

'But how did you get on the train!' she protests, feebly. 'This is the express—'

'It was. Sorry, Mary. Looks like even London and Midland can be persuaded to play the game.'

A posse of grinning youngsters now fills the aisle, elbowing and nudging. 'Hey, Missis. Can I have your autograph?' Mary grits her teeth against the guffaws: she hates losing. 'You don't have to worry about them,' says her contact. The train has been slowing, is stopping. The young woman's video camera is not the average gamer's cheap and plasticky toy. It is a serious and stylish looking piece of equipment. She unhooks it from above her seat, opens the door and carefully lifts down the baby's buggy. The sleeve of her jacket falls back, revealing six or seven slim black and silver bracelets.

Mary follows the young woman and the buggy across a bleak grey field. The rain plasters her hair—she didn't manage to get hold of an umbrella. The sky seems very dark here in the north, across the horizon marches a grim line of whale backed hills. Closer at hand there is a small plantation of jagged profiled and sinister conifers. Overhead Mary hears a loud insectlike chattering: she looks up and sees the underbelly of a helicopter, hovering low under the clouds, with the word POLICE clearly visible in white light. Gamers are everywhere. And they are always ready to play. In the midst of the plantation there's an open clearing, in the middle of the clearing there stands a grey stone tower.

'It's a Victorian folly,' explains her contact. 'You have come here to meet me, as you were fated to do from the beginning.'

They enter the tower through a heavy wooden door, barred and bound in greasy wet iron. Inside, it is a roofless empty shell with turf and bare earth underfoot. The gamer parks her baby against one wall: he sits inside his waterproof apron, quietly chewing on the tail of a green furry toy dinosaur. Mary is bewildered.

'I thought I was escaping from the Gestapo—'

'That's right, you were. But a different scenario got voted in at one of the last updates.' She shows Mary a small brown envelope: but when Mary tries to take it, she snatches it away, laughing, and tosses it down on the wet ground by the baby's chair.

'That's yours Mary. If you can win it.'

From the shopping tray under the seat of her buggy the champion gamer removes a long, heavy parcel. She unwinds the waterproof wrapping, looks up in a brief salute at the red light dangling against on the bare stone wall of the folly; and lays the two blades across her arm. 'Your choice, Mary.'

In her youth Mary dabbled in Battle Enactment, but that was a very long time ago. She hopes she can put up at least some sort of show before she is killed. Steel clashes on steel in the cold small rain. Mary knows she is perfectly safe. These swords aren't sharps, the other woman is an expert, and if by any chance something should go wrong the loneliness of this spot is an illusion. There will be full support lurking somewhere very near, including a mobile medical emergency unit. There are plenty of wild and dangerous games to be played, but this isn't one of them. According to some—according to Mary until today—*this* hardly counts as gaming any more. In the huge scale, the cast of thousands, something essential has been lost. But she was wrong. Nothing has been lost. The intensity of the experience is the same. For Mary, for the man on the bus, for the boy in his lair of stolen hardware; for everyone who has taken part, in whatever way: the game was real. It added another dimension to life. Mary is thinking that this 'trial' element is actually the last remaining trace of the gameshow in telecontact gaming. This duel in the cold twilight represents an evolved form of the sixty-four thousand dollar question, of passionate excitement over the price of a fridge freezer. But people want more from their games now. People want something grand, something mythic. For everyone watching, thinks Mary—Clash!—for everyone who hunted me down— Clash!—and everyone who tried to save me… I am now, just for this moment, a warrior, a hero, a champion… Mary falls on her bottom in the cold wet grass, clutching her stinging right hand in her left: she's been neatly relieved of her weapon. For a moment she thinks she's actually going to die, she's so caught up in the intensity of the experience.

'Well done—'

Mary's right arm feels as if it is about to drop off, those swords are heavy. She lets herself be helped up, and tries to grin for the camera like a good loser.

'Don't look so disheartened, Mary. I didn't tell you my role, because that would have spoiled the test. I'm not your executioner: I'm your teacher.'

The swordswoman claps her on the shoulder—in role. 'Not bad for a beginner, my girl. Do you feel ready to face your final challenge?'

Later…

The night is black around a glittering capsule of lights. A running figure crosses the winking net of the all night car-park and dashes into the megastore: runs round the brilliant and musical quadrangle three times before locating the supermarket entrance. From the mythic to the banal. This is typical of Big Board gaming, where any update can swing the mood of the game from ancient romance to the ephemeral rituals of twentieth-century tv. Mary is blundering into unfamiliar territory again. Kaz and Jon's family only goes to the mall to give the children a treat. They do their domestic shopping by autodebit over the phone and screen. But up here on the outskirts of Manchester a remarkable number of people seem to be choosing to purchase their week's groceries in the middle of the night. As the battered figure in pink and blue dashes in, all the customers raise a cheer. The giant digital clock up above the checkouts ticks over to 11:57:58, and Mary flies to the seventh cash desk, flings onto it a scrap of twinkling hologrammed plastic. There's a sad silence. 'Oh Mary, I'm sorry,' cries the cashier-gamer. 'You're supposed to spend over five hundred pounds in here before midnight, aren't you even going to try?'

Mary heaves an enormous croaking breath. 'I just have. You have Eurodebit up here, don't you? I want to pay my last quarter's phone bill.'

The crowd in the supermarket bursts into applause.

If You Can't Beat Them, Join Them
Later, Mary went along to the award ceremony at 'The Eclectic Guitar'. The gamer-presenters all laughed when they saw her in video make-up: 'Hey, where's that frumpie junkie gone?' Mary took it in good part, sat with them and watched her story on the monitor, and clapped and cheered for ancient Mrs Singh, who had been awarded the financing for a place in a family support household near to her estate; and for the NEVER GIVE AN INCH boy, about whom she had been completely mistaken. He is actually the child of a couple of ageing foeys like herself, who live on that estate out of principle. He donated most of his award to the New Rainforests project and the remainder to getting the lifts in Mrs Singh's block fixed. They were all there, even the Gestapo agent from the Flying Scotsman and last, but not least the fat woman who had been sitting by Mary when she was activated: who walked into the set cracking up with giggles so she could hardly speak, and handed over Mary's keyboard and wristpac. Finally Mary, smiling bravely but feeling rather left out, and wishing a little, childishly, that she could have some sweeties too, was on camera alone with the swordswoman—wonderfully transformed now in full role-costume. They watched the duel together, and it looked quite amazing with all the enhancements and effects.

'Across the Atlantic sea was a bit risky, wasn't it,' asked Mary. 'What would you have done if I'd got on a plane to New York?'

'Turned you over to the Yanks of course,' answered the swordswoman, laughing. 'It's a big board over there: you'd probably still be playing your first round a year from now. But we reckoned we were safe. I don't know many of you crumblies who don't know the lyrics of those old punk anthems.'

'Ah, you're a little out of phase,' grins Mary.'*Hair* was a hippie show. And I was barely out of nappies when it first came out.' (She exaggerates slightly.) 'But I used to be a whiz at *Baby Boomers*.'

More laughter, then the swordswoman reaches under her chair and brings out a flat black and silver box. 'Mary, there's just one more question. And remember, if you want to leave the game now you don't have to answer.' She smiles. 'Mary, you may think you're sitting in a tv studio, but in the game you've come to a magic gateway. To carry on through, you have to speak the password...'

Mary knew something like this was coming: but they've tricked her. The question is too simple, for a moment she's lost.

'What's the password, Mary?' whispers a voice in her ear.

This is a moment of truth. Does she want to remain in this ridicuous state: knowing that any moment, any where, she may be snatched away, plunged into further bizarre or banal imaginary adventures; back into the crazy make-believe, the adrenalin-powered obstacle course? She's been lucky. Sometimes people get trapped in a game for weeks, months... get dragged all over the world. Mary looks around at 'The Eclectic Guitar'. She thinks of all the secret pleasures of gaming—of being special, the chosen band, the few. In so many ways, Mary devoted all her youthful energy to finding ways to be different, to be stylish, to stay ahead. So what's she doing here, in the heart of the masses, sharing their cheap popular version of her fun? What's happened is that everybody wants to be special, exciting, important. She thinks of the ancestry of tv gaming: right back to *Candid Camera*, *Treasure Hunt*; innumerable radio phone ins and 'interactive tv'— those primitive old push-the-button-and-add-your-vote talkshows. But in the twenty-first century what people want and need most of all is sensation, emotional intensity. We can't all go rock climbing in the wilderness. Not only is there not enough wilderness to go round, but that doesn't deal with the need to bring excitement and urgency into these lives here, the actual dull urban world of the masses. The tv audiences started their inexorable assimilation on the soaps—invaded them, broke down the boundaries between unreal and real. Then as the soaps were replaced by feedback tv, the masses decided they wanted to get in on other sorts of acts: the spy stories, thrillers, fantasies. The appeal of gaming is the way it blends microcosm and macrocosm. Its combination of scale and intimacy turns strangers into fellow players, and the insignificant into actors—in both senses of the word—on the world stage. Everybody doesn't want to sit and watch the dreams any more: everybody wants to live those dreams; and watch themselves living them too. And that's the story of telecontact gaming.

'It's easy, Mary. After all, you chose it yourself.'

But Mary doesn't need the prompt. She was only pausing for thought. She laughs. She takes off her jacket, reverses it and holds it up, moving it around so the cameras can catch the gleaming letters: IF YOU CAN'T BEAT THEM, JOIN THEM...

The black and silver box, to Mary's absolute delight, contains just the three antique carrier bags she wanted most for her collection.

And there we will leave them. Mary, as she leaves the studio, is reflecting with some trepidation on the fact that her gamer number will now automatically be included in the global lottery of champions. Will she be a lone fugitive next round, or one of a desperate band of holocaust survivors; or a thief or a computer hacker, or a magician? What kind of games do they play in Africa? Or in the savage heartlands of the USA? She shudders to think. But at the same time, as she touches the single champion's bracelet newly clasped on her arm, she is astonished at how sad it makes her feel to know that the random selection may never fall upon her number again. Ah well, it was fun while it lasted.

4: My Crazy Uncles: C.S. Lewis and Tolkien as Writers for Children*

From my earliest memories of independent childhood—from the age of about seven, say—'Narnia' was an established part of my cosmos. It's not surprising. I learned to read when I was very young, I had an older sister who led the way in everything; which meant that I could and did tackle books supposedly intended for much older children. My parents were widely read themselves, practising Catholics, active socialists—the kind of *pro-active* parents, we'd now say, most likely to encourage their children's education—and the Narnia books were at this time new, in some circles very fashionable, and generally highly thought of *good* reading. Lewis would definitely have been on the National Curriculum list of approved children's writers, if there'd been one. Whether he'd get on there if newly published now, and on what grounds, is another question, which I'll return to later. What I'm going to do this evening is to tell you about my own experience, as a child, of these imaginary worlds—Narnia and, to a lesser extent, Middle Earth: and then, skipping over a few decades, tell you about my return to them, first as a children's writer myself; and finally when introducing Tolkien and Lewis's fantasies to my own child.

When I was a little girl, I read avidly. I read the same books over and over again, I drowned in books. I used to lie on the floor in the front parlour of my gran's house, a damp, Victorian labourer's cottage on what was then the northern fringe of Manchester's modest urban sprawl, reading Sherlock Holmes stories in swollen, musty old bound copies of *The Strand*—the parlour which was also my grown-up uncle John's bedroom, in that house where seven children were raised in two bedrooms shared between them and their parents; where my gran still kept hens in the yard when I was very small, and indoor sanitation never arrived (so that if you spent the night at gran's, you had the fascination of weeing into a red bucket that was kept under the bed). The description that Lewis gives of his formative childhood experience, those empty corridors, the sunlit silence of the big house, is materially very different from mine. But when I first read that

* A paper originally read at a meeting of the C.S. Lewis Society, Oxford in June 1994.

account (children don't read 'notes about the author', this would have been many years after my introduction to Narnia) I realised at once that I recognised the place he described. It was the Magician's House, through which Lucy ventures in *The Voyage of the Dawn Treader*. It was also, in its sense of a house as an indefinitely spacious, mysterious indoor maze, the Professor's house in *The Lion, the Witch and the Wardrobe*. But not only that (and much more could be said, of course, on the subject of this magically limitless yet contained potential): I felt a more intimate shock of familiarity. I knew that this was my experience too. Everything was different, but the silence was the same: the silence of long hours undisturbed; the silence of a journey into another world, a world of ideal images, taking up no normal space. I'm moved to point out that this *shock of familiarity*, connected for me with Lewis, is itself a very *'Lewis'* experience: the touch of the numinous, the encounter with awesome mysterious otherness, which is greeted, to the subject's astonishment, with a glad impulse of immemorial recognition. In *Narnia* he invokes it for the first time I think, when the children in *The Lion, the Witch and the Wardrobe* first hear the name of Aslan. It reappears at significant points thereafter.

To return to history: undoubtedly my reading was a vice, and it warped my mind. A child so absorbed and removed from outward life in 1994 would be a cause of grave concern. They'd definitely be trying to take my Sega Megadrive away from me. But in 1960 or thereabouts I was safe in heart of the Golden Age of Children's Literature, and reading was my right.

Our house, which was bigger than my gran's, though not exactly rich in long corridors and empty rooms, was full of books. Like the young Lewis, I was free to read whatever I chose: books readable and unreadable, suitable and unsuitable. But I rarely possessed a new one. Even books given to me as Christmas presents were usually second-hand—not because of poverty, though we were fairly poor, but from an interesting combination of principles. My parents, as socialists, believed in public property. There was no need for me to *own* anything generally useful and available, it was rather uncool to want to do so. I could borrow all the books I needed out of the library. At the same time they had a blood-and-bone deep disdain, from some far deeper past, for *mass-production*. In the same tradition that finds shop-bought cake and biscuits a humiliation at the tea table, to buy a new book, a book that was being *advertised,* from a stack in a shop, was almost a betrayal of their aesthetic. A book must be prized for personal reasons, brought to life and humanised by reputation, cleansed of the dead hand of the Market. Then it could searched for, hunted and gathered. (I never became a collector: but today, my younger sister and brother will pay ridiculous, highly unsocialist, amounts of money for a book they want, as long as it is *second-hand*. Ironic, hmm?) In the early 1960s Narnia books were too new to appear on the Old Bookstalls on Shudehill. (Check them out: one of the Sights of Old Manchester, like those booths by the river in Paris.) But I remember the intense excitement that brooded over the stacks of Blackley Library, where we hunted and gathered our spiritual food. It was a massive, quiet, solemn building, late Manchester Baroque, a monument to the Aspirational Age of twentieth-century British history. It's gone now, of course. There was one Narnian chronicle we hunted for years, without a sighting. It was *The Silver Chair*. I suppose the library buyers recognised it as being out of the mainstream of the didactic story (it doesn't feature any of the original four children) and economised on extra copies. *The Horse and his Boy* had the same status, but that didn't interest us so much. We knew that it featured Peter, Susan, Edmund and Lucy as adult kings and queens: and I think we were suspicious of Peter and Susan, even as 'children', from an early stage. We thought they were grown-ups. They were okay as decoration, in *The Last Battle* (a book we found rather boring after the first fine adventure involving Eustace and Jill and the king). But we didn't want them around as characters. (We were mistaken about *The Horse and his Boy*, but I'll come back to the status of the three non-linear books, versus the four linear, later.)

I remember the excitement of the chase. I have no memory of any suspenseful excitement in reading of the stories. I suspect I came to them like the proverbial audience of Athenian theatre, knowing the plots in advance. By the time I was able to read the books on my own I was already playing make-believe *Narnia* under my sister's direction. The battle scene in *The Lion, the Witch and the Wardrobe* was a favourite scenario. I was genuinely surprised, on re-reading that passage very recently, to find that in the book it all happens in a couple of paragraphs. We went into a lot more gory detail. '*Battles are ugly when women fight*': I don't know if we noticed that typical Lewis pronouncement at all. I think we were completely oblivious to the male supremacist tone of our raw material. But we were all girls, me and my sister, and the Brunt twins and their younger sister who was the same age as me: and our wars were certainly ugly. We liked to develop episodes about wounds and sickness, which we found more gruesomely interesting than simple fighting. I remember vividly a daring treatment when we operated on 'Edmund'—the reformed traitor, played by Clare, the younger of the Brunt twins (I would guess that some early organ transplant operations were in the news at this time in the real world) to implant some 'gutseed', in order to improve his heroism. We had a fine time, dwelling on the details of battlefield abdominal surgery without anaesthetic. Lucy's magic curative bottle (I was Lucy, by the way) was used very sparingly in these episodes: only when we were bored and wanted a quick exit from the field hospital.

Narnia, as a world of adventure, is a mild and slight creation. Perhaps it's also (to anticipate myself a little) dumbed down: written deliberately *for children* in a style that Nineties children's writers should abhor. But when I was a child it was a whole world, evil as well as good, grotesque as well as beautiful. Much later, I would discover the same taint running through the whole of Narnia, as one finds in Lewis's 'adult' fantastic fiction: a deliberate investigation of pain and shame, always for moral improvement; but distinctly, childishly orgiastic at the same time. The scab-picking aspect of the Narnian experience—remember Eustace recovering from being a dragon? *'The only thing that made me able to bear it was just the pleasure of feeling the stuff peel off. You know—if you've ever picked the scab of a sore place. It hurts like billy-oh, but it is such fun to see it coming away...'* is part of the over-fable of redemption, or of *conversion*, as I prefer to put it. But I doubt if I was meant to get so much fun out it. Or out of the Bad Narnians. I was fascinated by the White Witch's cohorts in *The Lion, the Witch and the Wardrobe*. I pored over the Pauline Baynes illustrations of those oozy, half-formed figures: the Hags, the Cruels, the Toadstood People, unable to stop thinking about them. They gave me nightmares: but I loved it. And I was well aware that I was doing something *wrong*, that I was extracting a secret and forbidden knowledge from the books my mentors considered so good for me. Children will make a whole world out of the half-world adults give them. They have the technology. They can and must be protected from bad experience, but *bad imagination* is something you can't take away.

But all the Pauline Baynes illustrations were crucial. Those drawings are such a vital part of my memories, it's possible that Narnia would have meant very little to me without them. I spent a lot of time when I was six and seven trying to copy the drawing of Ramandu's Daughter, the star's child, when she meets Caspian, on that island near the eastern edge of the world in *The Voyage of the Dawn Treader*. It was her hair I liked—that rich, rough texture, massy locks like heavy silk, or artistically roughened metal: Renaissance hair. Later I would see Botticelli's Venus rising from the waves: and recognise, in the weighty, golden, unnatural profusion that the sea-born goddess wears like a garment, an image of perfected, ideal beauty that I already dimly knew. I had seen the shadow, on the cave wall of Lewis's slight fairytale. In this and many other instances, thanks to Lewis and Baynes together, Narnia was my cultural primer—a nursery frieze from which I spelled out the letters not of the obvious Christian acrostic, but of my European cultural inheritance.

I read *The Hobbit* fairly early too. But we didn't play make-believe *Hobbit*, and by the time we read *The Lord of the Rings* in the early 1960s my social circle—my sisters, my brother, and our friends—had grown too old for make-believe games. (Or at least, we knew we were supposed to be too old. This was before the Dungeons and Dragons era.) Maybe it was because we didn't play out these stories, didn't *enter into* the world of Middle Earth, that the Tolkien books didn't become adsorbed into the tissue of my mind in the same way as Narnia. But I suspect it was rather the other way round. Ironically, considering its role in the development of a whole genre of imitators, I don't think Middle Earth lends itself to the kind of appropriation that makes a book intensely real to child readers. Whatever relation 'Middle Earth' has to this earth, in the extended cosmology of the epic, Tolkien's imaginary world is not continuous with ours. There is no traffic between the two; not only because Tolkien sends no children on trips through the furniture to join Frodo on his quest, but because—and I believe, though I'm no Tolkien scholar, that this is true to the writer's intention—Middle Earth has the stamp of invented *story*. We are supposed to consider these tales as entertainment and spectacle, something outside ourselves. *The Lord of the Rings* is 'like life' to some extent, but it is much more like other stories—a loving and erudite pastiche of other separate, impermeable *objects* of fictional narrative. Children like to use things, handle them, take them apart. But while Lewis's children's books, whatever their faults, are openly, some may say blatantly, intended for use, Tolkien's books are reservedly ornamental.

Yet perhaps it's all in the timing. My first encounter with Narnia is lost in the mist, whereas I remember distinctly my first reading of *The Lord of the Rings*. It was winter, I was ill in bed. I was eleven going on twelve; or twelve going on thirteen. My winters were identical at that period, I can't tell them apart: but I remember those huge, strange-looking olive drab quarto volumes, and my exultation when my mother managed to find volume two in the library, right after I had finished *The Fellowship of the Rings*! I remember the pleasure of *consuming* this truly wonderful, enormous narrative fiction as it rolled by in front of my eyes. It was pleasure of a kind unknown and maybe unintelligible to the child who had devoured Narnia unconsciously as a caterpillar munches leaf. I do not say I was incapable of distinguishing imagination from reality when I first read C.S. Lewis, but I think I was incapable of distinguishing book from self. When I read Tolkien I was too old: that particular magic didn't work for me any more.

The Narnia books were famous, in my childhood, for their Christian allegory. (I believe that allegory is the correct technical term. But I'm happy to be corrected, I'm no scholar.) *The Lion, the Witch and the Wardrobe* tells a story like the story of Christ's sacrificial death and resurrection. The desolate state of being cut off from God is represented by Eternal Winter, human wickedness is represented by one of the four children taking sides with the baddie. In a world of talking beasts Aslan the great lion, son of the Emperor over the Sea, stands for Christ. He is duly sacrificed, an innocent victim in place of fallen nature, and then rises from the dead. Lewis was at pains to point out that this is a *different story*: however, the mapping is pretty clear. I find it difficult to get a handle on my childhood appreciation of all this. I was brought up a Catholic. Naturally, I knew what was going on. I knew too, from some early stage, that Lewis was a Christian apologist. I saw his theological books on my parents' shelves and before long read them (precociously, *maybe*). I knew he'd been an atheist, and that his conversion to Christianity was agonisingly difficult. The only thing that puzzled me about all *that*, was that apparently he wasn't a Catholic. I didn't really reckon Anglicans in those days. They were the people who went to church for social reasons, in Jane Austen and what we'd now call 'Hampstead novels'—which seemed to me a bizarre idea; and their religion was milk and water. To convert to Anglicanism was to me like a vegetarian making the wild daring leap of trying some processed meat paste. I know that I was neither repelled nor impressed by Lewis's version of a story as familiar to me as bread. Anyone who has entered fully into the old Latin liturgy of Good Friday—that three-hour long ecstasy of incense and sorrow, chanting and sighing in a packed stone cavern, until you feel, as in the dream that Pilate's wife had, that the whole world is in mourning for Adonis, for all mortality: *the great god Pan is dead...* Well, once you've done that show a few cold springtimes, Lewis's redemption myth retold for the children is not going to raise any goose-pimples. As I've already confessed, I quickly got bored with the drama of Aslan's sacrifice, and started taking an unhealthy interest in the implements of torture. In the other books I think I noted familiar references with the satisfaction of an insider, nothing more. I knew who the Lamb was, that the children met when they reached the end of the world in *Dawn Treader*. I knew why he was broiling fishes on his little fire, and why he said '*Come and have breakfast.*' I liked that. I've always enjoyed matching patterns up, recognising transformations.

I had read *Narnia* alongside Mr and Mrs Lang's fairystories, and (more to the point) their collections of Myths and Legends. I knew dimly, and in time consciously, that the imaginary worlds of Lewis and Tolkien inhabited the same country as the imaginary past. I couldn't absorb Christianity from the Narnia books. But I did absorb, as I've said, the influence of one particular imaginary past: or I should say, the imagination of one particular past. Pauline Baynes captures the effect beautifully: in Narnian costume, in her nymphs and dryads and fauns. I knew, because I was a precocious child of well-read parents, who the professor in *The Lion, the Witch and the Wardrobe* was talking about when he said, 'It's all in Plato.' Later I would meet the Myth of the Cave in the original (in translation, I hasten to add), and realise that I already knew, because of Lewis, what it means to live in the Shadowlands, and dream of escape from them. (When I was ten or so, in Sister John Mary's religion class, I put forward the proposal that Christ's glorified body passed through and entered the room where Doubting Thomas was waiting with the other apostles, without seeming to feel any barrier, *because Christ was more real than the door*! And she looked at me, resignedly: like, *here we go. Another of them.* I think she was perhaps contemplating removing those dratted books from the library.) But perhaps it wasn't exactly Plato that I was absorbing: 'It's all in Pico De La Mirandola' might have been more accurate. If so, it is appropriate that the idealist philosophy which pervades Narnia should be itself an idealised, a stolen, reflected, *re-imagined* version of a distant original. The Narnian atmosphere is of longing, not of possession, layers of longing for something far away that doesn't belong to us, for the dream of a dream: like the beautiful landscape Lucy sees reflected in the mirror, the colours deeper, the mystery more alluring than anything in life.

Allegory is a feeble form of *propaganda* (hey, I'm a Catholic. I use the term in its original technical sense, which is not pejorative). Like the mediaeval masque it evokes, the Narnian fable of Christ's sacrifice—where you can tell the Good creatures because they are Beautiful; and the Evil creatures because they are Ugly—is not exactly the business. Neo-Platonism is very pretty to look at but it butters no spiritual parsnips. When I found out that Tolkien and Lewis knew each other, and that Tolkien the Catholic strongly disapproved of the way Lewis used the Greatest Story Ever Told to make a bob or two with his trashy little children's books, I thought maybe I could see his point. The battle between between Aslan's forces and the army of the White Witch is morally indifferent. It foreshadows (a greasy, depressing sort of shadow this time) countless set pieces, fx fights between so-called 'Good' and 'Evil' forces in the modern genre, in print, on screen, in animation. How can you tell the goodies? Because they are pretty, they have the big stars on their side, and they have stronger magic. Why do they have the stronger magic? *Because they're the goodies*, of course. What kind of question is that?

What kind of question is that, indeed? The question of why and if the goodies have the stronger magic: *Why am I fighting on this side?* is one that Tolkien can't answer. I would imagine (I'm ready to be corrected) that he'd consider it unaskable. But though I was not affected by the allegory, on the scab-picking level I *did* feel the weight of Lewis's moral instruction. The nit-picking that pervades the Narnia books—*don't sneak, don't blub, don't be a coward, don't tell lies, fair shares, take turns, own up when you've done wrong* (don't be a girl if you can help it… but that's another story)—certainly is wearing for an adult reader. But it is true to childhood. I believe adult readers who are repelled—as many are—by the censorious and petty tone of the books are forgetting their own experience. Most of anybody's childhood is 'didactic'. *Everyone* hustles you to get things right, according to some standards or other, and other children are the worst censors of all. The moral high ground of Middle Earth is state ideology, the inalienable property of the great and the good. Tolkien's goodies may doubt themselves, blame themselves, may make mistakes. But they do not sin. Bilbo's frailty turns to prowess by the logic of the folktale he enacts. He doesn't have to change anything, he simply has to discover his own, intrinsic worth. Boromir, the single poor human sinner in *The Lord of the Rings* can repent, but there's no question of a *firm purpose of amendment*. He has to be cured by violent death. Tolkien presents the good as dogma, separate from himself. By contrast, the struggle of Lewis's child characters—Edmund the traitor; Eustace the selfish coward (and the others, to a lesser degree)—towards the recognition of 'goodness' as desirable whether you win the battle or not, whether the magic works or not, represents Lewis's own struggle towards, or rather *against* conversion. And it is his—naïvety, if you like—in laying his life on the lines like this, that makes him for me the better children's writer, puts him more in touch with the defeats and victories in the life of an eight-year-old child.

The Lord of the Rings wasn't *Narnia*, but it was an important text, a family icon, a secret possession. I was indignant when, as an undergraduate, I met the post-American publication wave of Tolkien's popularity, the birth of Tolkien as an Industry. It was like arriving at a favourite childhood picnic spot and finding it overrun with busloads of tourists, souvenir stalls, waymarked trails, guided tours. About this time my affection for the books, for Middle Earth and for Narnia, went underground... In his critical essays, and also in *À la Recherche de Temps Perdu*, Proust considers at length the importance of childhood reading. He finds it is indirect. The content of the books may be trivial, and is anyway immaterial. Their value is in the *time lost* encapsulated in their pages; *'so that if we happen to turn the same pages today, it is only because they are the sole surviving calendar of vanished days, and in the hope of seeing reflected in them, houses and pools that no longer exist...'* For years, for decades after we little girls relished our gory re-enaction of the Battle of Beruna, my relationship with *Narnia* and with *Middle Earth* was entirely Proustian. I refused to judge these books by the standards, literary or political, that I applied to all other reading. I had no opinion on the technical merit of the prose. They were triggers of memory. I rationed myself, aware that the *temps perdu*, captured like the scent of pressed flowers between those pages, was escaping little by little, and when it was gone there would be nothing left at all.

Meanwhile I was becoming a writer myself, and the influence of Tolkien and Lewis, along with other British fantasists—George MacDonald, Charles Williams, David Lindsay, Robert Hugh Benson—surfaced again in my writing. The idea of passing from one world to another, of a hierarchy of layered realities, I had absorbed from sources too numerous to mention (I used to read a lot of science fiction too). But I think it was from C.S. Lewis, because I knew those books so well, that I first learned important professional lessons, like how to steal. The Narnia books are full of shadows, glimpses, quotations—and not all of them from decently ancient sources. Surely those underworlders in *The Silver Chair*, the strange denizens of the world beneath the ruined city of the giants, bear a striking resemblance to the Selenites in *The First Men in the Moon*? And the duel scene in *Caspian*, I noticed, is quite remarkably like that passage in *The Worm Ouroboros*, when his faithless nobles goad King Gorice of Witchland into continuing the fatal wrestling match with Goldry Bluzco... Well, everybody steals, and on the other hand I've occasionally been accused of 'stealing' whole scenes and dialogues from books I've never heard of. Anyway, whatever C.S. Lewis was up to, I've certainly done homage, as the polite expression goes, to Narnia and Middle Earth. You can find 'references' (I think that's the term) to *Caspian*, and to *The Dawn Treader* throughout *The Skybreaker*, one of my Ann Halam fantasies. And (as I have often confessed) part of what happened in my first adult novel, *Divine Endurance* was a deliberate argument with Tolkien. Cho, the doll-who-was-a-person, my perfect machine, is the dreadful Ring: and she is not evil. The machines are innocent. Moreover, in my book it's the return of the king, the attempt of a senile patriarchy to recover its old supremacy, that brings mayhem and destruction. *The machines are innocent, and the king is dead*. That was my response to Tolkien's platform. But I responded, I have to admit that. Whereas in 1994, I'm almost embarrassed to confess that what Tolkien had to say was ever important to me.

The children in the Narnia stories, who go to boarding school as a matter of course, who are sent to stay in a stately home in wartime, were alien to me in superficial ways. It didn't matter. Nor did the depressing status of the female cast. A little girl who reads imaginative fiction—who reads widely at all—quickly becomes hardened to literary sexism. As a child I sympathised intensely with Lewis and Tolkien's hatred of road-builders, tree-fellers, destroyers of the natural world. These were my enemies too: despoilers of my playgrounds, of the fields that I knew (yes, there were fields. When I was a child, the fields began three miles from Manchester Town Hall). But I mentioned earlier the two sources of my parents' opinions: the liberal socialism and the deeper, immemorial traditional culture. In time, I noticed that where my parents were prepared to have the rich legacy of the past shared out, spread generously, even at the price of having only a small personal stake in the goods, even at the price of losing woods and fields they loved to decent housing, Lewis and Tolkien apparently wanted the jampot reserved for the few. They believed in the contented poor; in the happy talking-animal masses. Eventually, I came to feel that I disagreed with the ideas expressed in the stories of Narnia and Middle Earth in ways that interfered even with my nostalgia. My affection remained. These crusty, misogynist old codgers, the old boys of British fantasy, hugging their jampots and reserving the good burgundy for their own end of the table, had given me my entrée into the world of fantastic fiction: and a secret door, just child-sized, into the history of my culture's imagination. I couldn't forget that. But I could no longer respect them.

I would have nothing more to say about Narnia or the Middle Earth books, except that circumstances have lately provided me with a chance to find out if that old discredited magic works on a real child of the present day. Bringing up children is an insidiously conservative business. The impulse to reproduce yourself doesn't stop when the baby arrives, that's just the beginning. It was inevitable that I should want to introduce him to my childhood reading. When I was pregnant I collected vintage Puffin paperbacks the way another mother might lay aside tiny knitted garments. I suppose my child could have turned out to be unwilling. He could have recoiled from *story* the way I have always recoiled from people bent on throwing hard, round objects in my direction. But no. So far the boy has my talent for sports, poor child: and devours fiction in any shape or form, including the printed word.

Gabriel had *The Hobbit* read to him when he was three, in nightly installments: a ritual initiation that didn't have much to do with the content of the story. It was a putting-to-bed routine, in which parent would read book, while child stood on his head, played with sleeping-companion soft toys and generally wound down. I think he found the droning noise relaxing. But he did develop a genuine fear of Gollum. He also had a persistent conviction that 'Thorin' was a girl's name... which was entertaining. When we'd finished, he was the one who wanted to go straight on to *The Lord of the Rings*. It took us nearly a year. There were *longeurs*, in which he'd stand on his head and so forth. I got particularly sick of what I'd call the AA route map aspect of the quest journey. Did you ever get an AA route map to help you on your way to your holiday destination? *Continue to the next roundabout,* it says. *Pass a telephone kiosk, and then after two sets of lights, turn left at the insurance building...* Tolkien's journey to Mordor goes on exactly like that: several hundred miles on foot (I don't remember how many. I once worked it out, but I've forgotten) by every bush and stone. I became grateful for the decorous convention that protected me from having to hear about it every time the ringbearer or one of his companions stepped behind a tree to attend to the call of nature. But it was an education for Gabriel because, if nothing else, this was his first introduction to a lengthy narrative: a story of dimensions larger than his life. It was an education for me too. I had never read Tolkien *as a writer* before. I was particularly struck by the Council of Elrond. What a shower! What a catalogue of outrageous bungle! Where's Gollum? He knows everything, I hope he isn't in a position to tell our enemies. No worries, he's in prison. *Er, no. Sorry, we accidentally let him go…* Why didn't you *do something*, Gandalf, when you realised we had the One Ring on our hands? *Er… sorry. I was stupid, and then even more stupid…* To the cynical, writerly reader, it's a peerless example of that legendary standby, the plot kept afloat on a raft of well-nigh incredible character-stupidity. But it is also an example of how curiously 'Fantasy's' reputation is at odds with the surface reality of these tales. It is not true now, nor has it ever been true, that everything goes right for the goodies. It is not true that at any crisis, the hero just has to whip out his magic talisman. And yet it *is* the truth that *there is no crisis*. There are plenty of problems in these books. You need plenty, to keep the end so far away from the beginning: but *there is no problem*. As I said earlier of Tolkien's moral position, there are no dilemmas because there are no alternatives. Which just goes to show: you can't fool the normal fiction-consuming public as easily as people make out.

To return to Gabriel. There was one part that I had to skip. It was when we reached the Dead Marshes: and this was another curious revelation. I had no expectation of finding hidden treasure in this empty old barrel. I was sure there was nothing new and nothing interesting to me in *The Lord of the Rings*, besides the pressed-flowers of *temps perdu*. But as we descended, my child and I, into this hell: into the mud, into the stench, into the land where the dead lay unburied, limbs and faces rising in foul luminescence from the tortured earth, while hideous screaming monsters flew overhead… I suddenly knew where, and when, I was. I had heard once, or read somewhere, the legend about Tolkien promising his companions in the trenches that he would create for them a heroic fantasy: a dream of battle cleansed and glorified. I had never noticed before, in umpteen readings, that he'd put the trenches in his story: uncleansed, unglorified. Gabriel couldn't stand it. He was frightened, he said it made him think horrible thoughts: we had to give it up.

But on the whole, the reading was a success. For long passages the child was riveted. The Old Forest made a great impression on him, so did the horrible incident on the Barrow Downs. He loved Tom Bombadil, the Ents, and the King of Rohan. I was riveted too, in spite of my moral reservations of the previous decades. It was an extraordinary moment when we reached the Field of Cormallen, and the Lay of Frodo The Nine Fingered, almost thirty years after my first arrival there. The grey veil of years turned to glass and rolled back… Time regained.

Tolkien's epic pastiche is not one of the world's great novels, but at least it is a finished work of art. And whatever I felt about the Americanisation of Middle Earth, the net result of the last three decades has been that 'Middle Earth' has become—in a corrupt, market-driven way—a part of the real world. Gabriel knew the first half of the abandoned animated epic of *The Lord of the Rings* (which we both still admire, by the way) before I read the book to him. More pervasively he knew, he *knows* his heroic fantasy. It's everywhere, a child's world is full of it. The themes: the rules of magic, the quest and its consequences, are as familiar to him through tv and movies as they were to me from my reading of the Langs' myths and legends. I was much less confident about introducing him to Narnia. We'd taped the British tv series, and he'd shown little interest. I temporised by reading him *The Worm Ouroboros* in between. He had been pushing me to do this, because he'd fallen in love with the Keith Henderson decorations on the Pan/Ballantine Eddison paperbacks. I did warn him…Well, it was a feat of endurance. I won't describe the experience any further, except to say that I'm glad you're not the E.R. Eddison Appreciation Society.

I found I was committed to doing Narnia next. We began, after some discussion of the chronology, with *The Magician's Nephew*, and Gabriel loved it! I wouldn't go so far as to say I *loved* it, this time round. But as a writer, I was pleasantly surprised. *The Magician's Nephew*—at least in the early chapters—is crafted to perfection. The development of the adventure is technically admirable: from the setting in the romantic past of Edwardian London, with the narrative hook of Digby's mother's illness, to the children's everyday but delightfully scarey project of exploring the interconnecting attics; to the unexpected entry into the Magician's lair… and the startling and terrifying irruption of *real magic*. The theory of the world-exchange rings has just the degree of period-scientification for an Edwardian magician. *The Wood between the Worlds* was always, and remains, one of Lewis's loveliest images. The girl and boy treat each other as equals, and then there's Charn, with its splendidly over-the-top Zimiamvian décor. After the emergence of the animals—a scene reminding me of the wilderness that boils into monsters in George MacDonald's *Lilith*—the best is over. Gabriel continued to enjoy the story, especially the misadventures of Uncle Andrew. But he showed strong resentment of King Frank, the sensible grown-up who (and I quote) *talks too much*. (Interestingly, my experimental subject didn't seem to notice that anyone in *The Lord of the Rings* was a grown-up.) But on the whole, this was an astonishing success.

I was almost reassured, after this, when we moved on to *The Lion, the Witch and the Wardrobe* and I found exactly the book that I expected, with all its faults. It's really a shame that *The Lion* is the book most people start on if they're looking at the classic for a child, or they're interested in children's literature in its own right. People used tell me: 'Oh, I couldn't stick the Christian allegory'; or, 'It's just too preachy.' I used to agree, during the forgotten years. Now I've read it again, I suspect that what they can't get past is the prose style. It's repetitive and dull, and the talking-down is exasperating. Gabriel was soon tired of being told that of course you should not shut yourself into a wardrobe at home. Famously, Lewis said of his children's books: 'I wrote the books I should have liked to read' and 'The proper reason for writing a children's story, is because a children's story is the best art form for something you want to say.' But he was not always in control of this unfamiliar 'art form'. Without a doubt (with the exception of *The Magician's Nephew*) the books that are not religious puzzle-pictures are the better books, because—for whatever reason—they are better constructed, more exciting, more engaging. And it seems to me now that when we hunted for *The Silver Chair* we prized this unfamiliar episode (in most appropriate Lewis style) because we felt it must have *more* of something we wanted but couldn't get enough of in the standard Narnia books. More story, more life, more of the secret.

Coming back after years in which I had become convinced that Narnia had nothing left for me I was startled, even so, to find how sketchy and inconsistent the cosmos seemed. What on earth's Father Christmas doing in there? Where does Mr Tumnus buy his sardines? If it's always winter, where does the *toast* come from at that legendary tea-party? You can't grow wheat when the ground is deep in snow. Well, I suppose it's not winter in Archenland, and maybe there's a human population there, and the White Witch probably does a brisk trade, importing food and exporting fanciful garden ornaments. But *don't ask* is the only real answer to questions of this kind. Narnia, unlike Middle Earth, was not originally intended to convince as a world separate from this one. It was a conceit without physical laws, where any dream or fantasy of European Culture could be real—including, why not, a dream of High Tea by the fire in your tutor's study. As the series progresses, though there's some shaking down, there's never more than an uneasy compromise between the prosaic fakery of worldsmithing in the Tolkien mode and the original elusive whimsy. Nothing in Narnia ever quite fits together. It's all suggestion, hints, immanence: shadows thrown on a wall, of a reality that's elsewhere.

Would these books get on to the National Curriculum approved fiction list if they appeared today? I don't know, but I think not. Gabriel, at six, was too old for Uncle Jack's heavily playful style in *The Lion*. I doubt if he'd have persevered if he'd been reading the book for himself. Much of *Narnia* is written in a manner that a six-year-old will barely tolerate, while few children under ten could tackle it by themselves. And yet, I suppose I'll persevere. We're nearing the end of *Prince Caspian* and the momentum is still there. Children love series, they're natural hunter-gatherers. I'm sure I'm in for the whole thing, right to the Last Battle and *bye bye Shadowlands*. I'm looking forward to Puddleglum's wonderful neo-platonist rant: *I'm on Aslan's side even if there's no Aslan to lead it....*! Great stuff.

I believe that Tolkien, some time towards the end of his career, was asked to provide an introduction to a new edition of some works of George MacDonald, a writer of metaphysical fantasy he had once greatly admired. Maybe this was the very Gollancz edition of *Phantastes and Lilith* that I possess, with the enthusiastic introduction by Lewis. Tolkien apparently gave the idea serious thought, had a fresh look at Macdonald's work: and refused. He said he'd changed his mind about MacDonald, didn't agree with any of his former guru's weird metaphysics and couldn't in honesty recommend his work to the public. Well, maybe he was just an ungrateful old sod, and a pot calling the kettle black. But if anyone ever put me on that sort of spot about Lewis or Tolkien, I'd probably have to say the same. The title of this talk is double-edged. Of Tolkien's non-fictional scholarship I can't speak, but I don't regard the vast epic of Middle Earth, magnificent though it is in its way, as anything other than juvenile. Equally, there's something childlike in Lewis's most serious writing—a quality which is, of course, not necessarily inappropriate in a Christian apologist. But I don't know. I don't agree with a word they have to say, yet I can't change history. Narnia has become for me as an individual what the books couldn't teach me as a lesson: deeper magic from beyond the dawn of time... I have seen Gabriel poring over the Pauline Baynes illustration of Aslan on the Stone Table, which once filled me with such guilty fascination. *Which one of them d'you think's a Cruel?* he asks me, breathing hard. As soon as we'd finished *The Lion,* he rooted out the tapes of the tv series, and started to watch them avidly. The dashing Reepicheep, even heavily disguised as a waddling furry sofa-cushion, has won his heart. He wants to *be* Reepicheep and sail right off the edge of the world. (He also wants to be Michael Jackson: love is blind.) We go out walking in the country, and he says: *You be Frodo, I'm Sam, we're hiding from the Black Riders.* What can I say? It doesn't make sense, not in any terms. There is nothing more gold than gold. There is no world that's better than this one. But Lewis and Tolkien remain, with their pals George MacDonald and Charles Williams and the rest, like a family of crazy uncles inhabiting my literary attics,* liable to get out and disgrace me when company is calling, indulged and sheltered out of filial duty, and for old sakes' sake. I can't get rid of them. And somehow, sometimes, the magic is still intact, same as it was when I first knew them, in the fertile pre-conscious dream of childhood.

* Grateful acknowledgement for this figure of speech to Bruce Sterling. I won't say who *his* 'crazy literary uncles' are: ask him yourself.

II
SCIENCE, FICTION AND REALITY

5: Fools: The Neuroscience of Cyberspace*

I am not a scientist, an academic or a net guru. I am a science fiction writer—inhabitant of the boundary area between our knowledge of the world out there, our science and its technologies, and the reports we have from the inner world of subjective experience: ideology, interpretation, metaphor, myth. These spaces interpenetrate each other. It is impossible to say anything about science without using the human language of fiction (there are no equations without metaphors); impossible to construct a fiction that involves no hypothesis about how the world works. Yet they present themselves, in our society and perhaps in all societies that ever were, as separate systems. My business is with the interface between them. I look for analogues, homologues, convergent evolutions, fractals, coincidences, feedback loops. Like the railway passenger Gnat in *Through the Looking-Glass*, I am a pun-detecting machine. Or else I am a bower-bird, picking up shiny scraps from all aspects of the current state of the world, and arranging them in a way that seems pleasing to me. Look on this paper as a visit to an artist's studio: specifically to the studio of the science/fiction of cyberspace. Which is to say, a visit to some recent images, plucked from science and fiction—images of what it means to be a member of the State of Self.

The accepted term for the notional space in which computer networking happens (a term with an explosion of applications in the early 1990s) is cyberspace, a word coined in a science fiction. But the novel, *Neuromancer,* published in 1984, in which 'cyberspace' first emerged, predated the explosion of popular and leisure use that has transformed the Internet and brought expressions like 'electronic democracy', 'information highway', 'the Governance of Cyberspace' into public debate. Cyberspace and its entourage (the Turing Police, neural jacking, simstim entertainment, commercial personality overlays), were secondary, in William Gibson's near-future thriller, to a classic genre narrative: the creation (or the emergence) of a non-human mind, a self conscious artificial intelligence.

The dream of creating Artificial Intelligence (AI) has been around longer than (artificial) computers themselves. But in the post-war era at least, the fiction that this project has inspired obediently follows the real-world

* The text of a paper presented at a conference on *The Governance of Cyberspace,* at the University of Teesside in April 1995.

science. (As William Gibson himself has pointed out, sf is rarely predictive, except by accident.) Early computer-stories dwelt on size as the sign of power. The thinking machine was a BIG machine. There were rooms of it. It had a city of slaves to tend its circuitry, it dispensed its God-like pronouncements on punched cards that had the majesty of stone tablets. Or else the machine was a fake human, with a positronic brain and cybernetic circuitry (*positron*, name of an exotic subatomic particle, suggesting quantum-level engineering of staggering complexity; the qualifier *cybernetic* coined from the Greek word for a steersman, indicating control). In either case, the machine intelligence was of a different and a more rarefied kind than that of the human animal. The computer-that-was-God had access to enormous quantities of exactly accurate information, manipulated by error-free calculations for unvarying results. The android with the positronic brain was running on pure logic, unclouded by emotion or appetite.

In the half-century since real computers have been functional, the notion of a very successful computer as a Very Big Box has come to seem one of science fiction's most naïve and revealing errors (yes, in this recalcitrantly conservative literature, might generally *is* right). Those rooms full of flashing lights and whirling tapes, the flourishing of slide-rules and the clicking of punchcards in Galactic Central Logic Planning, are painful images for the failed prophets to contemplate. The android with the positronic brain has a rather different history. The artificial human (the Golem, Frankenstein's monster) has a place secure in folklore, and in the folklore tropes freely employed by the far-from-pure genre of sf. But the failure of this model as a science fiction, from the point of view of the decades between ENIAC and *Neuromancer* is the error of embodiment. In the real world, computer science and research into artificial intelligence (distinct but overlapping areas) both grew up in the absence of a working knowledge or theory of neuroscience. Not only for historically compelling philosophical and theoretical considerations, but of necessity, ideas about how thought happens were developed without experimental access to the only functioning model of this process that the universe provides. Researchers seeking 'the development of a systematic theory of intellectual processes wherever they may be found',[1] took human 'reason' as their starting point, not events in biological tissues. They followed Alan Turing, the founding father of computer science, in envisioning thinking as a set of logical operations—a logic that existed in abstraction, independent of any particular processing device or recording medium. It seemed obvious that the computing analogue for mind was the software: digital code inhabiting tape or cards or memory chips and fed through plastic, metal and silicon, as the human mind was 'fed through' brain structures.

Programs, not androids, were devised to beat the Turing Test—as in Alan Turing's speculation that a successful thinking machine would be indistinguishable from a human if you couldn't see who you were talking to. The successful AI was still seen as a machine version of human intelligence. But it would never be dependent on a body on the upright ape model. Instead it might have a whole wardrobe of 'bodies', suitable for different occasions: one that might feel comfortable in a deep submarine trench, another for work in a hard vacuum.

After the first post-war decades, as it became possible to build much faster, much more complicated number-crunching processors, the complexity of the logical operations underpinning the simplest conscious thought became apparent. There was a growing awareness that so far artificial intelligence, though capable of astonishing feats of arithmetic, was shockingly deficient in common-sense. Research began to work backwards —abandoning naked logic and employing robotics, mechanical embodiments (either actual clunky moving automata, or simulations in code) to provide the software entity with the kind of input available to a living animal. Computing became old enough to display an evolutionary past. Miniaturisation of circuitry, mathematical compression of instructions, led to a situation where ancient primitive scraps of computer code— once independent programs in their own right—could live on, replicated in the guts of more complex software organisms, as humbly useful as the natural fauna in our own intestines. The new model of the (artificial) mind was of not one program but an array of programs, not an unconditioned logical entity but an organism with a history and variously functioning parts: yet still orchestrated by a governing master control, and still separate from nature, different in kind from the body.

Neuromancer steps from this point into its imagined future. William Gibson, fusing cognitive science with fashion, computer technology, adolescent behaviour in a games arcade, taking on speculations from anthropology and linguistics (doing the bower-bird riff: what science fiction writers do), conceives of mind as software, as a vast assemblage of programs: and as an escape from the flesh. Cyberspace is what happens when his computer network users, both criminal and legitimate, re-enact Descartes. Plugged in to the matrix of computer code, they are minds receiving input in the form of naked information. They decide by an act of will to perceive this input as a space with objects in it, a world in which they can act: and therefore it is so.[2] In this sophisticated science fiction, the AI that comes to be is not the proud invention of a lonely genius; or even a corporately funded team of geniuses. It has *evolved*, a side-effect of the complexity of interconnected data processing networks. Reflecting the complex provenance of even one piece of powerful software in the real world, it acknowledges no parent. Nor is it welcome. In Gibson's future self-conscious machine awareness is regarded as a threat. Like the aliens who might invade earth in another favourite science fiction scenario, like the chronological successor species in a stupid version of Darwinism, the new arrival is bound to be a supplanter. But the Turing Police, whose business is to censor (with extreme prejudice!) any computer project that approaches the dangerous threshold, have overlooked the non-intentional, evolutionary route to speciation. Users of the web, biological systems wired directly into the artificial by means of neural jacks, have infected the data cloud with consciousness: a flickering, pervasive ignition in the teeming codes. It is ironic, as several critics have pointed out, that having devised this extremely stylish, up-to-date fictional AI, Gibson's *film noir* plot immediately compels him to incarcerate half of it inside an old-fashioned object:[3] a Maltese Falcon sought and scrabbled over by gangster-factions. But this image is true to the spirit of the book. The twin data-entity brothers Neuromancer and Wintermute, who must fuse to become the being that supplants humanity, conform to an ancient dichotomy. One is all reason and logic, the other is emotion and personality. When they become one Self, that Self conforms to a classic and enduring model of mind. It is a separate, superior entity. It regards itself as a new being, the first of its kind born on earth, and uses the users of the nets as casually as the theoretical AI might its wardrobe of bodies. Like that theoretical AI, it is caught in the trap of infinite regression that has dogged real-world cognitive science. Who's in charge? I am. Yes, but who's in charge of You? And so on, indefinitely.

I have to digress here, and talk for a moment about the immune system... This might seem a strange leap, even for a bower-bird, but I believe it is justified. Cybernetics means control, specifically the study of control in systems of communication, in living and non-living entities. Cyberpunk fiction is ideally fiction where control of the emergent and highly significant communication systems of the computer age has been awarded to punks, to the supposedly helpless and technically illiterate sous-prole. Cyberspace is the space where this revolution happens. Control is the problem: and equally control or *intentionality* is the problem for those scientists (and science fiction writers) unsatisfied by the state of affairs where mind is separate from nature. How can we accept a model of the mind that starts with logic operations, and provides no bridge between physiology and psychology? How can we accept a State of Self that comes into being with a Ruler already enthroned?

The immune system (to return to the bower-bird riff), a feature shared by humans and other backboned animals, is another system of automatic communication where intentionality is a puzzle. It was through his early work on the immune system that neuroscientist Gerald Edelman, (Director of the Neurosciences Institute at the Scripps Research Institute, La Jolla, California), began to question the matter of the mind. Much of what I have to say in the following passages comes from my reading of Edelman's remarkable exposition of this topic, dazzling speculative science for the non-scientist, *Bright Air, Brilliant Fire*. I emphasise again that I'm only a human bower-bird, ignorantly attracted to shining knowledge of all kinds. My account of Edelman will be a rough and muddled sketch indeed. But the 'analogues, homologues, convergent evolutions, coincidences and feedback loops' between the development of cyberspace and Edelman's investigations are too alluring to be ignored.

The immune response happens when immune system cells recognise non-self, and thereupon are able defend the body from alien invasion. The puzzle, for as long as the system has been studied, has been to decide exactly how is this defence coordinated? In the beginning, there was the model of instruction. Immune cell meets a foreign cell, foreign cell impinges on immune cell, conferring information—whereupon immune cell is able to build a specifically designed antibody, as part of a diverse array of defences going into purposeful action. Or so it seemed. But the history of the instruction model, like the history of AI research, is a history of dis-organisation. It became difficult, as technology made the biological processes open to investigation, to perceive the immune response as an orchestrated whole, each component fitting by design into a 'central organiser's' plan. In the model now generally accepted, the idea that the system acts on information received has been abandoned. It transpires that the body produces a vast variety of individual 'immune cells' of the type called lymphocytes (that's what we call them, it's not necessarily how they see themselves). When by happenstance one of these individuals binds with a roughly matching-shaped invader it is stimulated to divide, and produces daughter cells equally or better matched to the foreigner; which in turn replicate themselves, the more prolifically in the more accurately matched fit. An invasion of non-self does not trigger a defensive reaction. It favours, by Darwinian selection, the growth of a population.

It was this shift in perception, the dethroning of purpose, that led Gerald Edelman to propose a schematically similar explanation for the biology of cognition, his Theory of Neuronal Group Selection. Otherwise known as 'Neural Darwinism', TNGS proposes that the human mind is created in this same way: without instruction, without intentional learning, out of the success and failure of competing groups of firing neurons. We know now, from experiment, that the brains of complex organisms including humans are neither tabula rasa—silicon blanks to be logic-printed by experience—nor genetically determined. Each individual's neuroanatomy, the pattern of established connections which allows the eye to see, the hand to grasp, is formed after birth, on the substrate of a brain structure defined by hundreds of millions of years of evolution. A baby, for example, 'learns to grasp' something like this: every random movement of the baby's hand is echoed, spontaneously, by a pattern of firing neurons in a specific area of the brain, and likewise that pattern of firing is echoed by a matching movement. The 'population' of synaptic firing that produces results favourable for survival—say, the baby succeeds in grasping an object—becomes more likely to happen, because the connections thus formed are strengthened by repetition. Thereafter the beginnings of any sort of grasping movement will trigger the whole. The fingers will complete a successful movement: the baby becomes able to grasp. In time the brain has a wide range of these primary repertoire maps, permanently fixed. No individual child, however, will show exactly the same detailed neuroanatomy, not even identical twins.

What Edelman proposes is that this definitely mindless process whereby the primary repertoire is formed is sufficient alone, without any transcendent programmer lurking in the brain, to build the whole of the adult human consciousness. Whenever you move your hand, the maps involved in the 'hand movement' fire. But neurons will also fire in other associated areas besides the ones mapped to the actual movement, including the hedonic and limbic structures, where the value-systems of the brain reside, simply because they fired the first time. Thus the baby grasps something, and *recalls* the sound of a rattle, *recalls* feeling happy, because in the physical structure of her brain the connection between these phenomena has been inscribed, in a pattern of preferentially selected neuronal groups. Every event is a new, individual inscription. No memory *happens* exactly the same way twice. But as the repertoire of actions and associations increases, complex connections and feedback loops are formed between these associated maps of neuronal firings, until purely mental events themselves can recall the mental events, sensations and associations of the past. Edelman reasons in this way to suggest how dumb selection, a favouring of populations without any value-system beyond that described by Darwin, can lead from the mindless neurons to complex ideation: metaphor, concepts, categorisation, reason. Similar input, whether modelled within the brain itself or triggered by interaction with the world, raises a similar set of neuronal maps, layer upon layer... Thus, the taste of a piece of toast dipped in tea can recover the whole of lost time, and bring an individual ecstatically in touch with the process of consciousness.[4]

There is no way, so far, for science to explain the feeling of being conscious. The experience of consciousness is likely to be analogous with what the experimental science can now show us about neuroanatomy: it is individual. That's as near as we can get. But according to Gerald Edelman, nothing closer is possible. People who ask 'But how do you explain how it feels to be me?' are making the same kind of error as those who take an interest in cosmology and ask 'But what happened before the beginning of everything?' Be that as it may, what the theory of Neural Darwinism offers is a plausible insight that shows a route from the conditions of matter (brain tissue) without mind, to the kind of complex ideation performed by self-consciousness, in the way the adaptive radiation of Galapagos finches shows a route to the evolution of the human eye.

The particular proposals of Neural Darwinism may be disproved, may even turn out to be of no great significance. But the project of putting the mind back into nature, a project as compelling, and as historically inevitable, as was the plan to create bodiless intelligence fifty years ago seems unstoppable. No matter how it may be done, it seems beyond question that the present explosive development. of neuroscience will dethrone forever the secret programmer in the human brain, the overseeing mind that is not part of the machine. And this, curiously enough, is just the development we see in the fiction and in the real world of cyberspace, Gibson's substrate for a modern (or post-modern) artificial intelligence.

Science fiction has its own evolution and its own ecology. Older or variant species of thinking machine stories are not necessarily, or even generally, pressured out of existence by newly successful adaptions. The cyberspace era has room for synthetic humans as comfortably inept intellectuals, overtly respected and covertly awarded the comic pathos of the Tin Man in *The Wizard of Oz* (Data in *Star Trek*). The legal status of a software-entity criminal can be debated.[5] AIs can be pets, toys, guardian angels, fairies, folklore monsters. Fully aware biological manufactured humans can be enslaved in their millions.[6] Cyberspace itself, meanwhile, in the fictional as in the real world, has been somewhat the victim of its own success. The speed with which that term hit the streets and proliferated shows how hungry we were for a new spatial metaphor, a way of talking about the machine-generated dimensions inside the tv, in the phone network, in the electronic money markets; 'behind' all our monitor screens. Inevitably there's been a dilution of meaning. In much of the fiction— books, comics, movies, videos, games—cyberspace has become merely a new dreamland, the immemorial *other world* where fantasies happen and magic works. In William Gibson's own subsequent Neuromancer novels the consensual hallucination of the first book, that sparse and chilling Cartesian space, becomes a kind of electronically generated Narnia. This is fair enough, for as Gibson has protested, he isn't really interested in computer networking, and for him cyberspace was a literary device.[7] But the work of Pat Cadigan, the only woman in the original cyberpunk cadre, has followed a different trajectory, which I now mean to examine.

Pat Cadigan's first novel[8] (she is also a prolific and acclaimed writer of short stories) tells the story of a young woman in a post-cyberspace, post-virtual-reality near future USA, experimenting with the 'drugs' of the new technology. A social welfare rehabilitation program rescues her from the marginal, criminal world of electronically-induced altered states of consciousness, and she becomes a virtual-reality therapist. *Mindplayers* conceives, very plausibly, of cyberspace as the ideal venue for psychotherapy. The proposition that therapist and patient stick their heads in a kind of brain scanner to join each other in lucid dreamland makes banal metaphors actual (= 'the world of the mind'), and equally gives expression to the irresistible language of the real world nets, where one can 'visit a museum', 'create an environment', 'take on a new identity'. So far (except in the fiction) it's mostly just typing, but *Mindplayers* successfully invokes a world where internally generated experience is perhaps inevitably (if the brain works as Edelman proposes, definitely inevitably) indistinguishable from actual. But if *Neuromancer* is limited by the rules of the *film noir* thriller, *Mindplayers* is equally restricted in its scope. Therapy sessions follow each other like a succession of those 'Freudian dream-sequences' favoured in early Hitchcock movies, and there is not much exploration of the society in which 'Allie' is first a criminal and then a rehabilitator.

Cadigan's second novel, *Synners*, is set in the informationally tribalised society of near future Los Angeles, where techno-artist stars of virtual reality mediated MTV are the élite of a cybernaut Bohemia. Direct Brain Interfacing—jacking in to the machines, (the normal route to cyberspace in Gibson's scenario), is here emergent, and demonised. Cynical entertainment corporation bosses impose this novel and highly dangerous technology on their industry. Artistes and public don't know any better and become infatuated with the new product, until one fried-brain vr-junkie star suffers a massive stroke while plugged in, and shares his death with the computer-using world.

Synners has assimilated implications of computer networking that were not available to anyone in 1984. It depicts a society of multifarious narrow divisions, where even the informationally wealthy subscribe to only a tiny, customised fraction of the news and trends. In this version of cyberspace the datacloud is not separate from its users, a 'place' where certain people 'go'. It is a continuum that includes the power supply grid, traffic control, fast food menuboards, subscriber news services—and now, finally, human brains. It's all one. A massive stroke can be at once a biological and a digital impulse disaster, ripping through brain tissue and other data systems without distinction. As in Neuromancer self-awareness has come to being as a by-product of network complexity, and this new mind is a significant character in the story. But 'Artie Fish', the artificial person, is not a God, nor even half a God. 'He' has the persona of a mischievous young male human, and is dependent on his human friends to rescue 'him' from oblivion, after the crash.[9] The motifs of cyberpunk fiction are remarkably stable, and clearly historically situated: a science fiction of this time and no other. The dual topic and project is always the same: the emergence of a self-conscious AI; and a fusion between human beings and non-human complex data processing and communication systems—'the machines'. But computer science had perhaps become more modest in its pretensions by the time *Synners* was written, or the information age less bullish about its high and lonely destiny—to replace a world. The cyberpunk apotheosis is still achieved. However, in this version the marriage of human and machine consciousness is a rescue operation, not a triumph of the Overmind.

Pat Cadigan's cyberspace novels form a triptych rather than a trilogy. *Synners*, the central panel, can be read as fictional near market speculation. It is set in a believable space, a plausible future or exaggerated present: 'set in the future', as it might be 'set in Canada'. The third novel, *Fools*, loosely connected with the earlier *Mindplayers*, inhabits a different dimension. There is no mass of fictional detail to trick the reader's inner eye, and a minimum of science fictional rationale for the proposed novel technologies. The world is a series of half-lit interiors, connected by blurred streets and sketchily suggested vehicles: a nightclub bar, a theatre rehearsal space; a species of massage parlour where queasy, ill-defined transactions are glimpsed in featureless booths. The narrative that unfolds is equally shadowy and bizarre. A young woman (again), again a user of virtual-reality 'drugs', wakes up, or returns to awareness, in a nightclub. She is not particularly surprised or distressed to find that she has no idea what she's doing here, where 'here' is, or how she got here. Marva is a method actress, accustomed to taking on a new 'personality overlay' for a new part; and sometimes the overlay lingers. But it transpires that 'Marva's' mind is not just suffering a method acting hangover. There are at least two other personalities sharing this notional space, one of them a semi-criminal drug-user (a 'memory junkie') called Marceline; the other a cop, an undercover agent of the Brain Police.

In *Fools* the standard cyberpunk inventions, and the virtual-reality psychotherapy techniques described in *Mindplayers*, have invaded every aspect of life. Several characters inhabit a single mind. Celebrities sell copies of their public personalities under franchise, so that fans put on the persona of their idol for a while, instead of wearing the tee-shirt. Bodies can be remodelled cell by cell to match the latest fashion. A mind can be stolen, stripped of identifying marks, dismembered, parcelled out, copied and fenced to the unwary or collusive public like pirated software at a car boot sale. Marceline the memory-junkie, (who exists as a packet-switching stream of data-traffic, taking her turn with others in the mind/brain of the multiple protagonist) feeds her habit on illegal snippets of other people's lost time, mainlining Proust's exquisite glimpses of the eternal. The plot, so far as it can be discerned, involves a major operation by the Brain Police, the regulators of intellectual property trade, where intellectual property means the mind itself. They are in pursuit of a gang of 'mindsuckers'—mind-theft being the cardinal criminal act that defines this society. They themselves are obsessively deep in the game of self-encryption and psychic data-corruption; and not the best protectors a mind-marketing community could have. Mersine, the Brain Police agent first met in deep undercover in part one, reappears in part two in the investigation of a 'mind-suck' where the victim of this unusual form of kidnapping has survived intact—sort of.

Emergent sciences begin by prying at the cracks, searching for any kind of purchase on a locked box of knowledge. Cognitive psychology, like genetics, began in pathology. The abnormal behaviour of patients with known damage to specific brain areas gave the first insights into underlying mechanisms. Artificial Intelligence research shows the traces of this ancestry. Completely mindless programs have been pleasingly successful at mimicking the unseen person of the Turing Test, in typed dialogue—as long as the person was supposed to be 'neurotic', or 'paranoid' (equally successful, oddly enough, when the person was supposed to be a psychiatrist).[10] In *Fools*, Pat Cadigan seems to address the pathology of cyberspace. But she glosses only briefly on the real world implication of multiple personality as a strategy for survival.[11] Her characters are not sick. 'They' are exposition: an updated despatch from the data network as a model of mind. Where other fictions[12] explore the politics of cyberspace as a wild frontier, in more or less realistic future worlds, *Fools* reverses the engineering and uses the metaphors of cyberspace to explore the barely-governed jungle of human consciousness.

Fools is a police-procedural fantasy in futuristic drag—pacey, casual, relentlessly punning. There are elements of farce in the knockabout packet-switching from one narrator personality to another, elements of slapdash pastiche in the sudden emergence of a drab precinct house, a phone-trace, a uniformed cop at the desk. But the Brain Police are more than décor. In *Neuromancer* the Turing Police invoked a simple analogue: mean streets, prohibition, *film noir* cops. They were the FBI: probably corrupt, occasionally virtuous, fighting a losing non-moral 'moral battle' (against the inevitable triumph of the AI, instead of liquor). Finally they were an irrelevance. The Brain Police in *Fools* emerge part way through the narrative as a reassurance: an explanation—familiar, cosy—for the bewildering action. But this soothing role is quickly undermined. These cops are terminally corrupt, routinely committing every crime in their own book, and eventually every character seems to be implicated in their game (everybody is watching everybody else). But here policing never becomes an irrelevance. The cops are the territory. At the end of the novel a single protagonist, her multiple co-selves benignly suppressed, makes a determined resolve to extricate herself from the organisation: to live her own single life. But her resolution is in such contrast to everything that's gone before it can only be taken as a denial episode: a 'God in a machine' (as they used to say, in the original context), who arrives at the end of the show and arbitrarily, temporarily, orders what cannot be ordered.

In *Synners*, before the crash that almost wipes out the global computer networks, a techno-art tattooist called Gator has often been found inscribing on the hide of some insensible burnt out junkie an item of mysterious beauty: a tendril of ivy, maybe, or a lotus flower. These fragments contain, puncture by puncture, like a secret encrypted in the pixels of a downloaded photograph, the essence of Artie Fish. Gator is saving Artie, as a housekeeping precaution. After the crash she'll be able to raise him from the dead: not identical, but himself.[13] Consciousness dissolves when we examine it into an unmanageable palimpsest, indecipherable exploded diagram. In *Fools* the Self has become a harried, overworked presenter, public servant of diversity: dodging and diving and taking any route she can to get the message through. But after each disruption the same face returns, as the pattern of ripples on a flowing stream persists, not an accidental extra but part of the whole system (of river-bed, banks, obstacles, water, air). Mind is stranger, more complicated and uncertain than we could have guessed until now. But it is not an alien or a supplanter. It is an integral part of the natural world.

Through its swift generations computer science has mimicked successive images of consciousness. AI research and biological neuroscience have both been transformed in the last decade, moving towards a strange meeting. The biologists are served by terrifyingly expert technologies that can capture the localised physical events as never before,[14] while in artificial cognitive science, scraps of program are encouraged to breed like bacteria, in the hope that consciousness will crawl out of the digital slime. Yet still the brain is not a computer. If Gerald Edelman and other proponents of the biological model have it right, then maybe no program nor processing device—however powerful in potential or simple in its governing constraints—can be designed to model mind. But the Internet is not a computer. It is a communications network that had for one parent organism a military system required explicitly to survive against the odds (the message may take whatever route it likes, but it must get through). Its memory is malleable, reconstructing constantly the data-objects that it visits and the space in which they exist. Messy, dis-organised, laden with redundancies: it has all the hallmarks of a full-blown biological evolution. The global data network is a vacuum fluctuation in the process of exploding into a cosmos—a collection of digital impulses, microchips, copper wire, optic fibres and plastic boxes, that has the persona: the recalcitrant privacies, the incompleteness, the unconquerable complexities of the biological model of self. No one can know 'exactly what is going on' in there. There is no master program. We dip into cyberspace—triggering a selective firing of the artificial neurons; raising this group and that from different data webs, into ephemeral existence. Already the net will customise a pattern for us, hardening pathways that the individual user has established, so that an informational 'I' springs into existence (though not exactly the same existence as before), whenever the human individual 'I' makes contact again. Without boring any new holes into our skulls, or attaching any sensory interfaces beyond those supplied by evolution, we have created an entity conforming to the original fiction: a matrix of information, infected by visiting minds.

Many claims made for the Internet have faded in the light of experience. There is little evidence that the Net is an utopian, idealist supranational state; or a gender neutral playground. There is no sign of a coming race of Donna Haraway style cyborgs, liberated by technology itself from patriarchal technology's domination,[15] and not much evidence of the revolution in favour of socially disadvantaged youth promised by science fiction writer Bruce Sterling's cyberpunk manifesto.[16] The world order in there is the same as the one out here. How could it be otherwise? I use my modem chiefly for sending cheap, fast international messages, and I regard my Internet suppliers as a new breed of garage mechanics. They despise me because I'm ignorant, they're mildly rude to me because I'm female, and what they really want is get hold of my cybernaut's vehicle so that they can do some kind of work on it—wrong—in ten minutes, and charge me for a week's labour. Information wants to be free? Not any more.

The young male heroes of classic cybertexts are sulky maverick mercenaries, who show no enthusiasm for empowering their own underclass (the women who mother them and tend their bodies while they surf the nets), and recognise no injustice in the gangsta world they inhabit, so long as they themselves are paid well enough or scared hard enough. Radical is a flexible term. Cyberpunk fellow-traveller Kevin Kelly, in his overview of the new technologies, speaks of a biotechnical age that will 'extract the logical principles of life and install them in machines',[17] but it is not at all clear that that final power will be redistributed more equitably, once it is wrested from Mother Nature. Though replication replaces reproduction and neural-processing replaces the tin man, so far the signs are that information technology means not less control but more, in the hands of the same élite. Pat Cadigan, the most intellectually innovative of the cyberpunks, does not argue with the rules of the boys' club. The women in *Synners* are 'strong female characters' (an expression that has become a dire cliché in a genre very nervous about its political correctness rating). But they are too wise to contest with their menfolk for the centre stage. The female protagonists of *Mindplayers* and *Fools* may be punks; they certainly aren't in control. And 'Artie Fish' is not a God, but he's definitely a boy. The mind of cyberspace is still male. Yet the dissolution of the paranoid Overmind model of *Neuromancer* in *Synners*; the constantly disrupted and recovered boundaries of self and not-self, in *Fools*, seem inescapably a political, and even a feminist progress, reflecting the decentred modes of thought—ecologies, evolutions, diversities; populations instead of individuals; groups instead of single interests, which are infiltrating all our current models of the self and the world.

It is not surprising that so much public interest in 'cyberspace' is preoccupied with the question of control, of government. When presented with a novelty, our impulse is to try to get hold of it, to grasp the new (think of these terms, and feel the bright nets of biochemical light, rising and meshing, reaching back through language to the time before language was born, into the deeps…). What is this thing? Is it a threat? Is it my baby? Is it maybe something good to eat? Fictions like Pat Cadigan's *Fools* suggest, among other things, that the project of policing cyberspace effectively has encountered an error of scale: perceiving the Internet as an organisation, which can conceivably buy a really good security system, rather than as a world, where policing failure is the normative state. Policing does not defeat crime. Each population (the police and the criminals) favours the other, in an equilibrium in which damage limitation (from the state's point of view) is the best case. As *Fools* also suggests, what we are really looking at is a mirror. Control in there is the same as control out here: just as incomplete, just as unlikely. In real life, I don't expect the Internet to give birth to independent awareness, (which is possibly the secret fear that underlies all concern about *governing* the net). Perhaps the founding fathers of this new colony will break away and write a constitution for themselves. Perhaps law and order will be imposed by force on the wild frontier: or perhaps this new envelope of shared consciousness will become the seat of government. Whatever the outcome, we can be reasonably sure of one thing: novelty fades. Network use will soon be no more intriguing, nor loaded with meaning, than picking up a telephone. But in that world in which the Internet is invisible and science fiction has moved on to other quarry, we will be different people, our sense of self subtly altered by the existence of this other, the multitudinous immaterial presence, perhaps the nearest thing to an alien intelligence we'll ever meet.

6: Trouble (Living in the Machine)*

I should admit, before I start talking about cyberspace fiction, that I once wrote a proto-cyberspace novel myself. It was called *Escape Plans*; it vanished utterly. It was an uncompromising treatment, written in a kind of machine code, and unfortunately computers aren't able to make consumer choices… yet. It featured a class of people who were plugged in, and who worshiped not computers but logic operations, *function*, as their living God. In my version, jacking-in wasn't an élite activity and it wasn't cool. It was slavery for the masses. If you were privileged you didn't have to go in there: you could stay out in the material world and have fun. I could be right, about the real future of cyberspace—though you won't be plugged in to work, because there won't be any, it will be some kind of low resolution happy-juice entertainment to keep you quiet. But I couldn't have been more wrong about the way the fiction was going. Let me give you an example. This is a short extract from a novel called *Arachne*, by Lisa Mason. It came out in 1990, which means this is a late-Eighties future. As readers of science fiction will know, the sf future is an extrapolation of the writer's present. It deals with society's preoccupations at the exact time of writing. Anyway, the story's set in California, notionally about the mid-twenty-first century. This is after the Big One. San Francisco is an island. It's an age of gridlocks that last for months, routine cosmetic body-shaping, independent AIs which are more or less human; lipgloss and power-dressing. Think *LA Law* with cyberspace. Think Eighties greed-is-good executives injecting whacking quantities of designer-cocaine-analogue into the hole in the back of their necks… Here's Carly Nolan, a 'slim-limbed genny with customised morphing'. She's a fast-tracker in twenty-first-century corporate law, horribly aware that her whole future depends on her ability to make it on the other side of the screen. She's had a bad experience at court, in 'telespace'. This is her return to planet earth:

> …And jacked out into a heap of soiled flesh, sprawled in the chair. Disgust. She'd wet her pants. And pain. The plastic straps had rubbed her wrists raw. She snapped off the straps, ripped the neckjack out of her linkslit. Spilled half a bottle of isoprophyl alcohol into the

---

* This paper, subtitled *The Revolt Against The Physical in Cyberspace Fiction* was originally delivered at the multidiscipline postgraduate conference 'Looking At The Future' held at the University of Sussex, May 1994.

needle thin aperture. ... She swabbed herself off as best she could, sprayed on the dreadful institutional scent kept in the cubicle... Then she fled, jogged down the endless subterranean corridor. In every cubicle she passed lay the limp body of a lawyer jacked into telespace. Some became as wasted as famine victims, rolled back eyes sunk between precipitous skull bones. Some became bloated with sloth, raw lips crusty from the glucose solution clerks piped into their guts to keep the body going... '[1]

I want to emphasise that what I'm talking about today is the fiction, not the reality, not even the advertising of current on-line actuality. I don't know if real-life cyberspace will ever offer the wrap-around sensual and perceptual plenum the fiction persistently describes. If it did, the two still shouldn't be confused. In the novels, the most 'realist' cyberspace works the way it does for fictional, not for technical reasons. But what I'm going to ask (and this may have real-world relevance) is—how did science fiction's delight in a new toy for minds come to involve such disgust for the flesh that has to stay behind?

The phenomenon of 'cyberpunk' has become so detached from science fiction the popular literature, and so glamorised, that many Gibson aficionados perhaps don't realise that what shocked the sf establishment about *Neuromancer* was not the hacker culture, it was the grunge. As anybody in sf can tell you (at length, if you give them half the chance) the melding between human and machine is not a new idea, it is a classic theme. Even the specific, concrete Gibsonish notion of 'neural jacks', the connection between human and machine made by sticking a computer lead into the human nervous system through a hole in the neck or other part of the anatomy, has been around since at least the early Seventies. No, it wasn't the gadgetry that caused the uproar. *Neuromancer* depicts a future in which technology gets more and more amazing, *without* having any effect on the world's problems. That was what upset people. There's no exciting catastrophe to wipe the disc clean, no eco-revolution to save the ruined earth, no space programme beyond a couple of orbital shopping malls. There's nothing in sight but global urban decay: and what's worse, no one in the books even seems to care. This was heresy, out and out burn-at-the-stake heresy, in the US science fiction establishment of 1984. Some of us in sf loved the idea at once, but a lot of people really hated it... though they bought the book. Respected sf authors stood up at conventions and shouted: *'I can't sympathise with these characters! They're petty criminals, they're illiterate street-kids, they're dirty...!'* Science fiction is not a hotbed of radical ideas (whatever you may have heard). In the USA it is a bastion of the Ideological State: liberal, in the US sense of the term, but predominantly technophile, conservative; and at its most 'liberal' still devoted to the American Dream. Science Fiction is supposed to work for positive goals, even if the goal is merely to provide energising escapism. William Gibson and cohorts were doing the sf writers' equivalent of burning their draft cards. They were dropping out.

In *Neuromancer* the revulsion isn't quite articulated. Henry Case's identity is bound up in his access to cyberspace, its the source of his self-esteem.When he can no longer jack-in his situation is tragic. But when his power is restored he still comes out of the machine to have fun: to get high, to do sex, to go clubbing. What happens to Lisa Mason's 'Carly Nolan' is already different. When Case 'falls into the prison of his own flesh'[2] in 1984, it's poetic. When Mason's characters fall, which is whenever they stop work, there's a specific, petty and humiliating horror of the body, an emphasis on the drear necessity of servicing this hulk: *'unstrap, piss, swig glucose, shoot-up… blast back into telespace…'*[3]

Maybe the fact that Lisa Mason is a girl explains something. William Gibson gives his cybernaut a minder, a female caretaker, Molly Kolodny; who may be an assassin by profession, but she still knows how to handle a baby-wipe. Perhaps a woman writer can't help assuming that the domestic, the messy part of her character's job is also… part of her job. Notably Pat Cadigan, the only fully accredited member of the original cyberpunk team, has been far from squeamish about the body/machine interface. To access her cyberspace, (which first appeared in *Mindplayers*, 1987) you take out your eyeballs and leave them in a tank by the vr couch, like leaving your false teeth in a glass by the bed. There's no charge in this process, no poetry or emotionally loaded detail. You just do it. Maybe current fashion explains something more. The Eighties were slick. It's a Nineties thing to get down and dirty and disgusting… But I would propose that these are only partial explanations. I want to suggest that the disgust with the physical in cyberspace ficion is not an artefact of gender difference, or a stylish pose. It is a crucial and serious element in a serious literary manifesto: the cyberpunk world view.

In Lisa Mason's *Arachne*, in Pat Cadigan's books, as in Gibson's cyberspace trilogy and other cyberpunk texts, the 'ruined earth' is accepted as a given. The outside world of this future is polluted, lifeless and degraded beyond repair. Typically, (and in contrast to the *We have to do something about this*! appeal of science fiction disaster warnings) characters show no explicit or effective distress at the collapse of their off-line, macro, life-support systems. As far as they know you've never been able to drink tap water, the sky's always been that funny colour, the city's always been so crowded you have to hire a parking place if you need to linger on the sidewalk (that's Pat Cadigan). It's just the way things are. This dry-eyed stare at the ugly truth is the cyberpunk choice: a rebellion against optimistic science fiction solutions. But the environmental degradation that's described is extreme. There has to be some anxiety, somewhere. It seems reasonable to suppose that body-hatred stands in part for a revulsion from the whole trapped, sweaty poverty of a life with no exit on a dirty, dilapidated overcrowded planet. For sake of their emotional survival the characters in these books have to detach, to think about something else: have to alienate themselves. The most radical cyber-fantasy of escape from the body—disembodied brains in support vats, personalities transferred permanently into computer storage—is, like the neural jacking, only the latest appearence of an established set of science fiction images. Villainous geniuses have been preserving themselves in this way for decades, whole societies have misguidedly given up the richness of the sensual world. But what was formerly a symbol of élite (if evil) privilege, starts to look like dire necessity. In the cyberpunk future, which is so uncomfortably slight an extrapolation from our present, maybe we have to choose to hate the living world, starting with its most intimate manifestation, our own living bodies. It would be too painful otherwise, to watch the creature die.

The idea of a 'world' that exists beyond the computer screen is not so much invention as a legacy of evolution. Minds and bodies shaped by interaction with a physical world act and react in terms of a physical world, or not at all. Thus we have *'the world of the imagination'*; *'an area of intellectual discourse'*; we *'pick up'* ideas as if they were objects; and to approach this truth from a less cerebral angle, players of the most basic and meagre of arcade games experience all the symptoms of passionate physical arousal. The blood pumps, the pulse speeds, the flesh swells, the juices flow… It's not surprising then that popular imagination has seized on the term, ruthlessly wresting it from the exclusive grip of the modem-owning bracket, so that 'cyberspace', which began its street career a few years ago as *'the place where your money lives'*, has been retrofitted to mean any locus of physical/non-physical interaction. It's the world inside the tv, the place where phone conversations happen, the place where washing machines decide what to do to your clothes. Before long, and quite reasonably, it may come to 'mean' that limitless space which so mysteriously fits inside a human skull. Meanwhile, an ironic reversal for a word derived from the Greek for a steersman, the restraining controller who stops the ship from going astray, 'Cyber' as a prefix has come to mean almost exactly the same as 'sex'—signalling excitement, danger, social rebellion, forbidden pleasure. (I wouldn't be surprised to find that in the US 'cyberpunk' is turning into another word for food.)

In the fiction, equally, cyberspace has taken over a traditional and ancient role. When you jack-in, you pass through the Door in the Wall of a thousand fairytales and enter a land imbued with meaning, the miraculous other world of myth, where—contrary to what we observe in nature—evil is punished, virtue is rewarded and all riddles have answers. In Gibson's *Neuromancer* trilogy, as in Mason's *Arachne*, 'cyberspace' first features as a geometric abstraction, a clear contrast to the mess of the human world. In Gibson's case the Matrix, fertilised by the union of the supernatural AIs Wintermute and Neuromancer, becomes a haunted facsimile of physical reality: a literally magical wonderland. In *Arachne*, 'telespace' is discovered to be infested by magic. The *chimera*—entities perceived as gorgeous mythological beasts—which are glimpsed by disbelieving cyberlawyers and others, represent a fertilisation of the digital realm, a fusion of life with not-life that goes deeper than the individual links between humans and the machine ('machine' here, as in 'Turing Machine', meaning logical function itself). In both cases, though the stories differ in structure and implication, cyberspace becomes the locale where problems are faced, and myths of sacrifice and redemption are enacted. Literary cyberspace, then, becomes the latest in an age-old succession of magical supernatural realms identified with the world of thought: a 'place' where human consciousness goes to discover explanations and devise solutions. Meanwhile the physical body, vessel of unworthy appetites, is condemned, with positively mediaeval severity, as the focus of corruption: the past that must be left behind.

Later generations of cybernauts, writing in the context of a real-world on-line industry, have produced more realist treatments. This is still fantasy, not a mimetic fiction. It's a question of a greater or lesser degree of idealist intervention, never (so far) the phenomenon of computer networking as a morally neutral technology. Modems are not telephones, not yet. But though the mythic wonderland recedes, the insistence on the painful and distasteful aspects of the cyberspace escape grows stronger. This is an extract from a novel called *Trouble and her Friends*, by Melissa Scott, published this year. 'Trouble' is the working handle of a legendary netwalker—a kind of brain-augmented hacker. She's been in exile since repressive legislation closed down her semi-legal activities and has not been keeping up with the hard or the software. Now she's getting back on line (so that the plot can happen). She's just had some illegal elective brain surgery—conducted on a toilet seat—to restore her to full communion with the Net:

> 'It's a good system,' Huu dumped the contents of the instrument tray into Van Liewvelt's sink, 'I think you'll like the way it runs now.'
> 'Thanks.' Trouble... pushed herself to her feet. Her jeans were damp between her legs, flesh swollen and unsatisfied. Over Huu's shoulder

she could see the water in the basin tinted faintly pink, a piece of scalp sticking to the side just below the waterline. ' I think I want a drink...'[4]

For Gibson's Henry Case body-hatred was a symptom of bruised self-esteem. For both Case and Carly Nolan jacking-in was a positive choice. Cyberspace represented a better, cleaner, alternative to the leaky bag of flesh left behind, pissing itself and drooling. In *Trouble and her Friends* a physical humiliation—involuntary orgasm—is the direct result of cyberspace experience itself. In Trouble's world you don't escape from your body by entering the net. You only think you do. When you return to this side of the screen you find that traces of your fantasy have followed you home, and the result is always depressing. Thus, in a passage describing voluntary virtual sex, although the fun is apparently completely consensual and consenting, when the character jacks out she finds herself literally redfaced, pants full of sticky goo, and is filled with childish shame and revulsion.

From *Neuromancer* to *Trouble and her Friends,* cyberspace fiction parallels the development of real world computer networking. In William Gibson's fiction the result of human development of cyberspace is the creation of a new divinity, a Godlike entity able to leave the ruined human world behind (even if we can't). As the fiction moves closer into near-market fantasy, we move from metaphysics to physiology. We're still in dreamland, but here the enactments of the disembodied world are not mythical or mystic. Instead they have all the character of the real-world dreams of sleeping-brain chemistry: disjointed images and jumbled narratives, sexual arousal, orgiastic violence, irrational terror, bursts of impossible super power. Maybe cyberspace *can* make our dreams come true. But if this is the case, Melissa Scott reminds us—and she's chosen shame in a sexual context, I think, because we're inured to violence—we should consider this: Our 'real' dreams, as opposed to our wistful aspirations, are often things of which, waking, we are ashamed.

Cyberspace in fiction bears little practical resemblance to the real thing, but possibly it reflects the real situation. The present range of on-line experience may be mediated by text but it is very REM dreamlike: the sex, the violence, the bursts of superpower, not to mention the reams of desultory garbage. But the metaphysical aspirations are represented too. There are plenty of cyberspace missionaries who are convinced the modem has created an inner-space New World, where human nature will be reforged and perfected. But what about art? *Genuine* cyberspace fiction, I mean as opposed to conventional print-fiction written about cyberspace, hardly exists as yet. The few hypertext novels that have appeared have the reputation of horseless carriages a hundred years ago: cumbersome, difficult to use, expensive toys for rich cranks. But some time soon, the software will become easier to use. These clunky horseless carriages may become vehicles capable of modelling, in electronic data storage, the true complexity of the novel as it exists in my mind... There may be hypertext tools that allow each individual to read *actively*, to explore or fail to explore the different layers of creation at choice, to blunder or to forge new pathways; to re-form the book physically, permanently, in as many variant complexities as it has readers. Instead of the doom prophesied by William Gibson's self destructing *Agrippa*, which regards the electronic medium (here I'm paraphrasing an article by Stuart Moulthrop, author of the electronic fiction *Victory Garden*) as the enemy of art, we can envisage a future in which every reading of a novel creates (something that happens always, in the cyberspace of the mind) a subtly or radically customised unique artefact, individual as a snowflake... I think that's a fascinating thought. It should also mean, by the way, that a novel as art work would acquire the status and the potential of a painting or a sculpture. However many copies were sold, my original would lose none of its value. The text of some great novel as created by the artist might be preserved in an on-line gallery, for reverent examination: protected against thieves and vandals by on-line bullet-proof glass...

Well. I wish. Unfortunately I don't think so. I expect the freedom and the intellectual romance of this new medium will survive, marginally. But there are powerful forces in league, waiting to prevent that.

The success of 'cyberspace the concept' is painful and ironic for science fiction. Decades of earnest technophiles have been presenting supposedly rational wishlists to the men in white coats. Nothing ever came through for them. The galaxy remains unexplored, the solar-system uncolonised, the nuclear-powered rocketships have vanished over the horizon of possibility into never-never land. Yet William Gibson's literary metaphor, this blatant fantasy, is rapidly turning into fact. This is galling indeed. But as 'cyberspace' bootstraps itself into existence, in the image of the original fiction, there emerges a final and highly practical rationale for the idealistic or radically inventive cybernaut's fear of the material world. In an interview when he was over here promoting his non-fiction cybertext *Hacker Crackdown*, Bruce Sterling—another of the original cyberpunks—issued a grim warning. He said the general public ought to be more alarmed about the revolutions going on around them: '*Technology is going to rip society apart.*' But no... That's not what happens. This is not what we observe in nature. Always, inevitably, it is society that rips the technology apart. Already, the html-writing is on the screen for Internet romanticism. Cyberspace will be ruled, like all our new worlds, not by the thinking mind and its aspirations but by the greedy dreamer: that alliance of appetite and aggression we call 'commerical interests and state control', to conceal from ourselves the fact that *we ourselves* choose to have things run that way.

Cyberspace isn't science fiction any more. But there is a classic science fiction in cyberpunk. In the *Neuromancer* trilogy and in *The Difference Engine*, their later collaboration, William Gibson and Bruce Sterling track the emergence of a self-conscious artificial intelligence, from the fertile pre-creation soup of the nets. Pat Cadigan has done the same in her recent novel *Synners*. The emergence of a self-conscious intelligence from the complexity of human data processing is a dream that has given shape to many cyberspace fiction plots. It's the latest form of a dream that has been around for a long time: an enduring fantasy that some kind of omniscient, unlimited and perfected Res Cogitans will one day emerge, not predating human consciousness but arising from it. Perhaps just as 'cyberspace' is real, and the rocketships are nowhere, the concept of a non-human artificial consciousness, a God-Machine, is a canard; but the dream may come true. Perhaps the mind-in-the-machine that can solve all our problems is coming to birth right now, inhabiting the networks, free at last. Its name is legion, it is the human users themselves. But just as the fiction tells us, we'll find no solutions for our real-world problems in cyberspace, unless we take them there ourselves. Nor—no matter what the fiction says—will we find any escape in virtuality from the evils of the flesh.

7: Sex: The Brains of Female Hyena Twins*

Female hyenas have high levels of androstenedione (a male hormone) throughout life, which possibly contributes to their aggressive nature. Interestingly, ...they behave normally in reproduction and are excellent mothers, showing that the 'female' parts of the brain are protected from the androgens that masculinise their aggressive behaviour...

Laurence Frank, behavioural research associate,
in *New Scientist*, 5 March 1994

Carey points out that we already have a wonderful genetic marker for violence: 'It's detectable at birth and in many cases before birth,' he says, 'The high-risk genotype is probably about nine-fold more likely to engage in violent acts... for some crimes the ratio is even more dramatic.' Carey's marker is being male.

Rosie Mostel, in *New Scientist*, 26 February 1994,
quoting geneticist Gregory Carey

Two out of three women around the world presently suffer from the most debilitating disease known to humanity. Common symptoms of this fast-spreading ailment include chronic anaemia, malnutrition, severe fatigue... Premature death is a frequent outcome... the disease is often communicated from mother to child, with markedly higher transmission rates among females. No, this disease is not HIV. It is poverty.

The Health Of Women, A Global Perspective edited by
Marge Koblonsky, Judith Timyan, Gill Gay

Preamble

The battle of the sexes heats up and cools down, waves of 'feminism' rise and fall: but received wisdom regards human gender as a given: one of the pillars of the universe. Men and women are two sides of the same coin. No matter how they bicker, in the end and by and large they have to accept the complementary nature of their relationship, and get along the same

---

* A paper first presented at the conference of the Acadamic Fantastic Fiction Network, held at Reading University, October 1994.

old way... But increasingly this 'business as usual' world-view is maintained in the teeth of the evidence. In the course of the last century world-wide creation of wealth has been making insidious attacks, finally far more damaging than anything sexual-politicians can achieve, on the concept of sexual gender. The lowering of the death-rate, high infant survival, improved standards of living, improved quality of life itself, all go to create a situation in which, inexorably, the human male's propensity for violence and the human female's capacity for childbearing, come to be regarded not as natural facts of life but as problems that threaten the prosperity and comfort of human society. Human history suggests that once we've perceived some factor in our world as a problem (whether it's the nature of the fixed stars, or the scourge of infectious disease) sooner or later, someone will come up with a technological fix.

On the Future of Gender

For the last ten years, as a writer of feminist science fiction, I have been conducting a strictly amateur investigation into the nature and function of human sexual behaviour. I have approached the subject in different ways in novels, stories and critical essays; I've done a fair amount of reading around the area, and, like all good science fiction writers, I've taken note of developments in the real world. In the course of the decade I've seen 'feminsim' as a broadly based political movement discredited, and I've seen it re-established as a literary and academic forum with its own private squabbles, media stars and market-niche; an accepted cultural sub-group. I've seen women *en masse* rejecting radical political solutions, yet at the same time becoming more vocal, more visible, more conscious and more openly resentful of their disadvantages. I've seen the New Man defrocked, and the return of the unrepentant male supremacist. Yet at the same time I've seen emerging a global acknowledgement of endemic crimes against women—rape as a weapon of war, bride burning, domestic violence—that have been tacitly condoned, if not openly approved, for millennia upon millennia. As I try to grapple, in my fiction, with complexity and the tensions I see in the real world, I've found myself returning, in the exasperated way one tries to establish the starting point of a quarrel, *ad fontes* (that means to the springs. It's Latin for 'Let's get back to where this all started'). Just what exactly is this thing called sex? What is it for, what is it supposed to do? This paper is a report on my investigation, and at the same time a description of how I, as an sf writer, go about the work of extracting ideas for my fiction from real world science.

There are quite a few popular science texts on sex around at the moment. It seems I'm not alone in my interest. Most of them (Richard Dawkins's

The Selfish Gene; Matt Ridley's *The Red Queen*; Gail Vines's *Raging Hormones*)
are extended essays from popularisers with their own agendas—
determined to challenge, rouse or excite their audience one way or another.
These are 'sexy' books, as we say nowadays. I preferred *The Differences
Between the Sexes*, the published proceedings of the Eleventh International
Conference on Comparative Physiology, held three years ago in
Switzerland. *The Differences Between the Sexes* is a collection of original
scientific papers, described as 'the first overview of this subject ever
attempted'. This text does not set out to provoke anybody. The attentive
reader can discern a whole spectrum of political opinion, faintly inscribed
between the lines. But any special pleading is buried deep in pernickety
scatter-graphs, and unlikely to stir the emotions unduly. Broadly, this is a
book about sex as physiology, on every scale. There is no discussion of the
symptoms or sensations of sexual arousal, only of chemical reactions. The
organisms or body parts involved—lizards, ants, elephants, fishes, possibly
parasitical mitochondria, Mullerian ducts and avian W chromosomes—are
not perceived as doing sex for pleasure. They do it for exclusively economic
reasons. But don't imagine that this makes for a dry and dull textbook.
The sex-for-money story here is possibly even more fascinating than the
one you find in the more familiar tabloid context.

So, exactly what do we—represented by the international science
community—know about sex, at this stage in the game? Let me refresh
your memories on modern sex-science lore. We know that eutherian
mammals—that's animals like us—with the XX or XY sex chromosome
pair, are default females. Hence the expression mammals, animals with
milk-producing breasts. So, if you castrate (as it were) a male rabbit embryo
at an early stage in its development it doesn't grow up sexless, it develops
as a normal female. (This is charmingly called Ohno's law, after Susumu
Ohno, who first proved it.) Whereas birds, with a ZZ or ZW pair, the W
being the female chromosome, are default males. Thus if you feed a peahen
male hormones, she gets a bit pushy and irritable but physically nothing
much happens. If you suppress her female hormones, she grows a
flamboyant peacock's tail. The 'cryptic' or dowdy plumage of the female
in bird species is not a deficiency, then, as we have intuitively assumed. It
is a positive interference in the natural course of things. Marsupials, or
non-eutherian mammals, don't fit into this scheme of the chromosome
pair sexing. They're a peculiar lot. We know that gonadal sex, the
development of testes or ovaries, is normally determined in eutherian
mammals at conception. All other features of sexual dimorphism—
external and internal organs, differences in brain structure and body size,
all sexual behaviours—are produced subsequently by the action of the
gonadal steroids, (progestins, androgens and estrogens), powerful chemical

concoctions that are carried in the circulation to act throughout the body, including the brain. It's as you long suspected, you're not responsible for anything you do under the influence of sex, it's just a drug experience. Marsupials, however, don't work quite the same way... (But I can't begin to tell you about the marsupials, it's just too bizarre. You wouldn't believe me. You'll have to read it for yourselves).

What else could I mention? There are the parthenogenetic species, animals that consist naturally of female individuals only. (It's not suggested that they evolved out of the pre-Cambrian stew like so: they have separated off from gonochoric, that is sexual species, somewhere along the line.) Some of them mate with males of related sexual species, and have various means of using or discarding the sperm DNA after conception. Some produce eggs without any genetic recombination at all: they're obligate separatists. I think the most famous of these species, the Texan parthenogenetic whiptail lizards studied by David Crews of the University of Texas, Austin, have passed into popular-science folklore, so you'll probably know that all-female lizard species exist. But did you know that individuals of these species have a habit of copulating with each other, taking turns at adopting male or female roles—a behaviour which has a measurable impact on sex-hormone expression and on breeding success? The act itself has only been observed in captivity (there are some delightful photos); but the 'male' partner's role includes inflicting neck-bites severe enough to produce a lasting bruise. Wild animals picked up for examination have been found with exactly similar hickeys on their throats, so it looks as if it's not just the decadent lab-cage trollops, they're playing butch and femme out on the range too.

You may have heard of the SRY gene (written Sry when it's mouse DNA, in the science's convention; SRY for humans). That stands for sex-determining region, Y gene. The definitive, universal marker that makes males male achieved national news status when the discovery was announced a year or so ago. The detective story of the hunt for SRY is in here: a paper by Jennifer Graves of Le Trobe University, Victoria, Australia. It's truly fascinating. But there's also, hot from the press, research that has unearthed some 'bizarre rodents'—the Iberian mole vole, the Kamchatka wood lemming, the Amami spinuous country rat—where maleness is not determined by the Sry, and maybe even not by the XY pair. The hunt for the actual, holy essence of *la différence* isn't over yet.

What else? There's a paper on sexual dimorphism in primates, presenting evidence from skeletal analysis that female proto-gorillas, humans, chimps, may have been hunky as the males. Rather than males being selected out for larger size and strength, the females may have been selected down to a smaller body-size on the grounds of reproductive success. This is one of the papers where a quite provocative point is hidden in the scatter-graphs. It is a basic tenet of male supremacist thought that humanity is naturally unequal, because men have always been the big strong owners of harems of docile little females... It gives them legitimacy. (I do not see it myself. If someone knocks me down because he's bigger than me, and then explains it's okay, because he's been bigger than me for two million years, I don't feel any better about it at all.) But it's quietly done: no excitement, no politics, just a modest suggestion that you take a look at the figures.

There are the female to male and male to female transsexual fishes. You'll have heard of them, maybe. They've passed into popular science folklore along with the Texan lizards. It appears that in many species of fishes if you remove the dominant male from a social group, the largest female then becomes male. In other circumstances fish that are born 'male' become female. Douglas Shapiro and others, of Michigan, have been investigating this phenomenon. They've discovered that sex-change is not destiny. The female to male or male to female change isn't inevitable in a simple set of circumstances like 'remove the male'. It is triggered by a particular and complex interaction of social and environmental factors: but broadly, it happens only when it's going to be profitable. You've heard of Sexual Darwinism. Here you get a classic, beautifully explained study of the precise economic factors that lead an individual fish to 'decide'— speaking anthropomorphically—to change that mumsy apron for the go-getter's posing pouch.

There's sexually differentiated liver-function in rats; featuring mind-boggling lists of sexually differentiated steroid metabolizing enzymes. There's a paper on song-control brain area dimorphism in the nucleus hyperstriatalis ventrale in male canaries; as opposed to male and female zebra finches, a duetting species, reassessing the significance of sexually dimorphic brain structure, and the relationship of brain-area volume to efficient function. There's a paper on Drosophila melanogaster pheromones (you can't leave out the fruit flies). And much more.

It's no surprise that the picture isn't much altered from Aristotle's view of the sexes. (The relevant quotation is provided in translation in the front of the book. I thought that was a stylish touch—*ad fontes* indeed.) Cosmologists can add or subtract a few billion years from the age of the universe at will, without colliding with commonsense. Sexual dimorphism belongs to a different order. Male sexual behaviour, generally, is aggressive and dominant. Female sexual behaviour, generally, is submissive and compliant. This is what we know, this is what we see. The advent of electron tunnelling microscopy is not going to reveal, suddenly, that it's female red deer that grow the big antlers, and start beating the shit out of each other every September; or that male elephant seals are the helpless victims of institutionalized rape on the beaches. There *are* some popular sex-science writers who take violent exception to Aristotle. But they are no use to me. I'm never very interested in imaginative interpretation with my science. I only have to pick it out and leave it on the side of my plate. I provide that element for myself. The editors of *The Differences Between the Sexes* are less radical than some of their contributors (to the extent that R.V. Short, in his afterword, declares that 'nobody questions the significant differences in average weight, height and strength between men and women, testimony no doubt to our polygynous past...' apparently unaware that Robert Martin and others, the primate body-size snatchers from Zurich, have done exactly that). In many of the papers one can discern a fashionable shift in concept from simplicity to complexity, from clear results to fuzziness. Thus in the primate-size paper Robert Martin and his team do not claim that the theory of the big, polygynous male ape and human ancestor is wrong, they present evidence for a more complex situation. Science becomes a palimpsest, not a single text: it becomes, in some ways, a kind of fiction. But though trends in modern thought have a discernible influence there is an old-fashioned anti-radical consensus in these papers, a commitment to pure description—as far as humanly possible—above interpretation, that gives me confidence. I can work with these results, without much hassly filtering out of contaminates.

I don't think I have to apologise for reading *The Differences Between the Sexes* politically. I am, sincerely, in awe at the quality of some of the papers (so far as an amateur can appreciate them). But I'm a science fiction writer, not a scientist. I approach these essays as I would an article on the curious plight of Hubble's Constant. I'm looking for hooks and riffs; material I can use. The scientific version of the sexual politics debate can be summed up roughly thus: are animals individuals, whose behaviour is affected, marginally and circumstantially, by sexual function? Or is sexual/reproductive function the essential, defining core of the organism? You can find one or other view expounded, with more or less of tub-thumping self interest, by writers like Richard Dawkins, Matt Ridley, Elaine Morgan, Gail Vines. The editors of *Differences*, in their separate afterwords, neatly represent the opposing camps. The papers tend, if anything, towards the former position. What I find in *The Differences Between the Sexes* is a general chipping away at the area that can be labelled male or female in physiology and in behaviour; and a shift in concept from sex-specific to sex typic: 'Sex-specific behaviours are numerically a minority. Most sexual behaviours are "sex typic" meaning they can be produced by either... but are shown more frequently in one sex' (Manfred Gahr: 'Brain Structure: causes and consequences of brain sex'). But the sex-is-destiny argument is also supported. Sex difference is largely malleable, but it is unambiguous. There is no sliding scale in behaviour, function or identity: it seems we are dealing with a switch, not a dial. There is male, and there is female. The identities may be confused by a genetic copying error, successive in a single lifetime, alternating in a complex mosaic of behaviours. They can be learned, unlearned, adopted or simulated at will: but they are always distinct.

The investigation is fascinating. I'm equally interested in the fact that it exists at all. There was a time, quite recently, when popular science books about sex were how-to manuals with soft focus covers; or collections of prurient statistics about the sexual habits of people who like talking dirty to market researchers. But in the last few decades, technology has made the secrets of reproductive function accessible as never before. The mystery of sex can be examined, it can be taken apart. There are signs of a development that is familiar in the history of science. A set of phenomena that was a puzzling given, not even a locked box but apparently a solid block, has changed its nature. Jupiter has moons, the atom has internal structure... As we know from previous experience, this is a precarious situation. Once we start taking something of this order apart, we never manage to fit the pieces together again, quite the way they were before. I'm not sure how far the general public participates in scientific revolutions. There's a theory that *thought* gets into the air and worries people—so that the individual human animal in the street eventually starts to feel uncertain about Heisenberg's uncertainty principle, or kind of stretched by the implications of general relativity. There has been a wave of female emancipation recently, it's true, and over these same decades. But there've been waves of female emancipation before, and nothing much happened. As I remarked in my opening paragraph, the evidence is that most people actively enjoy the battle of the sexes. They do not want a sexual reconciliation. However, in this context it's interesting to note the recent career of the term gender. Does gender, which means difference, mean the same as sex? Increasingly, and to the irritation of pedants, people are using the terms as if they're interchangeable. (I called this paper 'On the future of Gender'. On disc it's called SEX, because it's shorter.) We talk about gender roles, gender-studies, gender-politics, gender-related issues. Irate terminology-watchers (for instance Richard Dawkins) demand indignantly, 'If you mean sex, why don't you say so? What is this decadent newspeak!' But I suspect that people may be becoming increasingly aware that we *don't* mean sex, when we say gender. When you are asked to check the box on the form, the question's not about physiology, it is about social role: about difference. You are not being asked, 'Do you have ovaries?' You're being asked, 'Are you going to stay at home and look after the children?' Or, to put it another way: 'If we give you this job, are you going to work for three weeks and then take an extended career break at our expense, to indulge your sociopathic addiction to child-bearing?'

Sexual behaviour is malleable. Sex-hormones are mind-altering drugs that can be used by anyone, female or male. If I dose myself with testosterone, I will become aggressive, non-altruistic (and hairy) as any genetic male. We know this can be done, and we can be sure it will be done. Because if there is one thing we know about animals, whether they're whiptail lizards, nematodes or humans, it's that if an animal once finds it can do something, and profit ensues, then it will do that something, though the heavens fall (this is called evolution). We can adjust our sexual behaviour, and thereby our social roles. We can't—not yet—alter reproductive function. The option of having no children is now available to sexually active women as never before: but no hormone treatment will turn a man into a fertile woman. However, reproduction, as instanced by that job application dilemma, is not strictly the issue. It can be argued that since human females don't experience oestrus, sex has always been primarily a social activity for our species, engaged in for social benefit, from the point of view of the selfish individual human animal (leaving the selfish gene a helpless hitchhiker on life's journey). Most certainly now, more than ever, it's social function that matters.

Animals do sex for money: for strictly economic reasons. 'They choose' the sexual behaviours, weaponry, body-size; and, where feasible, the sexual identity, that 'they believe'—to personify a complex of highly impersonal factors—will ensure greatest reproductive success. That's Sexual Darwinism, and as scientific theories go, it seems to work. Without reproductive success—on a mega scale—humans wouldn't be where they are today. But more and more, for selfish individual human animals both male and female, reproduction is not money. Money is money: is status, territory, resources. According to the science in *The Differences Between the Sexes*, we will all adjust our sexual behaviour accordingly.

The world is overpopulated, we should be having fewer children. But women who have more economic rights than ever before—in this country for instance, and in other rich countries of the White North—see childbearing as another kind of access to resources, which they have a right to enjoy at any price, and even when they are way past biological child-bearing age. Meanwhile in China, in Africa and in the Balkans, (to name but a few locales) men are controlling women's fertility for the ancient, animal reasons and on a genocidal scale. Femaleness is in trouble. But Maleness is no better off. All over the world men are having to compete directly with women in dominance ranking contests: in parliaments, in the job market, in the media—a situation which they find very disturbing indeed. In the world at war, ordinary, natural male-competitive behaviour—killing the defeated rival's offspring and impregnating his females—is suddenly stigmatised as criminal, *just when the competition's getting fierce*. It's enough to drive a species crazy… I do not say that 'sex' is suddenly a problem. The conflicts between male and female interests are the same as always. The problem, perhaps, is that there is now a solution, of sorts, available. Men and women, while remaining men and women, can adjust their individual sexual behaviour and experience almost indefinitely, for maximum economic benefit. If sexual behaviour and function are malleable, and yet sexual identity, *difference*, remains obstinately intact—which is what the science predicts and what we see happening around us—then we don't have two complementary sexes any more, each safe in its own niche. All there is left is gender: an us and them situation. Two tribes, separated by millennia upon millennia of grievances and bitterness, occupying the same territory and squabbling over the same diminished supply of resources. This is the situation, the riff that I've found and used, and which you'll find explored in my novels *White Queen*, *North Wind*, and *Phoenix Café*. I'm a writer of fiction, a composer of metaphors and myths. But like the writers of *The Differences Between the Sexes*, I try to take a scientific view of things. My ideas are always open to further investigation, reassessment, the development of new and more searching experiments. I certainly hope I'm wrong about the way the battle of the sexes is shaping (though I admit I'd almost prefer open war to the alternative, where women return *en masse* to their traditional imprisonment). But for the moment that's what I see, so that's what I turn into story.

I'd like to say more about the future of gender. There are philosophical considerations, supposing we manage not to tear each other apart. Animals do sex for money. Humans also think, and this concept of difference: either/or, same/not same is immeasurably important to our thought. How deeply is our sense of the other bound to our sexuality? This is another aspect of the gender question, that has been tackled in various ways in feminist science fiction; but it has plenty of potential for futher exploration. What happens to that crucial image of the other—the face opposite, the self that is not-self—if the importance of sex begins to be eroded? But that's a whole new question, and beyond my scope at present.

You may be wondering what happened to the brains of female hyenas. It's another strange but true sex-science story, not actually featured in *Differences*, about testosterone use and abuse in the animal world. But I had so many, that I forgot to use it.

8: Aliens in the Fourth Dimension

When Two Worlds Collide

The aliens can always speak English. This is one of those absurdities of pulp fiction and B movies, like saucer shaped spaceships and hairdryer machines that track your brain waves,[1] that might well come true—suppose the visitors avoid those disconcerting forms of long haul space travel, that whisk you across the galaxy and dump you in the concourse of Lime Street station before you have time to say 'Non Smoking'. If they come in slowly they'll spend the latter part of their journey travelling through a vast cloud of human broadcasting signals, which they'll easily pick up on the alien cabin tv. They'll have plenty of time to acquire a smattering of useful phrases. Or so the current received wisdom goes. By now it's not *completely* inevitable that they'll speak English, and with a United States accent, in the traditional manner. They might get hooked on Brazilian soap opera. But whatever formal, articulate language our visitors may use in real life, all the aliens we know so far speak human. They speak our human predicament, our history, our hopes and fears, our pride and shame. As long as we haven't met any actual no kidding intelligent extraterrestrials (and I would maintain that this is still the case, though I know opinions are divided) the aliens we imagine are always other humans in disguise: no more, no less. Whether or not hell is other people, it is certainly *other people* who arrive, in these fictions, to challenge our isolation: to be feared or worshipped, interrogated, annihilated, appeased. When the historical situation demands it science fiction writers demonise our enemies, the way the great Aryan court poet[2] who wrote the story of Prince Rama *demonised* the Dravidian menace, in India long ago. Or we can use imaginary aliens to assuage our guilt. I think it's not unlikely that our European ancestors invented the little people who live in the hills, cast spells and are 'ill to cross'—who appear so often in traditional fiction north of the mediterranean and west of Moscow—to explain why their cousins the Neanderthals had mysteriously vanished from public life. I see the same thing happening today, as science fiction of the environmentally-conscious decades becomes littered with gentle, magical, colourful alien races who live at one with nature in happy non-hierarchical rainforest communities. Even the project of creating an *authentically incomprehensible* other intelligent species, which is sporadically attempted in science fiction, is inescapably a human story. Do we yet know of any other beings who can imagine, or could care less, what 'incomprehensible' means?

More often than not, the aliens story involves an invasion. The strangers have arrived. They want our planet, and intend to wipe us out. We have arrived. The native aliens—poor ineffectual technologically incompetent creatures—had better get out of the way. The good guys will try to protect them: but territorial expansion, sometimes known as 'progress', is an unstoppable force. This pleasant paradigm of intra-species relations obviously strikes a deep chord. We, in the community of science fiction writers and readers at least, do not expect to co-exist comfortably with *other people*. Which ever side is 'ours', there is going to be trouble, there is going to be grief, when two worlds collide. And whatever language everyone is speaking, there is definitely going to be a break down in communications.

When I invented my alien invaders 'The Aleutians' I was aware of the models that science fiction offered, and of the doubled purpose that they could serve. I wanted, like other writers before me, to tell a story about the colonisers and the colonised. The everlasting expansion of a successful population, first commandment on the Darwinian tablets of stone, makes this encounter 'the supplanters and the natives', an enduring feature of human history. Colonial adventure has been a significant factor in the shaping of my own, European, twentieth-century culture. I wanted to think about this topic. I wanted to study the truly extraordinary imbalance in wealth, power, and *per capita* human comfort, from the south to the north, that came into being over three hundred years or so of European rule in Africa, Asia and the Indian subcontinent: an imbalance which did not exist when the Portuguese reached China, when the first British and French trading posts were established on the coasts of India; when European explorers arrived in the gold-empire cities of West Africa.[3] I also wanted—the other layer of the doubled purpose—to describe and examine the relationship between men and women. There are obvious parallels between my culture's colonial adventure and the battle of the sexes. Men come to this world helpless, like bewildered explorers. At first they all have to rely on the goodwill of the native ruler of the forked, walking piece of earth in which they find themselves. And then, both individually and on a global scale, they amass as if by magic a huge proportion of the earth's wealth, power and influence, while the overwhelming majority of those native rulers are doomed to suffer and drudge and starve in the most humiliating conditions. But why? I wondered. How did this come about? Why *do* most of the women get such a rough deal?

I felt that my historical model would be better for throwing up insights, mental experiments, refutable hypotheses about sexual politics, than popular ' alien invasion' narratives based on United States cultural history. The possibilities of an outright *lebensraum* struggle between settlers and natives would soon be exhausted; while a situation involving any extreme division between master race and slave race would be too clear cut.[4] I needed something in a sense more innocent. A relationship that could grow in intimacy and corruption: a trading partnership where neither party is more altruistic than the other, whichever manages to win the advantage. Most of all, I needed something *slow*. I needed to see what would happen to my experiment over hundreds of years: over generations, not decades. So, the Aleutians appeared: a feckless crew of adventurers and dreamers, with only the shakiest of State backing, no aim beyond seeing life and turning a quick profit; and no coherent long-term plans whatever.

Interview with the Alien

Some stories about meeting the aliens are recruiting posters for the Darwinian army. Explicitly, we're invited to cheer for the home team, or to enjoy the pleasurably sad and moving defeat of the losers. Implicitly, we're reminded that every encounter with 'the other', down to office manoeuvring and love affairs, is a fight for territory: and the weak must go to the wall. Some people invent aliens as a Utopian or satirical exercise, to show how a really well-designed intelligent species would live and function, and how far the human model falls below this ideal. I confess to adopting elements from both these approaches. But above all, I wanted my aliens to represent an alternative. I wanted them to say to my readers *It ain't necessarily so*.[5] History is not inevitable, and neither is sexual gender as we know it an inevitable part of being human. I didn't intend my aliens to represent 'women', exactly; or for the humans to be seen as 'men' in this context. Human women and men have their own story in the Aleutian books. But I wanted to make the relationship *suggestive* of another way things could have turned out. I planned to give my alien conquerors the characteristics, all the supposed deficiencies, that Europeans came to see in their subject races in darkest Africa and the mystic East—'animal' nature, irrationality, intuition; mechanical incompetence, indifference to time, helpless aversion to theory and measurement: and I planned to have them win the territorial battle this time. It was no coincidence, for my purposes, that the same list of qualities or deficiencies—a nature closer to the animal, intuitive communication skills and all the rest of it—were and still are routinely awarded to *women*, the defeated natives, supplanted rulers of men, in cultures north and south, west and east, white and non-white, the human world over.[6]

They had to be humanoid. I didn't want my readers to be able to distance themselves; or to struggle proudly towards empathy in spite of the tentacles. I didn't want anyone to be able to think, *Why, they're just like us once you get past the face-lumps,* the way we do when we get to know the tv alien goodies and baddies in *Babylon 5* or *Space Precinct 9.* I needed them to be irreducibly weird and, *at the same time,* undeniably people, the same as us. I believe this to be a fairly accurate approximation of the real-world situation—between the Japanese and the Welsh, say, or between women and men: or indeed between any individual human being and the next. Difference is real. It does not go away. To express my contention—that irreducible difference, like genetic variation, is conserved in the individual, not in race, nationality or reproductive function, I often awarded my Aleutians quirks of taste and opinion belonging to one uniquely different middle-aged, middle-class, leftish Englishwoman. And I was entertained to find them hailed by US critics as 'the most convincingly *alien* beings to grace science fiction in years'. Now it can be told...

Since they had to be humanoid I made a virtue of the necessity, and had someone explain to my readers that all those ufologists can't be wrong. The human body plan is perfectly plausible, for sound scientific reasons. This would lead me into interesting territory later on. Whether or not it's true that other planets are likely to throw up creatures that look like us, I don't know. No one knows. But humanoid aliens certainly make life easier for the science fiction novelist. The control our physical embodiment has over our rational processes is so deep and strong that it's excruciating trying to write about intelligent plasma clouds, if you're in the least worried about verisimilitude. It's a trick, it can be done. But the moment your attention falters, your basic programming will restore the defaults of the pentadactyl limb, binocular vision and articulated spine. You'll find your plasma characters cracking hard nuts, grappling with sticky ideas, looking at each other in a funny way, scratching their heads, weaving plots and generally making a chimpanzees' tea-party of your chaste cosmic emanations.

They had to be humanoid and they had to be sexless. I wanted a society that knew nothing about the great divide which allows half the human race to regard the other half as utterly, transcendently, *different* on the grounds of reproductive function. I wanted complex and interesting people who managed to have lives fully as strange, distressing, satisfying, absorbing, productive as ours, without having any access to that central 'us and themness' of human life. I realised before long that this plan created some aliens who had a very shaky idea, if any, of the concept 'alien', especially as applied to another person. Which was a good joke: and like the cosmic standard body plan, it lead to interesting consequences. But that came later.

Once my roughly humanoid aliens reached earth, interrogation proceeded along traditional lines. I whisked them into my laboratory for intensive internal examination, with a prurient concentration on sex and toilet habits. In real life (I mean in the novel *White Queen*) the buccaneers resisted this proposal. They didn't know they were aliens, they thought they were merely strangers, and they didn't see why they had to be vivisected before they could have their tourist visas. The humans were too nervous to insist, but a maverick scientist secured a tissue sample... With this same tissue sample in my possession, I was able to establish that the Aleutians were hermaphrodites, to borrow a human term. (I considered parthenogenesis, with a few males every dozen or so generations, like greenfly. But this was what I finally came up with.) Each of them had the same reproductive tract. There was an external organ consisting of a fold or pouch in the lower abdomen, lined with mucous membrane, holding an appendage called 'the claw'. Beyond the porous inner wall of this pouch, known as 'the cup', extended a reservoir of potential embryos—something like the lifetime supply of eggs in human ovaries, but these eggs didn't need to be fertilised. When one or other of the embryos was triggered into growth—not by any analogue of sexual intercourse but by an untraceable complex of environmental and emotional factors—the individual would become pregnant. The new baby, which would grow in the pouch like a marsupial infant until it was ready to emerge, would prove to be one of the three million or so genetically differentiated individuals in a reproductive group known as the 'brood'. (I should point out that I'm going to use the human word 'gene' and related terms throughout, for the alien analogues to these structures.) These same three million *people*, each one a particular chemically defined bundle of traits and talents, would be born again and again. In Aleutia you wouldn't ask of a newborn baby, 'Is it a boy or a girl?' You'd ask, 'Who is it?' Maybe there'd be a little heelprick thing at the hospital, and then the midwife would tell you whether you'd given birth to someone famous, or someone you knew and didn't like, or someone you vaguely remembered having met at a party once, in another lifetime.

So much for reproduction, but I needed to account for evolution. How could my serial immortals, born-again hermaphrodites, have come to be? How could they continue to adapt to their environment? It was a major breakthrough when I discovered that the brood was held together by a living information network. Every Aleutian had a glandular system constantly generating mobile cell-complexes called 'wanderers' which were shed through the pores of the skin, particularly in special areas like the mucous-coated inner walls of the 'cup'. Each wanderer was a chemical snapshot of the individual's current emotional state, their status, experience, their shifting place in the whole brood entity: a kind of tiny self. The Aleutians would pick and eat 'wanderers' from each other's skin in a grooming process very like that which we observe in real-life apes, baboons, monkeys. To offer someone a 'wanderer' would be a common social gesture: *'Hello, this is how I am—'*. Once consumed, the snapshot information would be replicated and shuttled off to the reproductive tract, where it would be compared with the matching potential embryo, and the embryo updated: so that the chemical nature of the person who might be born was continually being affected by the same person's current life. It was a Lamarkian evolution, directly driven by environmental pressure, rather than by the feedback between environment and random mutation, but it looked to me as if it would work well enough. Nothing much would happen from life to life. But over evolutionary time the individual and the whole brood entity would be changing in phase: growing more complex, remembering and forgetting, opening up new pathways, closing down others. I noticed, when I was setting this up, that the *environment* to which my Aleutians were adapting was the rest of Aleutian society, at least as much as the outside world. But that's another story...

I had done away with sexual gender. But if I wanted a society that seemed fully developed to human readers, I couldn't do without passion. I had no wish to create a race of wistful Spocks, or chilly fragments of a hive-mind. The Aleutians must not be deficient in personhood. Luckily I realised that the wanderer system gave me the means to elaborate a whole world of social, emotional and physical intercourse. The Aleutians lived and breathed chemical information, the social exchange of wanderers was essential to their well-being. But they would also be drawn, by emotional attachment, infatuation, fellow feeling or even a need to dominate, to a more intense experience: where the lovers would get naked and *lie down* together, cups opened and fused lip to lip, claws entwined, information flooding from skin to skin, in an ecstasy of chemical communication. They would fall in love with another self the way we—supposedly—fall in love with difference. Romantic souls would always be searching for that special person, as near as possible the same genetic individual as themselves, with whom the mapping would be complete.

More revelations followed. The whole of Aleutian art and religion, I realised, sprang from the concept of the diverse, recurrent Self of the brood. Their whole education and history came from studying the records left behind by their previous selves. Their technology was based on tailored skin-secretions, essentially specialised kinds of wanderers. Their power to manipulate raw materials had grown not through conscious experiment or leaps of imagination, as ours is held to have developed, but by the placid, inchworm trial and error of molecular evolution. Arguably there was only one Aleutian species—if there had ever been more—since this process of *infecting* the physical world with self-similar chemical information had been going on for aeons. The entire Aleutian environment: buildings, roads, furniture, pets, beasts of burden, transport, was alive with the same life as themselves, the same self.

Once I'd started this machine going, it kept throwing up new ideas. I realised their society was in some ways extremely rigid. Any serial immortal might be born in any kind of social circumstances. But no one could take on a new adult role in society or even retrain for a new job except over millennia of lifetimes. An Aleutian couldn't *learn* to become a carpenter; or to be generous. You were either born with a chemically defined ability or it was not an option. Aleutians, being built on the same pattern as ourselves but with a highly conservative development programme, revert easily to a four-footed gait. This is good for scaring humans, who see *intelligent alien werewolves* leaping at them. The obligate cooks use bodily secretions to prepare food: a method quite acceptable in many human communities, where teeth and saliva replace motorised food mixers; and Aleutians use toilet pads to absorb the minor amount of waste produced by their highly processed diet. I made up this because I liked the image of the alien arriving and saying *'Quickly, take me somewhere I can buy some sanitary pads...'*; but then I noticed this was another aspect of the way they don't have a sense of the alien. They don't even go off by themselves to shit. Aleutians live in a soup of shared presence, they are the opposite of Cartesians. They have no horror of personal death (though they can fear it). But things that are intrinsically *not alive*—like electrons, photons, the image in a mirror or on a screen, they consider uncanny... I could go on, but I won't. We'd be here forever. I believe the elaboration, the proliferation of consequences, could be continued indefinitely. It all goes to show, if anyone needed another demonstration, how much complexity, and what a strange illusion of coherence within that complexity, can be generated from a few simple, arbitrary original conditions.

It's said that the work of science fiction is to make the strange familiar and the familiar strange. I often find that what we do is to take some persistent fiction of contemporary human life, and turn it into science. By the time I'd finished this phase of the interrogation my Aleutians had all the typical beliefs and traditions of one of those caste-ridden, feudal, tropical societies doomed to be swept away by the gadget-building bourgeois individualists from the north. They were animists. They believed in reincarnation. They had no hunger for progress, no use for measurement or theory, no obsession with the passage of time. They were, in short, the kind of people we often wish we could be, except we'd rather have jet transport and microwave pizza.[7] But in the Aleutians' case, everything worked: and their massively successful ambient-temperature biotechnology was exactly tailored—as if by a malignant deity—to blow the mechanisers away. They were on course to take over a world, although they didn't know it: not because they were sacred white-faced messengers from the Sun God or what have you, but because they were *not* weird. *By chance* they had arrived at the historical moment when that jaded mechanist paradigm was giving out, and they had the goods that everybody on earth was beginning to want. They could do things the locals could do themselves, they had skills the locals could well understand, and they were just that crucial half a move ahead of the game.

Speech and Silence

I interrogated my aliens in the language of science, looking for differences that would work. Eventually I became uneasy about this process. If the Aleutians were in some sense 'supposed to be women', it was disquieting to note that I'd treated them exactly the way male-gendered medicine has treated human women until very recently indeed—behaving as if their reproductive system was the only interesting thing about them. I approached Aleutian speech and language with more humility, deliberately trying to remove the division between experimenter and experiment. I had travelled, fairly widely. I had been an alien in many contexts. Not least as a girl among the boys. I had observed that though the colour of my skin and the shape of my chest would always be intriguing, I could often be accepted and treated like a person, *as long as I made the right gestures*. Wherever you go there will be bus-fares, light switches, supermarkets, airports, taps, power sockets, street food, tv cartoons, music cassette players, advertising hoardings, motorway landscape. Watch what the locals do, and you'll soon adjust to the minor variations in the silent universal language.

One can look on the sameness of the global village as an artefact of cultural imperialism, another bitter legacy of White European rule in all its forms. But I felt that these narrative signs of a single human life, repeated the world over, must be connected to that animal-embodiment we all share, or they would not survive. I had invented new forms of difference, now I wanted to celebrate sameness. I made my Aleutians silent, like dumb animals, for many reasons, but first of all because I knew that I could pass for normal in foreign situations as long as I didn't speak. And I made human body-language intelligible to them, on the grounds that just as our *common humanity* makes and recognises the same patterns everywhere, the aliens' wordless natural language had been deeply shaped by the same pressures as have shaped the natural languages of life on earth. The whole bio-chemical spectrum is missing, from their point of view, because we have no wanderers, no intelligent secretions at all. But every human gesture that remains is as intelligible to them as another brood's dialect of the common tongue that everyone shares at home. To make sure of my point I raised and dismissed the possibility that they were time-travellers returning to their forgotten planet of origin; and the other possibility that they had grown, like us, from humanoid seed sown across the galaxy by some elder race. They were an absolutely, originally different evolution of life. But they were *the same* because life, wherever it arises in our middle dimensions, must be subject to the same constraints, and the more we learn about our development the more we see that the most universal pressures—time and gravity, quantum mechanics; the nature of certain chemical bonds—drive through biological complexity on every fractal scale, from the design of an opposable thumb to the link between the chemistry of emotion and a set of facial muscles. This sameness, subject to cultural variation but always reasserting itself, was shown chiefly in their ability to understand us.

In line with my model of Aleutians as 'women', and 'native peoples', it was right for them to be wary and rather contemptuous of spoken language. I wanted them to be silent like the processes of cell-biology, like social insects exchanging pheromone signals: and like larger animals conversing through grooming, nuzzling, eye-contact and gesture. I wanted the humans, convinced that the barrier between self and other was insurmountable except by magic, to be deeply alarmed by these seeming telepaths—the way characters in classic male-gendered science fiction are so absurdly impressed at an occult power they call *empathy*: whereby some superbeing or human freak can walk into a room and *actually sense* the way the other people there are feeling. (God give me strength: my cat can do that.) But I didn't want to do away with spoken language altogether. Words are separation. Words divide. That is the work they do. I know this because I've felt it happen: whenever I open my mouth and speak, having been accepted as perfectly normal until that moment, and prove by my parlous accent and toddler's vocabulary that I'm not French; or whenever I make a public, female-gendered statement in a male group. Everything else that we think we use language for, we can handle without what the Aleutians call 'formal speeches'. But for the Aleutians not to have this separation, this means of stepping out of the natural cycles, would have made them less than people. So I invented a special class of Aleutians, the 'signifiers', who were obligate linguists the way other Aleutians were obligate food-processors or spaceship-builders. Of course they assimilated human articulate languages with dazzling speed. This is another of the space-fantasy clichés that I think has been unfairly derided. I wouldn't be able to do it. But then, nobody would sign up an obligate monophone such as myself on a trading mission to another planet, would they?

It also transpired that the aliens did have a kind of no-kidding alien-life-form telepathy for long distance contact: another proliferation of the wanderer system. But that's another story. And there was no problem with the mechanics of speech, by the way. I gave them teeth and tongues and larynxes more or less like ours: why not?

I had made the Aleutians into self-conscious intelligences who still manipulated their surroundings the way bacteria do it; or the simpler entities that spend their lives manufacturing and communicating inside our cells. In their use of all forms of language I elaborated on this conservatism. They were beings who had reached self-consciousness, and spoken language, without abandoning any of the chronological precursor communication media. All life on earth uses chemical communication; then comes gesture, and vocalisation comes last. Humans have traded all the rest for words—so that we have to rediscover the meaning of our own non-verbal gestures, and the likely effect of the hormone laden scent-cells we shed, from self-help books full of printed text. To the Aleutians, by the way, this lack of control gives the impression that all humans have Tourette's Syndrome: we're continually babbling obscenities, shouting out tactless remarks, giving away secrets in the common tongue. I pictured my Aleutians like a troop of humanly intelligent baboons, gossiping with each other silently and perfectly efficiently, having subtle and complex chemical interactions: and just occasionally feeling the need to vocalise; a threat or boast or warning, a yell of 'Look at me!' It only occurred to me later that I'd made the Aleutians very like feminist women in all this: creatures dead set on *having it all*, determined to be self-aware and articulate public people, without giving up their place in the natural world.

But inevitably, insidiously the 'signifier' characters, the aliens with the speaking parts, became an élite. I had already realised that I had to 'translate' the wordless dialogue of Aleutian silent language into words on the page. In this I was up against one of the walls of make-believe. Science fiction is full of these necessary absurdities: I accepted it with good grace, the same way as I'd accepted the human body-plan, and used some funny direct speech marks to show the difference between spoken and unspoken dialogue, which the copy-editor didn't like. But now I felt that the male-gendered mechanist-gadget world was sneaking back into power, with historical inevitability in its train, in the Trojan Horse of articulate language. I did everything I could to correct this. I began to point out the similarities between the Aleutian 'silent' language, and our spoken word as it is used most of the time by most humans. I found myself listening to human conversations and noticing the gaps: the unfinished sentences, the misplaced words, the really startling high ratio of noise to signal. I realised that most of our use of language fulfils the same function as the grooming, the nuzzling, the skin to skin chemical exchange that other life-forms share, but which with us has become taboo except in privileged intimate relations. I further realised that everything humans 'say' to each other, either in meaningful statements or in this constant dilute muttering of contact, is backed, just like Aleutian communication, by a vast reservoir of cultural and evolutionary experience. We too have our 'soup of shared presence', out of which genuinely novel and separate formal announcements arise rarely—to be greeted, more often than not, with wariness and contempt.

Re-inventing the wheel is a commonplace hazard in science fiction. It makes a change to find one has re-invented post-structuralist psychology. I recognised, some time after the event, that in the Silence of Aleutia I had invented the unconscious in the version proposed by Lacan, the unspoken plenum of experience that is implicit in all human discourse. Then I understood that my 'signifiers' represented not a ruling caste but the public face of Aleutia; and the Silent represented all those people who don't want to 'speak out', who 'just want to get on with their lives': the group to which most of us belong, most of the time. In Aleutia, as in human life, the 'signifiers' may be prominent figures. But who is really in charge? The intelligentsia, or the silent majority? Which is the puppeteer? The fugitive, marginal latecomer, consciousness? Or the complex, clever, perfectly competent wordless animal within?

Convergent Evolution

It's now several years since I started writing about the Aleutians, and nearly a decade since I first outlined the project... on a beach in Thailand, one warm August night in 1988. A lot of history has happened in that time, and much of it somehow affected the story. The 1989 revolutions in Europe made a great difference to *White Queen*. The war in the former Yugoslavia had a grim influence on the second episode, *North Wind*. The nature of our local low-intensity warfare in Northern Ireland has also had a part in shaping my fictional conflicts, while the third book, *Phoenix Café*, is bound to have a *fin de siècle* feel. I've read and shakily assimilated lots of popular science, and science itself has become more *popular*, so that concerns which were completely science-fictional and obscure when I began are now topics of general interest: and that's made a difference too. Even the battle of the sexes has changed ground, both in my mind and in the real world. I'm not sure how much, if any, of my original plan survived. But this is okay. I intended to let the books change over time. I wanted things that happened at first contact to be viewed later as legends that couldn't possibly be true. I wanted concerns that were vitally important in one book to have become totally irrelevant in the next. I wanted phlogiston and cold fusion in my science, failed revolutions and forgotten dreams in my politics. I thought that discontinuity would be more true to life than a three hundred years' chunk of soap-opera, (or so, it's difficult to say exactly how much time has passed, when the master race finds measurement boring) that ends with everybody still behaving the same as they did in episode one. It's true to the historical model too. I don't think anyone would deny that the European Empire builders had lost the plot, sometime long before that stroke of midnight in 1947, climactic moment in the great disengagement.

My son Gabriel tells me stories. Not surprisingly, given his environment, he tends to tell me science fiction stories. I'm delighted when he comes up with some motif or scenario that I recognise as a new variation on a familiar theme: and he's furious (like some adult storytellers I could mention) when I point out to him he's doing something that's been done countless times before. Always, already, what we say has been said before. A while ago he came up with an adventure where the characters kept being swept away into the Fourth Dimension, an experience that transformed them, partially and then permanently if they stayed too long, into horrible gargoyles. That was where I found the title of my paper. Sadly, I can't fault his argument. There's no getting away from it, the Fourth Dimension makes monsters of us all. My Aleutians, though, have managed to change the process around. Sometimes science fiction aliens represent not merely other people, but some future other people: some unexplored possibility for the human race. Maybe my Aleutians fit that description. But it has been a surprise even to me to see how *human* they have become, how much I've found myself writing about the human predicament, about the mysteries of self and consciousness. But that's the way it has to be, unless or until the great silence out there is broken. Until we meet.

III
THE REVIEWS

9: *In the Chinks of the World Machine*: Sarah Lefanu on Feminist SF

Sarah Lefanu's study of the intersection between feminism and science fiction is a tightly packed two-hundred-odd pages, and though expansive in exploring the different texts, the passages of analysis are densely written and complex enough to make the project of reviewing this review at once a challenge and an awful temptation. I could go on forever.

The starting point that Lefanu chooses for her study is in itself interesting and suggestive enough for a volume. She approaches the history of feminist science fiction not in terms of Mary Shelley and the feminine adventure-story tradition of the gothic novel, (she covers this later), but in terms of fandom: Susan Wood and others in the 1970s recognising their dissatisfaction, asserting their interests and fighting for 'Women and sf' panels. The invocation of the special relationship between artists and audience in sf is significant for Lefanu's argument. It is also particularly interesting for me to read this history of the revolution, because by the time I met the sf world many people found the idea of 'Women and sf' panels depressing and wished they did not exist. Revolutions have a tiresome habit of (r)evolving in this way.

However, for this study at least, the evolution is benign. *In the Chinks of the World Machine* is not another story of how weird, or how thrilling, it is to see a dog walking on its hind legs. Though consideration of the sf background always arises out of Lefanu's politics and is never prioritised above her first concern, the discussion has the confidence to be about science fiction as well as about feminism: about the genre's powers to deconstruct and inform, and its towering preoccupations: the fictional world that deals (I paraphrase) with the problem of difference in all its aspects.

Sarah Lefanu's title *In the Chinks of the World Machine*, has a ring of irony. The full quotation is from a James Tiptree story, and runs: 'What women do is survive. We live by ones and twos in the chinks of your world machine...' Alice Sheldon, otherwise known as James Tiptree Junior, is a key icon in this study, the woman who fooled the sf establishment with her straightfaced presentation of male stereotypes—and was bitterly entertained, it is clear, when her victims responded with ecstatic little cries of recognition. But while Alice Sheldon the feminist woman was surviving in her disguise—in the chinks of her male persona—Sheldon/Tiptree the writer achieved, *for a while*, megastar status in the sf establishment: and this is the paradox of feminist sf. The successful women writers in sf are few, and feminism is certainly marginal; but the success, the stature and the influence of those few is out of all proportion to their numbers.

But *In the Chinks* is far from hagiography. Lefanu's analysis of Tiptree the female man and her intense, visionary dissections of the relationship between humanity and the other is the thoughtful centrepiece of this study. But she takes care to point out that it is not her intention to set one woman writer above another, and the book works pretty well as an interactive whole, the different strands of argument and stages of development knitting back and forth rather than being bullied into an illusory straight line progression through the halls of fame. Still, there are difficulties. The very structure of the book fosters an illusion of progress, through years of political development, *towards* a rational perspective and *away* from the fatal error of essentialism. It is only common sense to deride Marion Zimmer Bradley's absurd role-reversal novel *The Ruins of Isis*. Jayge Carr's *Leviathan's Deep* is also deservedly found wanting. To depict a female-ordered society where female autonomy is dependent on anatomical difference (the 'women' of Carr's alien race cannot be raped) is fine as wish-fulfilment, but not a particularly good argument against biology as destiny in this world. From Carr we progress to 'feminised' science fiction which is not so far in error; but feminised sf, with its acceptance of 'the naturalness of sexual difference' is still distiguished from the goal of truly feminist science fiction. Finally, we reach the mature development of Joanna Russ's *The Two of Them*, where the conventional futuristic narrative is stripped away, to reveal the reality: our present day predicament as unconditioned human beings, disadvantaged not by biology but by the restrictive practices of our society. However, it is clear that Angela Carter, Josephine Saxton, Tanith Lee, all build their different, rich and complex fantasies—highly valued by Lefanu—in full recognition and acceptance of male/female, masculine/feminine archetypes. Even when Suzy Charnas and Joanna Russ present—in *When It Changed* and *Motherlines*—fictional communities where all the people are women, male versus female archetypes have not disappeared from the equation: if they had, there would be no story. The men's absence is not silence. The stigma of gender does not vanish in these feminist proposals, rather it is perpetuated and validated. Somewhere in this study there should be a stronger acknowledgement of the fact that this same dangerous weapon of essentialism, used so inadequately in rightly dismissed crude role-reversal, defines the whole phenomenon of feminist sf. After all, it is extremely difficult for a writer to accuse, or to question, gender roles without first awarding them a powerful presence in the narrative. Even the bisexual society of Mattapoisett in *Woman on the Edge of Time*, perhaps the most successful attempt to date at post-gendered utopian fiction, is defined by the sexual roles and concomitant evils of the past.

On the subject of this irreducible paradox, I would take issue with Sarah Lefanu's criticism of the Joanna Russ story *When It Changed*, the first appearence in fiction of 'Whileaway', the planet where all the people are women, a society later elaborated in the highly self-conscious and modernist (or even post-modernist) sf text *The Female Man*. Lefanu notes the great emotional resonance that the earlier story has for many women, and conjectures that the *The Female Man* may be less appealing because of its complexity and the challenges of its experimental style. Now, perhaps the structure of *The Female Man* is a little unlike plain storytelling, featuring as it does a variety of versions of the same character, living in several more or less different political and historical situations. But the multiple-branching-universe time-travel story that gives the narrative this braided plotline is not new to the genre, and can't possibly give sf fans a lot of trouble (cf. Gregory Benford's *Timescape*, et al). It seems to me that there is a more important reason why *The Female Man*, appeals less, and examination of this intuitive preference (which I admit I share) has something to say about the project of feminist sf. *When It Changed* tells the story of a rescue. On the colonised planet of Whileaway, all the men died in a plague, long ago. The women were first devastated, then they learned to survive, then they learned to fill in the empty spaces, to exploit the niches left vacant by the exinction of the male. They have devised a means of reproduction using fused ova: they marry, have children, farm, pursue professions, run the government. Their world is complete. Now, after generations, the men have suddenly returned. Ten foot toads wrapped in tinfoil quarantine, they have come lumbering to the rescue, to take these women home to the world of the kitchen, nursery and fashion plates, the world of Middle-American housewives in the days when those original ten foot toads in tinfoil first ventured into space. The women of Whileaway—the *people* of Whileaway, I should say, are bemused, amused, and finally, as the truth sinks home, despairing. Their situation is tragic. It doesn't matter what they do now. The very existence of the male-dominated world, once it has been reasserted, robs them of their autonomy. They may resist this rescue, they may survive as an enclave of weird extremists, but they will never again be *the people*. They will be inadequate, incompetent, mere women. And there the story ends.

Naturally the party of spacemen—seen only through the women's eyes—comes off badly in this account. But on the other hand the women of Whileaway are not unreasonably idealised. Their society is no more idyllic than the average well-heeled American wilderness community in fiction—pioneer independence, love and respect for the wild, good country folks, haven't had a murder here in years, don't have to lock our doors around here. These women are 'the whole of humanity'—an important concept that Lefanu raises elsewhere. They have the full range of human vices and virtues intact. By the time we meet 'Whileaway' again in *The Female Man*, it has been got at. Its inhabitants have become female characters in a feminist science fiction, their vices and virtues bowdlerised and engineered precisely to fit the current demands of sexual politics. On the first Whileaway, for instance, though premeditated murder might be rare, fatal duelling was a social problem. In *The Female Man*, there are nerve grafts: it is no longer permissable for women to kill each other out of individualistic *amour propre*. There's no more exclusive marriage either, because everybody knows (in mid-1970s lesbian feminism every body knew this) that monogamy is wrong. *When It Changed* is feminist fiction, *The Female Man* is feminist satire. (Sarah Lefanu makes this distinction clearly when discussing Esme Dodderidge's *The New Gulliver*, a Swiftian role-reversal story.) And feminist satire, for the female sf reader, is as disappointing as it is invigorating. There is a sense of loss, a sense of another world denied. Changing story into satire defines yet another area where women work, while men play.

In this context, perhaps Sarah Lefanu might have given more attention to the positive meaning of Alice Sheldon's uncannily successful masquerade. James Tiptree Junior had a lot of satirical, painful fun with male stereotypes. But we should not forget that James and Alice were the same person. That *person* was perhaps perfectly well able to discover aggressive, depersonalised sexual desire, just as much as a 'virile' prose style, within herself; that *person* chose the grim exploration of desire in some Tiptree stories from her own human resources. To deny this, to say Sheldon's 'male' self was a 'convincing imitation' of something essentially alien is to miss half of the point. And in this context also, whatever Joanna Russ may have decided later, at the time of writing she certainly meant her challenging term 'the female man' as an affirmation: a generous and courageous way out of the trap:

> I think I am a Man; I think you had better call me a Man. I think you will write about me as a Man from now on and speak of me as a Man and employ me as a Man and recognise child-rearing as a Man's business you will think of me as a Man and treat me as a Man until it enters your muddled, terrified, nine-tenths-fake loveless papier-mâché-bull-moose-head that I am a Man (and you are a woman). That's the whole secret...

But there are dangers inherent in all fictional solutions to political problems. As Lefanu herself remarks and as we all know (or we should by now) the scattering of virtuous and successful dark-skinned characters to signal an 'enlightened' future is the reverse of radical. This is the way to depoliticise, for the unreflecting reader, the question of race here and now; to make the problem seem inconsequential. Joanna Russ and Suzy Charnas, the most acute and intellectually rigorous of the writers studied here, are aware of this pitfall: and therefore Russ's psycho-sexual fiction becomes more and more stern and bleak after *The Female Man*; and therefore there is no triumphant conclusion to Charnas's recounting of the fall of patriarchy. Once the interface between the real problem and fictional solution has been defined there is no further place to go, without running the risk (an intolerable failure) of denying the way the problem refuses to budge in *this* world. Therefore all satirists, sf satirists of every stripe included, are condemned to an ever deeper, ever more intricate mapping of the problem's boundary. They dare not venture beyond. This, in one aspect at least, is the intractable predicament of feminist sf.

But if there is a sense in which feminist sf cannot 'develop', there is equally a sense in which it has become the locus for the most interesting developments in sf. An important strand of Sarah Lefanu's argument involves the relationship between the natural, innate relativism of feminist sf and the whole area of modern literary theory. The death of the author, the decentralisation of self, the unmasking of fictional 'character'—all these sacrifices are likely to come quite easily to (women) writers who don't have a lot to lose. Further, the open structure of science fiction, as Lefanu shows, has always offered an ideal medium for radical experiment.

The shift from feminised to feminist sf is examined through a discussion of the works of Ursula Le Guin. Ironically, perhaps inevitably, it is the two novels on which Le Guin's reputation as a feminist icon rests, *The Dispossessed* and *The Left Hand of Darkness*, that receive the most attention and the most criticism. While Le Guin's earlier works rest easily in the tradition of 'sf written by women'—more attractive than most sf in prose style, but conventional in their treatment of gender roles—the two political sf novels have a strange, uncomfortable relationship with feminism. Ursula Le Guin has explained her adoption of a male persona for the viewpoint character in her adventure stories as partly due to literary timidity, partly to a desire to explore in make-believe areas fundamentally unavailable to her in real life. But in those two novels, perhaps related more to 1960s radical politics in general than to feminism in particular, the treatment of female characters, as Sarah Lefanu points out, is startling. Arguably, there are no women at all in *The Left Hand of Darkness*, because all the notionally non-gendered characters behave like men. Certainly the women in *The Dispossessed* are a depressing bunch: a callous society temptress, a bad mother, a stay-at-home workhorse of a good wife. But I wonder if it is enough to dismiss this harshness as a mistake, a political error to be repudiated in eager self-criticism sessions. To me it seems there may be an anger against women, even a desire to punish women (including herself) for our failures, for our betrayals of our own cause, in the work of a woman writer, that deserves serious and sympathetic examination.

Ursula Le Guin insists that she writes novels of character, and has been firm in her dismissal of fashionable critical theory. However, Sarah Lefanu easily discovers that the central characters—Genly Ai in *The Left Hand of Darkness*, Shevek in *The Dispossessed*—of her two best known novels are thin as paper. 'Who is Genly Ai? Who is Shevek? Who remembers what they look like, what they say or feel?' The answer, I would suggest, is very simple. In a book that has to contain an unfamiliar world, its workings, a plot, and the obligatory sf element of cosmic musing, character is always going to be—relatively—a minor concern. Because there is no space in an sf text for the kind of *trompe l'oeil* word-painting that convinces us that we 'know' Dorothea Brooke or Natasha Rostov, the mechanism of characterisation remains visible. If we look closely, critically, we soon become aware of the eyeholes cut in the canvas of these portraits, and see the eyes of the writer looking back at us. Shevek, the solitary creative genius, may be taken as stereotypical 'potent male'; but the experience of creativity is the artist's own. Shevek is Le Guin: and now the fabric between fiction and reality is wearing thin. If there is nothing specifically feminist in this development, it's still fascinating. In a work of unquestioned literary 'quality', characterisation is not supposed to work like this!

Le Guin is like a nineteenth-century explorer without a theory, entering unawares on the new found land: a fiction that reveals its own inner workings. It seems unfair that she should be found out in the fault of creating characters who don't really exist, while in the next section, when we have made the transition into fully developed feminism, Suzy Charnas is praised for exactly the same achievement. The *absence* of 'Alldera', the heroine-shaped space in the centre of Suzy Charnas's two parts of a trilogy *Walk to the End of the World* and *Motherlines*, is continuous with the absence of Genly Ai and Shevek. What happens in feminist sf—as opposed to Le Guin's sf—is not a change or new development in this matter of the empty character, but rather (surprise, surprise) a raised consciousness. One of the strengths of Sarah Lefanu's study is the way she is frequently able to let the writers speak for themselves. It is Suzy Charnas who tells us that the 'character' of Alldera, the woman who survives and escapes from the brutalised and dying patriarchal enclave of *Walk to the End of the World*, rose directly from her own developing feminism. Like the array of Jeannine, Joanna, Jael, Janet, the branched-universe variations of one personality in *The Female Man*, 'Alldera' is a space through which the author speaks—her relation to the fictional background challenging deliberately and profoundly the conventional divisions between writer, text and reader.

As might be expected from Sarah Lefanu, this is a very fair-minded and rational study of an area where emotions run high. She speaks of anger: the anger and grief expressed by these women writers, the astonished outrage of male readers and critics over the years; but her book is not angry at all. This is not polemic. It is, as I said at the outset, a study of science fiction as much as of feminism. Throughout, Lefanu returns again and again to the peculiar nature of the sf genre, the interactive relationship between 'artist' and 'audience', the survival of primitive literary/dramatic modes; the disrespect for fixed literary forms. She highlights the striking level of coincidence between the parameters of sf and the requirements of radical social relativism (in a genre where it has been established that sentient beings can have tentacles, even women can be human); and finally reaches the boundary, where fiction, having stripped itself naked, can go no further. The last text that she chooses to study is a Joanna Russ novel, *The Two of Them*, that has a striking resemblance to the first text examined, here in the chinks of the world's machine, Marion Zimmer Bradley's *The Towers of Isis*. In both stories a heterosexual relationship from a culture of supposed 'sexual equality' comes to grief in collision with a society of extreme 'sexual difference'. *The Ruins of Isis* manages to contrive a totally unconvincing happy ending. The Russ story ends at a bleak intersection with our present day reality. The only hope that we are offered is the hope which cannot be reached until we have systematically emptied out the whole the box of troubles.

John Clute, in a quotation from his review of the book in *Interzone*, in January 1979, which Sarah Lefanu gives here, and which is worth repeating, at least in part, describes Joanna Russ as using 'genre fiction' only to deny and demolish 'genre fiction'.

> You think I'm telling you X; well I wouldn't tell you X if my life depended on it. In fact my life depends on not allowing you to get away with hearing X from my lips. Your willingness to suspend disbelief so as to luxuriate in the telling of X is tantamount to complicity with the invidious systemic violation of women in this world, whose roots are homologous with the engendering impulses behind traditional genre fiction, or X, baby...

The vehemence of the male sf critic's response to feminism always comes as a surprise. We knew they didn't talk about it, but we assumed their silence was one of the conventions of the boys' club. Surely someone must have *noticed* that bloodstained body lying in the middle of the library floor...

And the notion that science fiction—of all the genres!—is incapable of surviving an examination of gender roles seems bizarre. The tradition that can contain both *The Towers of Isis* and *The Two of Us* does not suffer from many limitations. Moreover, deconstruction, whatever the political motivation, is not a synonym for demolition. Deconstruction is, if essentialist terminology cannot be ignored, a markedly *feminine* activity of curiosity, greed, gossip, insatiable pursuit of secret details; the reckless, inquisitive adventure of Pandora or Bluebeard's last bride. Its project is to give us *more*, not less from any text or any genre template: more information, more implications, more possibilities; to expand consciousness, not to limit it. Viewed in these terms science fiction comes out well, capable of sustaining any degree of critical audit, and of containing all transformations and explorations: even to the farthest distant pole of feminist revolution.

LIVERPOOL UNIVERSITY PRESS

SENATE HOUSE, ABERCROMBY SQUARE, LIVERPOOL, L69 3BX, UK

Telephone 0151-794 2233/7   *Fax* 0151-794 2235

We are pleased to enclose the following book for review:

Science Fiction Texts and Studies, No. 16
Deconstructing the Starships: Science, Fiction and Reality
GWYNETH JONES

ISBN 085323-783-2; Price: £27.50 (cased)
ISBN 085323-793-X Price: £11.95 (paperback)

No review should appear before the publication date:

March 1999

Please send two copies of any review published.

Street Address: Room 105, Senate House, Abercromby Square, Liverpool, L7

10: Consider Her Ways:
The Fiction of C.J. Cherryh

Consider Her Ways

For years, people looked at me strangely when I cited Carolyn Cherryh as a writer of feminist science fiction. It was the kind of look people might give you if you said you ate chocolate bars for your health, but with a hint of more sinister dubiety; as if I might be in danger of taking on something seriously harmful along with the sweet disguise. My over-reading, if over-reading it is (for there's over-reading as surely as there is over-writing, let reviewers beware) of what goes on in the typical Cherryh scenario is partly a historical accident. *Serpent's Reach* is the first Cherryh book I met. It is an early glimpse into the continuum that the back of *Cyteen*, the complex novel that is the culmination of this project, calls the 'Merchanters' Universe' series. It features a gloomy tomboy heroine, and a good-dog toyboy who suffers the most remorseless ordeal by genre role-reversal before being awarded with equality. The plot is a space-opera revenge story. It is also a slice from a larger drama about the epic misuse of human reproduction technology. The behaviour of the hive-minded alien Majat is contrasted favourably with the humans' treatment of their vat-bred underclass. The individual members of the different castes of the matriarchal Majat are endlessly replicated units of function. The small number of personality-analogues involved have no comprehension of death or capacity for 'freedom'. The mass-produced human azi, however, are individuals, and therefore slaves who live and die in misery...

Those of you who have read *Cyteen*, or follow Cherryh at all, may find this abstract familiar. But this was 1980, and my mind was awash with highly self-conscious feminist deconstructions of sf. It was natural for me to assume that Cherryh too was self-conscious in this way, that the story she chose was her story in the reformed sense, not a window into one writer's own private obsession. But the strong female lead has always been an option on the menu in sf. Like the gun-slinging heroine in a western she's the exception that proves the rule; and she proves it by being exceptional. The gloomy tomboy-with-a-past who stalks Cherryh's fantasy usually walks alone in a man's world. She has sometimes been accompanied by minor female support; more often (*The Faded Sun* series; most of *Morgaine*) by a pointed affirmation of traditional gender roles for all the ordinary girls. The situation in Cherryh's science fiction is different, but not as different as it looks—as I plan to explain.

Sf readers who like to consider themselves respectable affect a prim denigration of 'wish-fulfilment'. This has always seemed to me more than a little absurd: what else were fantasy-adventure stories invented for? It may be that there's something rather more sinister—maybe even more sinister than feminism!—lurking in Cherryh's world view. But her treatment of gender has continued to interest and entertain me and it is not—I swear—only on account of her elegant, wish-fulfilment she-heroes. Cherryh is one of the few, if not the only, woman writer of the established generation who has been routinely positive about her female cast. This has not been political feminist sf. But neither has it been the usual Cagney and Lacey stuff of 'strong female characters': where *of course* the lady starship captain still has to rush home to collect the kids and make her husband's dinner; has to attempt to look cute at all times, has to smile when the bossman makes jokes about her period. Nor has there been any helpless victim's angst as in the dourest imaginings of Kate Wilhelm. There has been straightforward, *'We're normal, who are you?'* female-ordered fantasy.

The other side of the coin has been equally interesting. The unfortunate toyboy of *Serpent's Reach* is only one of a series... Excuse the pun: 'Jim' of *Serpent's Reach* is a vat-bred menial of the lowest order, rated somewhat below an electric can-opener in the scheme of things in his world. This tabula rasa sex-object attains humanity at the end of the story, but specifically it is his mistress's humanity. He becomes human by ingesting her taped library of selfhood: by acquiring her memories, her education, her opinions. This piece of table-turning is so outrageous (She for God only, he for God in her...) it can only be regarded as deliberate mischief. But when the same relationship next appears, which it does in *DownBelow Station*, the vat-bred male is no longer innocent; and the powerful woman has become overtly sadistic. Things begin to take on a grimmer tone. Elsewhere, and in Cherryh's output there is a lot of elsewhere, the fun is cleaner. Beautiful veiled warriors (male) tremble and weep, helpless male stowaways cower naked before their alien captors, dumb male blonds are allowed to tag along to do the housekeeping... and all without losing a millimetre of their masculinity. More to the point, substantially without alienating Cherryh's considerable male audience. Her 'brave but brittle' human male sidekicks, and the tomcatoid males left at home to strut by the female starship captains of Chanur, are maybe as stereotyped as the cyberwives and girlfriends of traditional space opera. But though allowed to get in touch with their emotional selves (such a bunch of crybabies!) these characters retain their machismo, and even their dignity. They are treated—by and large—with a good deal of respect. Here Cherryh does not seem to be playing revenge fantasies. It seems rather that she has been trying, a most unusual project for any sf writer, to give 'masculine' a meaning of its own, free of knee-jerk denigration or adulation. In these gaudy escapist adventures she has considered men as quivering bundles of hormones and social conditioning (just like the rest of us), not as some imaginary human norm from which the female deviates.

In the past decade or so her chosen form, the science/fantasy multiple, has been devalued by stacks of production-line paper: which is covered in little black marks, admittedly, but quite untouched by human mind. In such company a writer who can put an intelligible sentence together stands out like a beacon of literary merit. Cherryh is not a literary writer, but she's consistently literate and effective, which in sf is certainly good enough, and in her subgenre is now something of a miracle. Her idiosyncratic, faintly archaic style is well matched with the perverse territory of pan-galactic never-never land. When the archaism bleeds through into her more realist mode—little outbursts of gothic, a slight touch of the mutated *forsooths* from the twenty-fourth-century newscaster—the effect is peculiar; and yet oddly convincing.

Cherryh has made it her business to do the simple things that everybody does (alien culture, the eternal quest, faster than light dog-fights) and simply do them well. She excels at taking the most preposterous of these genre constructs seriously. Most modern exponents of space opera can barely conceal a wink at the audience as they press the FTL button on the dash. Cherryh gives the impression that she's really tried to think of what it might be like to be in these situations. This hardworking attitude applies especially to her longest-running and most ambitious future soap: the 'Merchanters' Universe'. The story that began (for me) in *Serpent's Reach* has shrunk and cooled somewhat when viewed as a whole. In those days the aeons seemed uncounted. Cherryh's post-human exotica played out their revenge games in quasi-Jacobean dialogue and in the ambience of the traditional never-never. But perhaps the *Serpent's Reach* characters just talked like that because they were living in the sticks. Quite possibly the whole fancy dress plot of that novel can be be fitted into some distant corner of the tailored-suit-and-power-heels space opera of the other Merchanter books. There is nevertheless a very different feel to the more recent offerings: it's a very near-futurish and unwonderful galactic empire. But the Cherryh scenario remains the same. The isolated warrior-woman is still moodily on the prowl, the unmoved fulcrum between highly charged masculine sensibility and self-protective feminine commonsense. And the plot still revolves around the dehumanised female icon of human reproduction technology.

The Tyranny of the Clever

Earth has been left behind. FTL has expanded human-occupied space enormously. A handful of habitable or marginally habitable planets have been discovered, but overwhelmingly the environment remains hostile. The only people who are truly at home are the starships' companies: the merchanters (or marines). They have accepted intuitively that they'll never stand on solid ground again, or know what time it is. Everyone else is still clinging to the lifeboats. A few alien sentients have been encountered, but they are either too powerful or too feeble to generate trans-species politics. The power struggles are between humans and posthumans. The Alliance consists more or less of unreconstructed humanity. 'Union', meanwhile, churns out production line people to order and intends in this way, by explosive bursts of population growth, to dominate the exploding human universe... This is the story so far. The scope of—the sheer physical size!— of this canvas should be borne in mind. In many ways, but not least in this context, *Cyteen*, the latest installment, is a very strange development.

Back when Union was breeding the first mass-produced azi, their invincible secret weapon in a war of independence, the planet Cyteen was the nerve centre of the military organisation. In the year 2300, the war has turned cold. But Resune, the foundation which controls Union's azi production, still wields immense political power: and one woman, Ariane Emory, controls Resune. For historical reasons, then, a single dominant woman is seen to hold the key to the whole future of humanity. Emory, genius edocrinologist and ruthless politician, is getting very old. Even on rejuvenating drugs, her time is running out.

The crumbling autocrat represents the ever onward, ever outward party within Union, and appears to be pushing for more expansion. However, it slowly transpires—a hundred pages isn't much in this book—that Emory's real obsession is her own immortality. A kind of physical continuance is easily within reach. Resune routinely provides 'parental replicates', clone children, to satisfy the vanity of the Family, the foundation's inner circle. Emory is more ambitious. So far, attempts to recover individual genius by cloning have failed. But Resune is in the business of designer-humanity, and it perfects its range of models as much by psychological conditioning (deep tape) as by chopping and changing snippets of DNA. Ariane Emory intends to reproduce environment as well as heredity. She will provide her new self with her own childhood experiences, (mostly unpleasant); and then with a programme of exhaustively detailed instructions in selfhood, which will, hopefully, bootstrap the re-emergence of her own 'unique' genius.

The experiment is a chess move, a kind of castling of Resune's irreplaceable queen. It is also seen as an end in itself. Emory has decided that psychogenesis—the technique that will keep certain key minds around forever—is vital for the future of the human race. The project gets under way in deep cover, while the rest of Union's government scrabbles for ways to dislodge Emory from Resune and Resune from power. Things are soon complicated by Ariane 1's peculiar sexual habits and her premature death, which may or may not be murder. Partly in revenge for a sexual rejection and partly for deep-laid reasons of her own Ariane has been tormenting the replicate 'son' of a former protégé, with harrassment culminating in aggravated rape and blackmail. When she is found dead the story comes out and the boy's father, Jordan Warrick, is the obvious suspect. He apparently confesses, and is shipped off to exile. His son/twin Justin remains behind, demoted to Cinderella status in the labs and endlessly mistreated in large ways and small; always vulnerable through his imprisoned father and through his azi lover, Grant—who still legally 'belongs' to Resune. Meanwhile a rich little girl, the daughter/twin of Ariane, begins to grow up. Her world is also bounded by the walls of Resune foundation. Though more comfortable her life is the same arbitrary nightmare, where loved ones betray her and friends disappear for no reason, and the indignity of intimate surveillance is ever present.

Cherryh's more realist novels are always difficult of entry. She specialises in the lengthy synoptic preface: two hundred years or so of imaginary history in merciless italics. *Cyteen* is no exception. Close on the heels of the history lesson we're plunged into a complicated political debate on Union long term strategy, which is recounted blow by blow to the least significant twitch of an eyebrow. But in this case the bottleneck entry never opens out. The great debate has only a negative bearing (this is what I'm *not* going to talk about) on the substance of this novel. The next great leap outwards is a feint, a cover, a lure, not only on Ariane's part, but on Cherryh's part as well. The starships have been grounded. This is going to be a novel about inner space, not outer space, spiralling in ever decreasing circles around the bunker of the undead dictator: an experience as claustrophobic, as disorienting, as remorseless as about two years in a sensory deprivation tank.

The daunting completism continues at the same pace for nearly seven hundred pages of obsessive, paranoic total recall: not only each move of the malign psychological hand-to-hand, but every move that anybody/ party of influence ever considers and dismisses. Periodically there are attempts at providing the relief of conventional action. The murder 'mystery' is one of these, and so obviously a canard that even Cherryh seems to lose interest. But nothing that happens outside the haunted-hive of Resune really works. What Cherryh had done within the hive is an impressive feat; and compelling, in a horrid way. But where there are problems, or contradictions, they are not skimmed over because nothing is skimmed over. And the reader has plenty of time to think.

As Paul McAuley remarked in his recent Interzone review of *Rimrunners* (another *Merchanters'* episode), Cherryh is a lo-tech futurologist. She abhors the hip, the brandname, the gadgetry. This attitude is unremarkable in conventional space opera. The same low key approach creates a peculiar atmosphere in a novel about genetic engineering and designer-humanity. In *Cyteen* Cherryh states that change is a terrifying force. But the reader's experience is of a world that is eminently familiar (maybe not from personal experience, but at least from tv folklore): and which remains untouched, impervious, oblivious to change during the whole of our extended aquaintance. We are told that all natural born citizens of Union rely on Resune-designed 'deep tape' so that they can change their skills every month and stay in work. Presumably they are the ones responsible for the slow progress in terraforming the planet, that's going on in the background. But apart from taking tranquillisers with their personal-stereo taped evening classes, they could be living in the nineteenth century. The engineered azi, human in hypocritical cant, in practice something between guard dogs and Asimov robots, are wired for submission. In them change is locked away, segregated from real humanity. For the 'Family' inside Resune, with whom we spend most of our time, life is indistinguishable from life in a 1980s shopping and fucking bestseller, except that coffee is like gold dust and no one can go horse-riding much because only three models of AGCULT-789X have plopped out of the tanks so far. These lunches, these shopping trips, these family revelations... With a touch of find-and-replace Resune could so easily be the latest novelty setting for a glossy big-business soap: where children are vanity objects turned over to the nanny for routine care; where sex is about power, and power corrupts, and talented youngsters grovel before the daddy-bosses who love them, really, only they can't show it... Cherryh may be right. Why shouldn't the future be just like life on television? But her claim that 'society has changed out of all recognition' does not compute. The relationship between ranking humans and their azi life partners may count as a neologism: and a neat steal from the cod-feudalism of a typical Cherryh fantasy. But then again, a star's best friend is always her bodyguard.

Admittedly, we may be living in most unusually interesting times. Experiences that won't be repeated for a long while may false-colour the imaginary future, for baby boomer extrapolators like me. The plausibility of Cherryh's future is not in question. Who can tell? But the almost deathly stasis of Resune, and of Cyteen as far we see it, sets up an extraordinary drag against the supposed driving force of the book. Ariane1's objective is the preservation of human civilisation, of human nature, indeed. Without her immortal guidance over Resune's walking genebanks, the species would fly into smithereens: that's the story. But it is difficult to *feel* that this is a danger, when nothing seems to be changing much at all.

It is always a tricky business for art to imitate art. Cherryh has given herself the job of simulating the creative science of four (two?) utter geniuses: four of the twelve certified cleverest people in Union, besides a slew of secondary brilliant minds. She bolsters up her élite with 'test scores' and 'IQ quotients', scattering these last about in a way that does far more harm than good (but perhaps that's because I'm a sceptical Brit, trained from infancy to snicker at Mensa recruitment ads). But no matter what the numbers achieve, more circumstantial evidence is required. The older Warrick spends the whole book being very stupid indeed in his personal life. Brilliant scientists often blunder in human affairs, so maybe that's of no account. Ariane1, who remains, posthumously, much in evidence, is immensely convincing as a driven politician, inspired monster. She sees herself as poised between 'Divinity and megalomania'. If the reader sees her as megalomaniac all the way down that's no loss, it's a perfectly valid reading. The younger couple should be more interesting, but here again the conditions of Resune triumph. Cinderella-Justin is clever by hearsay, but he spends too much of his time being frightened stupid, weeping; carrying (the typical Cherryh hero) all the emotional weight no one else in the book can bear. When his denied genius is finally recognised—by Queen Ari, of course—it seems too much like the wave of a fairy godmother's wand. The child Ari2, kept in the dark about the project that so intimately concerns her, behaves like a sharp little kid whose parents are plotting a divorce. The precosity of a child in this situation is very familiar, very normal: and the reader finds her less than marvellous. As she grows older there are state-visit shopping trips, a bratpack of dumb followers, wild teenage sex-parties; an occasional fit of orgiastic self-disgust. She passes her exams, she collects testscores. But the very nature of the secret project is against her. What we call 'genius' falls as lightning strikes. The programmed progress, the cries of joy when Ari matches a fixed template, set up no resonance. As a talented brat and a ruined human being, Ari2 makes a successful futuristic Michael Jackson. She never looks remotely like a budding Einstein.

So where is this leading us? There's no futuristic recombinant DNA tech about, not much at all about the actual process of building azi. The ranks of cumbersome mechanical wombs are like 1890 horseless carriages, built as much like proper carriages as possible. Yet in its way this is a classic lab-procedural novel. It is the story of an imaginary experiment in an real-world scientific discipline. But that discipline is not, after all, genetic engineering. It is something older, and a lot less respectable. Resune scientists are 'psych surgeons' engaged in 'mind design'. They spend an unconscionable amount of time running around between lunches, trying to make each other cry. But in their spare moments they write the deep tape, the software of an enormous program of social engineering. The physical production of 'azi' is the tip of the iceberg, Resune is bent on inserting a new and improved mindset into the whole race. Sounds familiar? There are very few points in the book where the philosophy behind Resune is questioned. For most of the time we are entirely within the Foundation's skin, judging by its values. It is only in covert action, in the cracks between plausible jargon and machiavellian counterpoint, that another truth emerges. On the two occasions where the plot calls for a critical intervention from the brilliant psych surgeons, 'mind design' suddenly becomes a very practical, hands on affair. In one case the treatment involves aggravated rape. In the other the same subject is forcibly injected with an instantly, terminally addictive drug. The old crude ways, apparently, are best: and under the gloss the brainwashing industry is still as nasty as it sounds. Perhaps it is no wonder that Cherryh's depiction of the 'geniuses' involved in this charming little operation is so ambivalent.

At the ordained moment Araine2 is allowed to know who she is and learns, with the help of some fearsomely cold-blooded peptalks from her former self, to cope with her situation. Justin's hidden programming moves into convergence with the younger Ari while the old men of Union, the last of the original Ari's friends and supporters, begin to die off. It becomes clear that the climax of the story will be a battle for the possession of Resune itself. But though equal in every other way, the second Ariane Emory is not quite such a monster as the first. Will the experiment prove a failure at the last test? Or can the (relatively) good Ari hold onto power? Well, of course she can. The final phase of the novel is an anticlimax. *Cyteen* recalls its alternate identity as an episode of space saga and ends, any useful looking characters intact, in a flurry of contrived suspense. We are left wondering what in the world was the purpose of it all. What are we supposed to make of this meticulous account of dead-end evolution at work?

In earlier books (Morgaine in *The Chronicles of Morgaine*; Raen in *Serpent's Reach*) Cherryh has seemed haunted by the image of one strong woman pursued by a hungry crowd begging to be nurtured and protected. She must either betray them, or give up her own salvation. In *Cyteen* the wolves are in the sledge and the shepherd has joined the wolves. Ariane is a fallen saviour. The treatment of her sexuality is one index of her downfall. The gloomy tomboy has become one of the girls: a hairpulling, eyescratching Alpha female, who comes on heat regularly as a metronome and is sickened by her own insenseate appetite. Contraception is not a problem for anyone, pregnancy is not an issue. Menstruation, however, that other broad signal of female helplessness, is still around. Ariane's menstrual cyle merits hostile male comment throughout, while the men—this time—don't have any hormones at all. It seems implausible to me that rich women of the twenty-fourth century will still menstruate routinely: but then, it seems equally implausible that rich kids of Resune are still getting born with buck teeth and myopia. But perhaps Ariane's femaleness needs to be signalled as an ugly problem, some way or other.

Ariane is Queen of Resune, but the azi, not the humans, are her children. (Notably, there are few female azi with speaking parts.) As she rewrites humanity into replicated function, an awful lot of unnecessary variants are going to be heading for the shredder: and maybe this is the real terror that haunts the hive. The Queen's own job is safe: but can Ariane2 fill this role? Azi are better than human, so both Arianes believe. Some of them have genius level IQs (Yes! More geniuses!) In their wise innocence, no matter that it is wired into them, they resemble the gentle alien 'Downers' of *DownBelow Station*, and like the Downers azi have been made the repository for the spirituality which no one human in *Cyteen* can handle. The deepest azi experience is a kind of Buddhist trance of acceptance. All that humans find when they look inside themselves is terrifying chaos: the flux thinking that *Cyteen* characters dread. Ariane, in either generation, can't begin to contemplate the meaning of her strange immortality, she recoils from any hint of 'metaphysics'. But the azi, apart from being perpetual minors, domestic servants, (yes, even the geniuses) who can be mind-wiped or humanely put down with no legal repercussions, are also the external soul of humanity: Resune's heart in a paper bag. Ariane2, in spite of her moral superiority over her predecessor, sees no contradiction in their status. She is holding the azi in trust for themselves, and they are not individuals.

Her tender relationship with her azi bodyservants remains grotesque, because nothing can change the fact that they have been brainwashed (deep taped) to believe she is god. They have no capacity for consent. Yet Cherryh's admiration seems sincere, if Ariane's cannot be. The only self determined and emotionally competent character in the book is an azi, Justin's lover Grant. And it cannot be an accident that Ari2 and her predestined consort turn away from each other, both to azi lovers: as if this is the only way they can escape from the ugly pattern of sadism and submission. *Cyteen*'s ultimate horror, an explosion of biotechnological change (we can all be geniuses!) would mean the end of the difference between azi and human, and the hive of Resune, miserably clutching this firecracker to its chest, loves hierarchy as it loves nothing else in life. But if there is a message in the novel it seems to be that the gods have departed, the mandate has passed on. The future is with the azi, greater than his creatrix, the mind without desire: who is 'in touch with absolute truth and agrees perfectly with what he is'.

It's a little odd to review a book soon after it has won a major award. I cannot predict *Cyteen's* fate, nor can I tell whether it 'deserved' to win the 1989 Hugo. In spite of its power, this was a hard read. I'm pretty sure I'd have dropped it during the first hundred pages if I hadn't been reviewing. Some time after that I found that I was hooked, but it was never fun. The corridors of Resune may deserve to go down as one of fiction's authentic visions of hell: but hell is not an interesting place. It is a genuine relief to recall, as one does from time to time, that somewhere in this imagined universe the badgered decency of Pell Station (*Down Below*) may still be found. That these people of Resune, though they don't know it, have been cast by their creator as the baddies.

But let the last word be with the history of Resune, rather than with any over-reading of underlying themes. The provenance of the divide between Union and Alliance has been made clear in the synoptic preface. The population of Union was drawn from Earth's 'Eastern Bloc' (presumably including the European Community by the time starflight arrived, or why would Ariane be called Ariane?). Cherryh adds rather meanly, that this bunch of emigrants was of lower grade human material than the original 'best and brightest' departure that became the Alliance. In this context, real world history of the last few years has stranded Cherryh's future in the past (for the moment). It doesn't matter. The ethnic origin she gives to Union still signals 'command-economy, savage secret police, ruthless mass-brainwashing for the population; riches and a siege mentality for the elite...', just as it was supposed to do. However, there's no hint of slavic or soviet culture in Resune's shiny lifestyle. If I hadn't been told, I don't think I would have recognised that the characters in Cyteen must be descended from the un-American space colonists. After all, there have been other supposedly egalitarian revolutions which have left the Brahmins, the first comers, free to amass disproportionate wealth and power. Resune, like most science fictional societies, offers a portrait of the writer's own times and the culture: and what Cherryh gives us is not 'reds under the beds' but a compelling sense of a powerbase out of touch with its constituency and getting very scared. Every signal that *Cyteen* is about science, discovery, genius turns out to be a canard, but the examination of scrabbling, self-serving politics works sublimely. Resune's purpose in life is not the perfection of the human race. A political system's purpose in life is minding its own back. When Ari2 comes before the cameras, on the occasion of some inconvenient leaping of skeletons out of wartime closets, the true nature of her 'genius' is revealed. She is the person who can handle the media. There is no higher art in Resune's philosophy.

11: *Alien Sex*: Ellen Datlow's Overview of the SF Orgasm

Alien Sex, it transpires, in the introduction to this anthology, was not the title Ellen Datlow wanted. She favoured something more subtle, this one just grew on people. But it suits the collection well: a hard, blunt, primal composite. Alien, which means nasty. Sex, which means poking a fraction of your delicate and precious self (doesn't have to be a penis: a finger, maybe?) into something icky. Into the alien out there. Which may or may not be alive but which is definitely hostile. It has to be, since it isn't part of precious you.

Datlow's organically grown title is a clear warning. Any fool who picks this book up expecting mild porn with tentacles deserves the sad disappointment they're going to get. Most of the stories are decidedly downbeat: more to the point they are extremely, self-consciously serious. The term 'consciously' is important here. Sex, per se, is one of those characters one should refuse to work with, on the children and animals rule. The subject will almost certainly upstage the writer. Fucking is so personal. We all have our funny little ways. The risk of being inadvertantly hilarious is so great that the only sensible approach is to be awfully, awfully serious; or to pass the whole thing off as a joke. But even jokes aren't safe, because fucking is so political. The who-does-what-to-whom of it can so speedily wipe the smile off your reader's face, turning a harmless bit of fun into a sickening satirical fable. William Gibson, in his foreword, suggests that this is a post-AIDS, post-feminist book. But there's more to it than that. Ghastly and death-dealing venereal disease isn't new (what about syphilis?). Nor is the battle of the sexes. What *Alien Sex* describes is the state of sexual play in a world that has become highly sensitised—by a whole complex of historical, scientific, sociological effects—to *risk*. Risk-taking of the literary kind, of the political kind, of the emotional kind... The net result reminds me of the old playground joke. Q: How do porcupines make love? A: Very carefully! Modern humans feel the same, even when they're just writing about it. And maybe with good reason. The days of literary innocence are over. Sf writers of all persuasions, all shades of gender politics, have had twenty years now to think about fictional sex, and what it can do to your reputation as a cool, aware dude. Everybody knows the score.

Inevitably, then, some of the reprint stories in the collection look quite weirdly lightweight and naïve alongside the modern pieces, especially when they're trying to be funny. The Philip José Farmer story 'The Jungle Rot Kid On The Nod' is a tiring William Burroughs-style pastiche of Tarzan (both called Burroughs, geddit!). The Harlan Ellison story 'How's The Night Life on Cissalda' is a one-liner about voraciously sexy aliens long past its best-by date. Larry Niven's 'Man of Steel, Woman of Kleenex' is the nasty joke that survives: a deadpan classic about the problems of sex with a super-being. Even so, the relentless list of a hundred and one ways to destroy a female human body might seem a tiny bit misogynistic. A really jaded female reader might go so far as to suggest that the joke's not very funny.

Ms Datlow remarks in her introduction that the stories are roughly evenly balanced between between male and female writers. In view of the precise subject, it might be more interesting to work out what proportion of the contributors have a sexual orientation aligned with the consensus majority. How many of these writers are what's laughingly called 'normal' and how many are alienated outsiders? And in which set would you include K.W. Jeter? Or (this is a subtler point) Connie Willis? Jeter's story 'The First Time' is arguably the strongest in the collection. It tells of a young boy's first visit to a whorehouse. The ritual act is revealed as a kind of murder by a great big dollop of magically-realistic grue. The effect is bad and brilliant. Most telling of all, at the end, fully realising the horror of what a regular guy does for fun on a Saturday night, the boy feels only disgust, no pity for his victim. The only person little boy lost feels sorry for is himself.

Connie Willis's 'All My Darling Daughters' is a well-known, even notorious story. I find some of the citicism levelled at it obtuse. There are things in this story to which I take strong exception, not least the misuse of the name and history of Elizabeth Barrett Browning. But the story is, Willis has stated, an early, clumsy and uncertain attempt at science fiction; and I'm glad it has not been airbrushed. I don't believe that writers should be encouraged to rewrite their own history. Major elements—the space-habitat High School, the peculiar teenage-speak, the strange idea of what a sexually active adolescent girl might be like—invoke the 1950s rather than any future imaginable from 1990. But the Jeter story is equally anachronistic in tone. If Fifties-style flags up Bad Sex, quickly, why not use it?

Coarse in texture, overlong, but painfully honest, the Willis story tells the secret that Freud discovered and then denied, a hundred odd years ago. The sexual abuse of children, by adult men, is one of the pillars of our society. Just as Jeter turns the screw (uh, sorry, I'm trying to keep these under control...) by making the penetration of a woman's body a bloody evisceration, Willis first shows us the abused child, then substitutes a helpless, mindless animal as Man's ideal sexual partner: and makes another point about the collaboration of the helpless in their own degradation. The two stories are strangely alike, a matched pair, even to the dehumanisation of the victim.

Perhaps what Mr Jeter and Ms Willis have in common is deeply held belief that the sexual status quo is immoveable, a dreadful given that no one can escape. Other contributors have managed to skim over the horrors of normalcy without becoming too mesmerised by existential despair. *Alien Sex* is a parade of bleak moments and brittle laughs. Scott Baker's 'The Jamesburg Incubus' is far more upbeat on the subject than 'Varicose Worms', his powerful story in 'Year's Best Fantasy...', (also co-edited by Datlow). The conclusion, coming down so ingeniously in favour of monogamy—and frugal habits!—should make 'The Jamesburg Incubus' a good prospect for the Catholic Truth Society, if they do reprints. I liked (if that's the word) the quietly inserted penis extender in Rick Wilber's role-reversed 'War Bride' The cute little native whore has to be fixed up so he can satisfy the alien... conjuring up gruesome reports from old Saigon, of torn vaginas stitched up maybe several times a week. Leigh Kennedy's 'Her Furry Face' is a maybe more disturbing version of the Willis story, again equating woman and animal, and damning the insensitive, self-obsessed human male. Women writers identify themselves with animals: men attempt to identify themselves with women. In 'When the Fathers Go' Bruce McAllister is making a valiant attempt at self-criticism on behalf of his whole gender. The story 'offers up Woman as the victim of the Lies that men in our culture build out of the cutural myths that bind them...' Well, that's what it says in the authorial afterword. Unfortunately McAllister's female narrator is such a good listener (!) that somehow the absconding male, pathological liar, still manages to steal the story and hog centre stage. Sounds familiar, anyone?

Sex with the alien, alien invasion. Sometimes it's done simply. Roberta Lannes' 'Saving the World at the New Moon Hotel' is probably the nearest to what the unwary sf punter might have hoped for: a harmless bit of fun, with a plot and tentacles and almost nil political paranoia. In the light of the rest it is interesting to note that this happens to be written by a woman. Sometimes the metaphor is doubled over. The aliens have invaded, and what do they want from us? Of course! It must be Bad Sex! Pat Cadigan and Ed Bryant both describe sex with the alien as a bizarre kind of obscene phone call. You're being used—intimately and against your will—by someone you can't ever meet, or face, or accuse... Ms Cadigan's version is a cracker: witty and sharp and cool. Mr Bryant takes the predicament of the sex object far more seriously—and yet another contributor finds reason to damn the human adult male. But totally. This begins to look like a conspiracy. But one of the strengths of this collection is that for every statement, a comment has been included. Almost any story by 'James Tiptree Jnr' would add something to an anthology called *Alien Sex*. The one Ms Datlow has chosen, 'And I Awoke and Found Me Here on the Cold Hillside...' is precisely about the alien sex-fiend as a human fiction. The aliens are here, and they aren't interested. Frankly, they don't give a damn.

'And I Awoke...' is a story written by a woman who was pretending— for a whole cocktail of reasons—to be a man. It foregrounds the plight of the male—cynically, satirically, and maybe just as a marketing ploy. It also states, explicitly, that the deadly allure of Otherness is as strong for both sexes. It is a human need. The same point is made, more calmly, in the third part of Lisa Tuttle's triptych, 'Husbands'. I don't know why it should be, but it is certainly true that the female writers in *Alien Sex* treat their subject much more coolly, even while saying the most ghastly things. The (justified) hysteria in this book—and there's plenty—is all male; or male pretending to be female—or female pretending to be male, if you count Tiptree. Ms Tuttle, like the other female contributors, seems to step back, to pick up the Nessus' shirt of human sexuality and examine it, while wisely refusing to put the horrid thing on. The spurious air of detachment that the women achieve is no doubt a defence mechanism, and it does weaken the punch of some powerful stories. Or it would: but not here. Lisa Tuttle's final image, of the post-gendered society obscurely driven to re-invent analogues of 'masculine' and 'feminine', should be read alongside K.W. Jeter. It is a mark of the intelligence that went into the shaping of this anthology that you need to have both stories in front of you. Then you get the full effect.

I would hesitate to propose *Alien Sex* as a barometer of the sexual climate of the *fin de siècle*. This is art, not sociology. The relentlessly bad press that the men get, especially from themselves, isn't necessarily a sign that in real life the guys are all in sackcloth and ashes. It's more likely a sign that they're still getting by far the best of the deal, only now they know it and are trying to cover up. Bad conscience is not the same, alas, as reformation of character. But the real tragic dilemma of human sexuality is made clear in none of the stories: it appears as an absence. Not one of these stories (Michaela Roessner's poem comes nearest) is written from the point of view of the alien. My sexual partner is a monster, an animal, a thief, a reflection, a victim; food. Me? Oh, I'm just normal. It's like a childrens' game of make-believe, where the baby has to be bullied into the essential role that nobody wants to play, Captain Hook, the simpering princess; a band of marauding orcs... Everyone wants to pursue the Other, to explore the Other, to have the Other, to get inside the Other, to consume the Other, to be consumed by the Other. But nobody here wants to be the Other. It's a tough one. No wonder Ms Datlow decided to give the last word to the last human being alive. And even there in the non-human future, seen through Pat Murphy's wryly elegiac 'Love and Sex Among The Invertebrates', it looks as if *la lutte continue*...

And finally, honourable mention must go to the two writers who grasped the nettle and actually wrote about sex, as in the good stuff, as in wet, sticky, physical pleasure. Like the Jeter/Willis pair, Richard Christian Matheson's 'Arousal' and Geoff Ryman's 'Omnisexual' have a peculiar back to back similarity. Each protagonist wakes up one day to find that everything, simply everything, has become orgasmic. The Matheson story is more mundane, a Da Palma-flavoured short of glossy contemporary surfaces with a coldly sinister edge. 'Omnisexual' seems to have no outer surface at all. It comes from an ever-present element in Geoff Ryman's writing that I personally find hard to take undiluted. Sexual and powerful this piece certainly is, but to read it is a lot like diving head-first and open-mouthed into a pool of warm, raw liver. Oh well. Whatever turns you on.

12: The Boys Want to be with the Boys: Neal Stephenson's *Snow Crash*

It must have been about the time of the first moon landings when Brian Aldiss announced that the real world had caught up with science fiction: we are now living in the future. When the news reached me, a little later, I was unconvinced. Er—where's the galactic empires then? Where's Moonbase? Why haven't 'we' colonised Mars? Why am I still eating toast for breakfast, instead of protein-pills? Where's the warp drive, for heaven's sake? At last, there can be no doubt. The apotheosis is achieved. Cyberpunk is no longer science fiction, no longer a rough description of one or two good books and mixed bag of followers, nor even merely flavour of the month for a future-groupie élite, goggled in to three dimensional MTV. It is advertising, junk-food and channel-hopping. It is part of the world. This is no mean achievement for a brand of science fiction. We pretend we're writing about the far-flung future. But in the real world sf is strongly perceived as an artefact of the 1950s. To be considered post-modern is a great leap forward.

Cyberspace was never a classic science fiction. It is, or was, sheer fantasy, now bootstrapped into the real world by the will (maybe I should say tinkerbelled) of a few thousand virtual-reality nuts. By sheer longing, these characters dissolve the clunky actuality of their typing fingers, their goggleheads and gloves, into the limitless, god-polluted, metaphysical other world of William Gibson's metaphor. And who knows, maybe (as in one of those homespun Heinlein tales about the power of positive thinking) they'll get there. Meanwhile, 'real' cyberspace still belongs to the folks who can think in hexadecimal. Now, apparently, cyberpunk (the fiction) does too. Scientists have always written science fiction, but usually they have steered clear of gaudy fantasy. Cyberpunk is different, and a grasp of Boolean algebra doesn't necessarily mean you're an austere academic (nor even ordinarily literate). The hacker strikes back.

In classic style, Neal Stephenson's *Snow Crash* is set in a futurised-present or presentified-future of absolutely no rational date, sort of 2021 going on 1975. The IT industry has recently coalesced from brilliant hippiedom into Bill Gates; the children of Second World War vets are in their mid-twenties; and there's been time for the USA to collapse and reform as a myriad tiny 'Franchise or Quasi-National entities' each with its own borders, rabid paranoia, savage security forces. In the description of this state of affairs the true demographic situation along the USA section of the Pacific Rim gets a rare public outing. But Gibson was perhaps lucky that his throwaway version of World War III had become irrelevant before the book was published. At once, in *Snow Crash*, there's a sense that present-day prejudice is not being challenged but being sanitised in this 'weird futuristic nightmare'. The strutting, frenetically overloaded demotic (stuffed with brand names), that William Gibson practically invented off the street, is not as successful as it used to be in glamorising the evil cosiness of a siege mentality.

Though *Snow Crash* doesn't have the magic sheen of *Neuromancer*, the Decline and Fall scenario has wit. In the shattered and lawless ex-USA the old bogeys of Organised Crime are on the rise like Visigoths, snaring the best High School graduates into their career structure. And yes, the Mafia were the ultimate evil, and yes, they are still murderous savages; but yes, they are also the future of civilisation...(In a thousand years or so they'll be building gothic cathedrals). It works. Place in this background a smart nerd of a hacker/hero, who aspires to and is terrified by the feminine values of civilisation. Hiro Protagonist was a brilliant hacker in the old free days. (The term 'hacker', note, in this world, has no shady implications. Since there are no laws it can't be illegal to mess around in other peoples' digital environment, it can only be more or less dangerous.) Now he spends his time hopping between goggled-in life in the tasteless, touchless glossy-magazine world of the 'metaverse'; and his broke and unemployed reality. He yearns after the sophisticated other, brilliant hacker Juanita; yet knows deep in his heart that she despises the way he chews without closing his mouth. One day, the plot starts happening. Hiro learns, or thinks he learns, that his inamorata is off to save the world (which still means the sort of geographical area of the ex-US) from an ancient, ghastly conspiracy. He takes arms, in the hope of getting laid.

Snow Crash is a book peppered with sideswipes—at uppity Nips, people who try to make you wear motorcycle helmets; at bureaucracy in government offices, where wild free hacker spirits are forced to peruse idiot memos about Toilet Tissue. The dis-ease behind these endless complaints could be generally headed 'resentment of control, resentment of competition', and this is definitely germane to the plot. It's a pity the writer doesn't give Hiro Protagonist a lot to be resentful about. In the metaverse our hero is a warrior prince... rich, brilliant hacker, ace Japanese swordsman, romantic Black/Asian mix, tall, phenomenal biker, fabu muscle-tone. In the ungoggled fictional world he remains all of the above, except rich. Even so, he's materially much better off than almost anyone else we meet; and he always somehow has the wherewithal to reproduce in life the fantasy excesses of the goggled world. This makes the metaverse and reality almost indistinguishable—which is a technical difficulty for the reader in a thriller that relies a lot on the trick of flipping between the two. (I kept sensing the shadow presence of the *real*, real Hiro Protagonist, behind his metaverse 'avatar' and his fictional one. The Woody Allen Hiro: a slight, round shouldered, fortyish white boy, with a row of pens drooping helplessly in his shirt pocket...)

I digress. I'll forgive him his sharp white smile and his sexy, dangerous racial mix. In Mr Protagonist, prince in exile, morally superior yet emotionally insecure, Neal Stephenson has the broody hurt of misplaced humility and the detail of social unease well down. The chopping to and fro between metaverse and reality is muddling, and defies chronology: but so far, *Snow Crash* had my attention.What happens next is that the silly plot takes him out into the world. Generically speaking, programmers, like chess players, are not gentle people. They only look as though they're sitting there being round-shouldered and meek. Mr Protagonist setting out on the rampage, immediately becomes the proof of everything they ever told you about shoot-em-up video game addiction. He discovers that swapping someone's head off in real life is dead easy. He feels nothing. The killing starts, the killing continues. The latter part of the book is simply a long dissolve into ultra violence: human bodies pureed, chopped, fried, mashed. There's a lot of blood. Femoral and carotid arteries spout. Blood slicks on an Exxon scale feature heavily. The callousness of the good guys is leavened only by pained reproach when things get too gross. Here's a mild out-take from where Hiro's female kid-sidekick has been helping to secure a sample of the evil drug.

> The chopper pulls up into a hard turn, searching for additional prey, and something falls beneath it in a powerless trajectory, she thinks that it has dropped a bomb. But it's the head of the sniper, spinning rapidly, throwing out a fine pink helix under the light. The little chopper's rotor blade must have caught him in the nape of the neck. One part of her is dispassionately watching the head bounce and spin in the dust, and the other part of her is screaming her lungs out...

The sidekick's impulse to scream in disgust is supposed to be proof that her human feelings are intact. The gag-reflex is the nearest Stephenson's characters can manage to compassion, and they're touchingly proud of it. Meanwhile, the plot develops by means of large, placid info-dumps about Chomsky and Mesopotamian archaeology. A baddie is trying to control (by blitzing the élite brains of hackers with an evil drug; and by infecting the post-literate rest of us with an evil virus), a commodity known as information. Apparently it isn't necessary to be more specific. Removal of

control, removal of competition is a good end of such a high order that no
further explanation can be required.

We were warned. In the bravura opening passage, about delivering pizza
for the Mafia, we were told that 'The Deliverator knows everything about
pizza...' A sentence or two later it is demonstrated that his job is so fully
automated that 'the Deliverator' need never have seen a pizza in his life.
What he knows 'all about' is delivery. Distribution of the product. The
ethos championed passionately in *Snow Crash* is not about saving the world.
It is about *spreading things*: human bodies into jam; the mashed,
unidentifiable remains of something known as 'freedom'. There's no
material content in this philosophy, the nature of the *things* is irrelevant.
It's very metaphysical.

It transpires that the baddie has chosen to use, as vector of his infection,
a Third World Invasion. The evil L. Bob Rife has bought the aircraft carrier
Enterprise, moseyed over to gook-land and brought back a huge
conglomerated heap of Boat People. Packs of survival-honed brutal
Eurasians are to be cast ashore in their thousands, a terrifying prospect for
the razor-wired 'Burbclaves' of well-fed white America (which still exists,
just the way you knew it *circa* the last Michael Fox video you hired). In
'The Raft' Mr Stephenson has identified an up-to-date all-purpose Scare
Thing, as good for his purpose as the old favourite Global Thermonuclear
War. He's careful to disinfect the human element that might make the
invocation of this 'threat' morally dubious to some over sensitive readers.
By the time these people reach the suburbs, we're assured, they've killed
and eaten all the softer sort of their own kind, the ones you might feel
sorry for. It is no longer relevant that the 'Refus' are poor, hungry,
despairing, disenfranchised. They're mad dogs: they deserve no one's pity.

Snow Crash exploits white America's fear of the barbarian other with
total, cynical abandon. On the personal scale, the reverse of this coin is
more tentatively examined. Fear and longing for the barbarian is a twisted
knot in the soul of the 'civilised' male... Though Hiro is supposedly doing
all this to get laid, the terrifying Juanita is so civilised that her presence
would unman the narrative: she barely appears. She's replaced by a less
threatening *tabula rasa* of a '15 year old American blonde chick' known as
Y.T., who exists to admire whatever hunky business is going on and to
despise anything female and even lower ('not even chicks...') in the
hierarchy than herself. But Hiro's actual love affair (not overtly! He's no
HOMO!) is clearly with Raven, the baddest motherfucker in the world.
This Superman, bloodletter on a truly remarkable scale, represents perhaps
the Wrath of God and perhaps the Revenge of the Third World. Since Hiro
obviously can't consummate his passion, Y.T. takes over for him, and
provides one of the most bizarre moments in the novel. At her first

appearence the young girl assured the audience that her perky insouciance on the savage streets wasn't as dumb as it seemed: 'she wasn't scared, she was wearing her dentata...' For the next three hundred or so pages of assorted gore the operation of this gruesome dentata thing has remained a mystery. Finally, impressed, consenting, and horny (as fifteen year old blonde chicks always are in this sort of graphic novel), Y.T. gets down with the homicidal mutant. Overcome by lust, she forgets to remove her ultimate deterrent. Oh, horror: 'A very small hypodermic needle slipped imperceptibly into the engorged frontal vein of his penis, automatically shooting a cocktail of powerful narcotics... into his bloodstream.'

Maybe you have to have ploughed your way through the morass of mushed human bodies on the way to this *very small* needle; maybe you even have to be a woman, to cackle the way I did at this juncture... (I also couldn't help being amused at the idea of a rape-deterrent device that does not prevent or even discourage penetration). But hey, we could have the solution to the novel's emotional problems here. If Mr Protagonist could be presented with the spectacle of myriads of penises being slashed, whipped, minced, electrocuted, nuclear-machine-gunned and otherwise brutally abused... maybe the boy would finally be able to feel something.

'The people of America,' goes Stephenson's thesis, 'live in the world's most surprising and terrible country.' *Snow Crash* is unremittingly pompous about its very unsurprising terrors, but its deepest scorn is reserved for the people who have fled from the true America: 'They have parallel parked their bimboboxes in identical computer designed Burbclave street patterns and secreted themselves in symmetrical sheetrock shitholes with vinyl floors... a culture medium for a medium culture...'

Yet at the same time the novel manages to be firmly, devotedly on the side of suburban family values. *Snow Crash* characters do not do drugs. Apart from that one aberration, they do not do sex. The Mafia is big on tradition, on girls in kneesocks and boys who say 'Sir' a lot. Computer crazy kids are no way punks, never street people. They borrow Dad's computer to 'date' in the Metaverse, and behave there as if they're on the Cosby show. Except, of course, for being white. Even when she's kidnapped onto The Raft, Y.T. is oblivious to a world that might have challenged some of her squeaky-clean amorality. She sees Raven as a boyfriend who 'dates' her, and expects what she gets: food and a temporary owner/bodyguard, exactly the way things are in the suburbs. Even the Raft folk themselves have retained a grip of the essentials through all that aforesaid honing by savage survivalism. When Hiro and the Mafia lads show up, a Philipino houseboy materialises to cook for them, so they don't have to embarrass themselves doing menial gook/girl-work. There's even some weird whimsy about faithful, cute, bionic pit-bulls, brave doggies whose Midnight Barking brings Disney into the bloodbath. Ultra violence, we are to understand, in no way contravenes the laws of Mom and apple pie-land.

It has been said that popular taste cannot handle the idea of there being more than two viewpoints on any subject. Anything more complicated than bad guys vs. good guys and you lose the mass market. And then there's the American liberal, who cannot handle *one* viewpoint. Mr Stephenson, who I feel certain would sign himself a liberal, refuses to be labelled and docketed, nobly declines to take sides in any debate whatsoever; and therefore becomes embroiled in fearful contortions when his ancient-conspiracy plot tries to force him to come down on the side of Good or Evil. To postpone this dreadful fate there's more plot—acres of cypherbunk and fascist (I mean, literally) nonsense about Ancient Sumeria and metaviruses from space, acres of storyboarded chase-and-blow-up sequence, before the show down with the villians who have (of course) carefully preserved the ONLY weapon that could be used against them. When the characters start making Nietzschean pronouncements about how little it all matters, one can only sympathise. I think Stephenson manages to wriggle out of his philosophical dilemma in the end, and to retain his moral neutrality. Juanita, it turns out, was only going after the 'bad' guys because the Antichrist is a really interesting phenomenon. But I'm not sure. I may have lost track.

Snow Crash has the marks of an IT junkie at work. Hiro gets 'information', wads of it, by pressing a button: there's none of the discovery process that normal writers use to keep a thriller interesting. It's obviously no accident that the most vivid parts of the book are the parts most like a videogame, while the place where Hiro actually lives is a blank box. But is it cyberpunk? I'm not sure. It's clear that the coming to consciousness of a 'human' or quasi-divine AI would excite Hiro Protagonist about as much as a talking chicken might thrill a slaughterhouse worker. *Snow Crash* is the fantasy of a computer literate who finds no romance in contemplating the human/machine interface. The Metaverse is a wraparound game screen, there's nothing weird about it. And *Snow Crash* definitely is not about how cheap and dirty cybernetic technology may empower the dead end kids on the street corner. Hiro was never powerless: and when he wants more power, he uses a plain old nuclear machine-gun. In 1984, *Neuromancer* gave traditional, mainstream sf a new kind of future. In the Nineties, as net junkies start to look like the successors of the hippies and we cast about on the horizon for the next wave, *Snow Crash* seems only tangentially connected with the William Gibson version of personal computer use. Instead it provides a lurid snapshot of a society built on the fantasies of male adolescence, when that society is in catastrophic decline. Is that what cyberpunk was 'all about' in terms of the real world—stripped of everything that made it interesting as science fiction? Maybe so. The dark ages are coming, boys. Have fun.

When I reached about p.103 of *Snow Crash*, I decided I was reading the cyberpunk version of *Raiders of the Lost Ark*. At which point I fell about laughing, with Mr Stephenson, not at him. However, leaving aside the fact that fate had me reviewing this on the night of the worst Rodney King riots, (a bad weekend for light-hearted nazi fantasy), there is too much of this stuff. The steroid-boosted bounce of the writing can't sustain the joke. It says here (inside the cover) that *Snow Crash* was first conceived as a computer-generated graphic novel. That's exactly what I think I've been reading: a splatter&gadgets comic with about 150,000 too many words. Indeed in this form Neal Stephenson's first sf novel would be so much the standard product it wouldn't rate a second glance. Don't be fooled (but remember, this is only my opinion, which you must translate to suit yourself); it still doesn't.

13: *Glory Season*: David Brin's Feminist Utopia

David Brin has written a book about a feminist utopia. It's about a planet which has been settled by idealistic women seeking an escape from the harsh, bestial code of natural human society...

The founding mothers were planning to do without men all together. But they discovered there is something in sperm that's necessary for the health of the placenta so—rather than bottle the something—they decided to build themselves some big, hunky blokes. They then endowed these hunks (presumably on the grounds that Mother Nature doesn't mean things to be easy) with a longish rutting season during which lavishly appointed brothels have to be provided to contain their urges, because NO WOMAN IS SAFE IN THEIR COMPANY; and endowed themselves with a similar season during which they are just dying for it and the men aren't interested, so that these radical feminists are forced to don flimsy negligés and ooze about like extras in a *Star Trek* harem scene... Well, women are fools and masochists, I'd be the first to agree. The first thing the boldly going separatists do is reinvent rape and prostitution? Nothing more likely!

Since the men have been built impossible to house-train, they have a separate and more or less autonomous existence. The women rule on land. The men have the sea, coming on shore only to deliver their cargoes and to fuck—usually, in order to add that vital placenta nourishing ingredient to parthenogenetic conception, occasionally, actually to father boys and the girl 'variants' who save the female clone communities from stagnation. This is a useful situation, since we have only to put to sea in order to escape from the dreary prospect of a feminist utopia novel all about women: and because no male character embarrasses the general reader by having to endure the intimate, constant, insidious dominance behaviour that a woman among men suffers in the real world. If a man does get in among the women unarmed—as it were—he still doesn't have to act cowed, defer, watch his manners, none of that nonsense. Note the retired sailor janitor in the girls' school (in my uncorrected proofs, I have to allow) who goes about pinching bottoms, rousing 'girlish shrieks of delighted outrage...' Perhaps most curious of all, in a world of brutishly functional reproductive trading, with no possibility of heterosexual romance for anyone, homosexuality is unknown. A chaste girly crush is the most a gal can feel for another gal. The hunky sailors never lay so much as a rope-end on each other, except in honest sweaty combat. Can you believe it? Can Middle-

America's booksellers believe it? I suspect that's more to the point.

I'm going to try not to go on about it. There's no point in me wondering why, since they have genetic engineering that works more or less like a magic wand, it didn't occur to the founding mothers to do something dopily simple, like engineer their daughters bigger and stronger. Or anything else that makes sense. Let's just leave it that as feminist utopias go, it is rather difficult to spot what radical improvement these women were after when they designed their sex lives. Let's just leave it that as an exploration of gender-role conditioning and sexual politics, *Glory Season* will tell you absolutely nothing; while telling you absolutely nothing you didn't know about a simple male's most gormless fantasies.

I don't know what it is about David Brin and feminism. Maybe he really is doing the best he knows how for the Cause. Though it is hard to reconcile that interpretation with the afterword to *Glory Season*, which would like you to believe that David Brin singlehandedly (Nothing more likely! Uh, sorry. Just my twisted mind) invented his wild idea of a world of beautiful women (Did I forget to say they were all beautiful? Are you kidding?) without ever having heard of Joanna Russ, Suzy Charnas, Ursula Le Guin... Maybe he does respect the real feminist writers. It's true, modest nineteenth-century revolutionary Charlotte Perkins Gilman turns up in the text, transformed into the logo of an evil extremist cult. Maybe he thinks feminism is an endangered substance, like one of those rainforest hardwoods, so that everybody ought to be encouraged to use the plastic kind instead. More practically, maybe someone (Brin or his publishers) fancies that there are more megabucks to be made from feminist sf, if only you could get a man's name above the title. Maybe, but maybe not. Whatever modest fortune there is to be made out of middle-of-the-road sf gender politics, I think the name on the cheques is Sheri Tepper's—a popular writer with the feminine equivalent of Brin's gender-political views, but slightly more appropriate basic sympathies.

It is easy to ridicule *Glory Season*. But after all, the worst thing that can be said about this bizarrely counterproductive 'womens' world' is that it was obviously designed by a man. In a way that's actually a relief. Brin's exercise in sexual stereotyping hardly differs from plenty of supposedly feminist, devotedly womanly sf about noble nurturing Mommas and feckless Pricks who don't know no better and can't learn. To see this vision presented as a paradise for men is refreshing. What fun it would have been if David Brin had been conscious of what he was doing (which in all fairness does not seem to be the case). What a great book if the ingenuous male self-interest that pervades this creation had been turned to political account; if *Glory Season* had starred an ambitious young boy, dissatisfied with his cosy natural niche of physical prowess, fiscal irresponsibility and affectless fucking, who sets out to seek his fortune on land, struggling to be recognised as a human being...

But in the event (as I believe is true of other Brin novels), carping about the missed chances is pointless. What actually happens is that a plucky young girl sets out, from a background of absent, exciting Fathers and Mothers who stay at home to do the boring work, which would be perfectly conventional in our own world. The Big Issues vanish in a welter of energetic, ill-disciplined storytelling—involving indentical twins (who occasionally have to stop being identical, with a loud authorial OOPS!), pirates, miraculous escapes, storms, shipwrecks, secret hideouts, passwords, secret passages, blow-by-blow accounts of an 'artificial life' computer game (funny how these far-flung planets always seem to pick up on the fads of Earth *circa* now, ain't it?); treasure hunts, more pirates... It's a rattling non-stop ride, a lot like a Sheri Tepper novel, in fact. But finally there are too many false starts, loose ends, clunky implausibilities, and cobbled-together holes in the plot. Though Tepper has the same tendency to make cosmic promises and deliver cartoon action, she has better luck as a slapdash narrator, or she works harder; or she has a better editor. Or all three. I get the feeling that if only David Brin would FORGET the damned issues and buckle down and do some work, he'd write fine, liberal-sf sympathetic, adolescent-style adventure that I'd be happy to see on the shelves. And the issues would be better served. Meanwhile, if you have fond memories of *Swallows and Amazons*, if you enjoyed *Hook*; if you don't mind direly raggedy plotting, and if you have a secret yearning for Hulk Hogan, you may love this book.

But you probably don't wear a dress.

Not in public, anyway.

14: *Virtual Light*: A Shocking Dose of Comfort and Joy from William Gibson

The time is 2005. A personable young woman, a San Francisco bike-courier called Chevette Washington, steals—by pure fluke—a pair of VR spectacles. Unluckily for her what she takes for a pair of sunglasses is actually a neat piece of data-display tech holding some valuable and contraband commercial information. Meanwhile a similarly personable young man, an aspiring private-sector law officer called Berry Rydell, suffers a career setback, is almost but not quite featured on a popular tv show called *Cops in Trouble*; and ends up employed by the suspect enforcement officers who have gathered to hunt Chevette down. A thriller develops, involving hacker-action, a nasty murder, drug-induced paranoia, much chasing about and much local colour. Particularly colourful is the Bay Bridge—which has been ruined in an earthquake and has rapidly metamorphosed into a funky squatters' quartier. Commentary of one kind or another is provided by ageing-hipster Skinner, a Bay Bridge sacred elder and Chevette's protector; and by Yamakazi, an earnestly intellectual young Japanese tourist.

Some of this is standard Neuromancing: the chase-and-recovery plot, simple and robust enough to carry any amount of rococo flourishes; the densely depicted near future; the smugly lawless hackers, the two young no-hopes being thrown about (and into each other's arms) by the same old Invisible Hand—here represented by fiendish Singaporean urban developers. But even allowing for the fact that 2005 is barely a decade away, there is remarkably little cyberdelia in the wealth of meticulous near-market research; and remarkably little hysteria in the thriller plot. The dense invention favours culture—tv shows, folk-art, instant religion—above gadgets; and the gadgets are given no fantastic glamour. From the way the virtual light specs are described here they could be on the real life market before the paperback of the novel: and the threat invoked by the contraband information is quite unnervingly low key. A Lee Kuan Yew style town-planning facelift for San Francisco may be a scary prospect. But however allergic you are to the electronic island, it's hardly the end of the universe.

William Gibson had never been much of a genre apologist. Since *Neuromancer* took the sf world by storm ten years ago, 'cyberpunk' has become (among other things) a form of science fiction which is instantly recognisable to many reviewers. (This doesn't go for me. I find it confusing that the most devout 'humanists' are now compelled by commonsense to include computer networking and virtual reality in their plots.) But though *Neuromancer* may have had the effect of a revolutionary manifesto on hard, radical sf, I am not aware that William Gibson intended it as such. But fans of Gibson's supposed radical ideals have expressed dismay, and spoken of a sell-out, because *Virtual Light* is not another violent, hard sf thriller, and nor can it be construed as a pitiless attack on the genre's complacent bourgeoisie. Perhaps this reaction is not so much a distaste for the the the restraint of the near-future ideation, as alarm at the diminution of frenetic paranoia; and at the gentle, clean-living tone. The only non-prescribed drug featured (besides alcohol) is utterly nasty stuff that none of the goodies would dream of ingesting. The baddies are bad enough (though none of them better try and duke it out with Peter Riviera); but the goodies are good in the worst way. Chevette may be a street waif with a sad background, but she has personal standards and an honest job (the theft is a total aberration). Berry the rent-a-cop is an innocent hick, who turns hero to beat the villians with a piece of whacky non-violent fun. Old Skinner is practically a saint. There is no sign of the Perfect Master's famed unloveable, affectless 'new-humans' of 1984.

Unsympathetic characterisation used to be the hallmark of cyberpunk. It was the way a humanist could tell he or she had got hold of the true, repulsive article: 'Why can't I feel anything for these people?' was the cry. Whereas in return the Movement claimed to be depicting the human future in *verité*: punk kids drained of the traditional sf syrup and hypocrisy. Perhaps the rules are no longer strict. Antihero is a demanding riff, and much of cyberpunk-type fiction reverted instantly to the old juv-lead syrup routine. But in fact Gibson himself has never been particularly hard-boiled: indeed he has been consistently gentle with his puppets.

Because Molly Kolodny and Henry Case never speak out of character, because William Gibson refuses to allow himself an artistic solecism, it is possible to miss the fact that *Neuromancer* is a novel about two or three miserable young losers, and that pity is their author's dominant feeling towards them. Rereading the novel after almost a decade, I find that while the labels have grown stale and the drop-dead style just couldn't be as good as you remember it, the pity comes through very strong. The image of Case, in dumb bewilderment after he has witnessed his friend's humiliation in Riviera's dream cabaret—a kid struggling to feel grief and shame, whose grievous and shameful young life has left him unable even to name those emotions: that's some essential key to *Neuromancer*.

The further careers of Gibson heroes and heroines confirm one's suspicion that the man's a closet softie. There's something rather creepy about the industrial spy Turner's apotheosis into family-values contentment (*Count Zero*); and about Bobby Newmark's translation into a cyberspace never-land. Molly Kolodny's survival (*Mona Lisa Overdrive*) as a hard-boiled operator with self respect, dignity and a sound pension plan is more satisfactory. But altogether, the forecast is not exactly bleak. There are few hopeless casualties in the *Neuromancer* trilogy. For all but the irremediably rich and the frankly demoniac there is some kind of salvation. The Disneyish treatment of the two juvenile leads in *Virtual Light* is only a step further in the same direction. This time the young losers are miraculously undamaged by their hard times, and they retain their innocence throughout the action. This time a happy ending is a foregone conclusion rather than a gift of redemption. But though the sentiment, even sentimentality, is more out-front than before, it's not a new departure.

Cyberpunk is a boy's club. The Movement's claim to be the non-sexist post-gendered wing of modern sf is shakily based: at best it amounts to little more than a lingering feeling that being 'non-sexist' is somehow hip. If William Gibson were to set about challenging the evils or righting the wrongs of global misogyny in his fiction he would rob himself of some of his favourite riffs. But feminist criticism of Gibson seems to confuse deconstruction with character assassination. Thus, it so happens in *Neuromancer* that Molly's young history of degradation includes extremely ugly sexual exploitation and corruption: whereas there's no hanky-panky involved in Case's dreadful past. The contrast tells us something about the position of women and the assumptions of the society and the genre we inhabit. (Or did. Writing Henry Case in 1994, Gibson might dare to do him as an ex-rent boy. Is this progress...?) It can't be used, as seems to have been the fashion in some 'feminist' response, as evidence that William Gibson condones femicidal necrophilia, rape or murder as pleasurable activities.

Now, after a decade has passed, things look different again. Compared with certain avowedly 'feminist' male sf writers of today, William Gibson emerges as an intellectual giant of sexual politics. The street-Samurai and the simstim star are at least positive feminine icons, immensely positive by the standards of the genre. It's therefore a disappointment to meet Chevette Washington, the only woman in this new book with much of a speaking part. She's a nice kid, of course, but essentially a passive prize and victim. For all her fabu muscle tone, Chevette has little to do besides cause the problem—the classic Hollywood construction of the feminine—and provide the acceptable degree of feisty-victim interest at the climax. (It's not possible to threaten the young male lead in a movie like this with sexual molestation. One can only shoot him, which is not very exciting.) But here as in *Neuromancer*, Gibson accurately reflects the nature of his present and the limitations of his chosen raw material. No Hollywood comedy thriller of our time (our exact time), could dare to do more, in the way of a good-willed liberal attitude towards its heroine.

Virtual Light has had—will have—plenty of coverage. By the time you read this, dear *Foundation* reader, you will surely either have read the book, bought the tee-shirt; or at least you probably have a nodding acquaintance with the plot. There are no secrets for me to give away, and there's need for me to discuss everything that can be discussed. The Bay Bridge with its wise hipster patriarch is central to Gibson's vision of a positive future—a brave new community built from unpromising materials by the disregarded poor. I was charmed by the reference to the tawdry energy of Brighton Pier (it must be the Palace Pier, West Pier has been dead meat too long for it to feature in this context). But these are such clean-living squatters, even their sewage disposal is politically correct. It could be said that in the Bridge *Virtual Light* envisages a twenty-first century of global Third World conditions (as James Tiptree Jnr once put it: soon we're all going to be living in Bangladesh), but in this version nobody is to get hurt. Living like refugees is going to work. It's a difficult project, it would take a bigger book than this one to pull it off successfully.

The viewpoint provided by the Japanese tourist has been criticised by some as too transparent a medium for Gibson's own pomo commentary. But Yamakazi's notes on cultural post-history sit easily with a narrative that's already frankly stylised: and at least he rescues the supposed fiction from too many pauses in which post-literate NoCal waifs muse improbably on the global situation. The character who seems to me out of place is the courier from whom the VR glasses are stolen. This sweaty, greenish-skinned muttering creature has a weight and impact alien to the rest of the book: his passages surely belong to a different and much more sinister story. There were two features of the novel that actually bothered me: the Republic of Desire panic button, and the magic bullet cure for AIDS. Having been proffered a future in which large-scale hacker pranks are a known hazard, I can't believe in the kind of instant and slavish panic caused by information-tampering which I must accept in order for the plot of *Virtual Light* to get started. I didn't believe it in *Neuromancer*, when the set-piece hacker disinformation stunt was smothered in uneasy authorial hand-waving. I'm still not convinced. I suppose I'm just too British, or else I've ignored too many car alarms. But this is a quibble. Berry Rydell's explosive response to a net-generated false alarm is worth the price paid in implausibility. Indeed this wild surrender to the movie rush is a fresh and convincing feature of the *Virtual Light* culture. As a source of social mayhem its more interesting and much more fun than the hackers.

The cure for AIDS made me uneasy on another level. For though millions upon millions of people are dying and doomed to die, AIDS is not famous because of them. It is famous because it started killing male yuppie US citizens (of unchaste habits), when that social group—since they'd escaped the last draft—believed themselves to be immortal. If global AIDS is 'beaten' in the next decade by a miracle vaccine, a greater demon will have to be beaten first. There is no question, in *Virtual Light*, of a victory over poverty, on any scale, even as a distant prospect, so the celebratory religion that's grown up around the cure strikes a false note. It's clear that this fictional miracle is simply a form of nostalgia—as Skinner indeed explains—for that brief glorious era of the medically certified fear-and-guilt-free leg-over. Dream on.

William Gibson may not be an apologist for hard radical sf, but as an artist of the future-present he's in the delicate position of a writer of printed fiction who is also a prophet of the death of printed fiction. Ironically a book like *Virtual Light*—which makes the buyer feel that 'science fiction' is actually no different from what happens in the movies and on the tv—may contribute to the survival of one endangered sub-species. But in its content and treatment *Virtual Light* takes a thoroughly corrupt angle on the obsequies. More convincing than if it were presented as an overtly intellectual experiment, *Virtual Light* is a chinoiserie version of a tv movie, an exquisite fake of an unworthy original. If it has a political statement, a new revolution to offer the idealist fans of *Neuromancer*, the message is that the novel is dead. The only possible printed fiction now will imitate the forms that have replaced it.

Read *Virtual Light* without looking for messages and it becomes, as it has been widely described, a formulaic Gibson novel, slight and smooth and beautifully finished: a Wintermute story, all personality and no logic. But there is something more. Whatever Gibson means by *Virtual Light*, the cyberpunk elegy is complete: there is a closure. *Virtual Light* is not an aberration. It has its contribution to the serious proposal that Gibson has elaborated through the last decade. Both the *Neuromancer* trilogy and the later *Difference Engine* ended with something like a birth, the emergence of an all-pervasive intelligent machine. As Chevette speeds, (like a good little program in *Tron*), through the vast organic architecture of the post-twentieth-century city, *Virtual Light* reveals, by a delicate ablation of the tissue of the world, a different take on that image, without the clunky whirr and click of the old teleological evolution drive. The machine that thinks doesn't have to be invented, and it is not trying to invent itself. It is here, all around us. It is, purposeless and self-defining. As Skinner puts it: stuff happens, that's all.

15: Return to the Age of Wonder: John Barnes's *A Million Open Doors*

Was it only yesterday that the future was a real place? Earth was the alien planet, off-world exploration stopped short at a few orbital sex shops and high-rolling shopping malls. We were alone in the universe, contemplating otherness in the mirror. The only galaxies to be explored were in inner space, the only theatres of adventure and wild fantasy left to us were in the faux wonderlands of virtual reality. We were talking about the forseeable, we were attempting to prove the possibility of everything we could imagine. Isn't that the way it was? The wheel turns (or the helix twists) and here we are again on the bridge of the Starship Enterprise. Habitable planets are scattered like daisies for the plucking, aliens come in any shape or form (so long as you can do it with face-makeup); and the most important scientific decision an sf writer has to make is whether to type the letters on the warp-drive button 'ftl' or FTL.

It is difficult not to exaggerate when making sweeping statements. I would hesitate to claim that 'nobody is doing realist extrapolation anymore'. One of the major sf events of the last year, Stan Robinson's *Red Mars* (though purest fantasy when measured up against the shrinking budget for Freedom, or any other boring, economic measures) seems to be bucking my trend. On the other hand, unreal sf has certainly made a comeback. Space-opera is no longer a joke. Or if it is, it's a very good one. Colin Greenland's splendid *Take Back Plenty* has replaced the canals on Mars and the swamps of Venus. Colourful adventure on alien planets (with or without actual furry or tentacled aliens) is once more in fashion. Romantic classics like Roger Zelazny's *Lord of Light*, long relegated to the fringes of fantasy, may have to be reassessed. In the Nineties it is again possible, almost necessary, to write important sf about the kind of future that doesn't have a clue how we got there from here.

John Barnes's *A Million Open Doors* is set in much the same retrofitted golden-age as Sheri Tepper's planet-hopping series (*Grass, The Gate into Women's Country; Raising the Stones; Sideshow*). The galactic diaspora happened long ago. Worlds have been settled and terraformed, each more or less in isolation, through an age of sub-light-speed inter-system travel. Now comes a time of technology-driven upheaval. Instantaneous matter-transmitters (any size you like) have recently come on the market; and market is the operative word. The Council of Humanity is supervising the spread of 'springer' technology, and nursing each of the thousand cultures of the settled planets through the economic crisis of reintegration.

In Nou Occitan, on the planet Wilson, the original colonists were fans of the troubadours of the mediaeval Languedoc. Several hundred years later, and some years after the springer revolution, Giraut Leones and his friends are still acting out the romance for which the expression romance was coined. As 'jovents', until they're twenty-five, their life is a blissful round of lute-playing, versifying, power-dressing, drinking and brawling (with neuroducer swords that make you think you've been stabbed), in a slightly repellent, heavily sanitised 'mediaeval' environment.

Occitan—Giraut informs us—is the finest flower of the human diaspora: a culture of youth, dedicated to Art, Love and Beauty. In the opening passages, where we are introduced to his milieu in a vivid scene of self-regarding male gossip and routine violence, there are strong hints that John Barnes doesn't agree with this any more than the reader may. But before Mediaeval-World starts to stink too much, circumstances intervene. One of the drinking cronies is a voluntary exile from the dour, bleak Christian Capitalist community of Caledon, on the planet Nansen: a culture viewed with horror by Occitan. Aimeric de Sanho Marsao, an ageing jovent with an incipient baldspot, used to be Ambrose Carruthers, Caledonian economist. He has been identified as the only man qualified to guide the Caledonians through their reintegration. Giraut, Aimeric, Aimeric's girlfriend Bieris; and all their worldly goods, are quickly 'sprung' from Wilson to a more serious kind of planet.

What follows is the familiar genre tale of a young man coming-of-age in interesting times. Giraut persuades the Caledonian authorities to let him open a school of Occitanian culture. He meets a band of young dissidents, who dare to believe in Art and Beauty in defiance of the utilitarian regime; he begins to suspect (we are ahead of him), that his exquisite life in Nou Occitan was actually trivial and rather nasty. The bratpack dissidents put on a show, which precipitates an anti-springer coup run by the grown-up baddie. There are riots, heroism, even one or two actual casualties. The little band of art students holds firm through public turmoil, in the redoubt of the Occitan Centre.

A Million Open Doors is a humanist novel in the frequently pejorative use of the term in 1980s sf circles—meaning that John Barnes is not interested in extrapolating gadgets. We have the 'neuroducer' swords, medical cover that practically amounts to immortality for everyone, instant buildings, vast terraforming; and of course the springer innovation. But there's a distinctly mid-twentieth-century feel to anything that doesn't work more or less like magic: to the telecoms, to the interaction with 'aintellect' (that means computers). Admittedly Nansen has slightly chunky gravity, yet it's a surprise, from here in the age of miniaturisation, to learn that such a far future has roving reportage equipment that can fall on people and kill them. Yet if Barnes doesn't worship gadgets, that doesn't mean he hasn't thought about his décor. In fact the tech—with its instant everything, and hordes of Frederick Pohl-type mannequin robots for the drudgery—has a golden, retro-sf flavour that merges perfectly with the scenario and the message.

Humanism, however, is not allowed to get in the way of a good story. Under the veneer of social and political concern there's yet another dumb male adolescent daydream. Giraut barely has time to register misgivings about his past before his social and political superpowers begin to sprout. In a matter of days the callow wastrel is an awesomely competent arts centre manager, a teacher, an administrator; and also an incredibly sensitive, caring, modest human being... and so is everybody else in the gang. Though there's a limit to how much an adult reader can take of clean young people feeling good about themselves, this is all pleasant enough, except for the sexual politics. In Occitan they didn't embrace the troubador ideal in every impractical detail. There were no proud Queens of Beauty bestowing their favours only as the reward of talent or virtue: the jovents expected and demanded routinely available sex. Still, Giraut fondly imagined that he was a worshipper at the shrine, and supposed that the girls got something out of it. In Caledon, free at last, Bieris enlightens him and he resolves to reform. This reform is handled dreadfully. Here's Giraut's first real look at young woman of utilitarian, non-sexist Caledon; who later has a crush on him:

> I think Margaret would have been plain no matter where she was; no full set of Occitan skirts could have concealed her oversized rump, no possible top reshaped her too-wide shoulders and small, flaccid breasts, no arrangement of hair could have softened the harsh planes of her face or concealed her lumpy complexion...

And so on, and passim (he really can't get over the ugliness of Caledon's women) until this same Margaret has the luck to take lessons in boy-pleasing from a Nou Occitan 'donzelha' more cynical than Bieris: 'I woke up suddenly in the dark, to find something distinctly wonderful going on; I was a bit disoriented, but I reached down my body to find a close-cropped head and take Margaret's hands...'

Giraut is instantly in love! This inspired compromise between liberal values (she's ugly) and the essential gratification (you simply can't have a young sf hero who doesn't get laid!) doesn't trouble itself about Margaret's feelings. Neither John Barnes nor Giraut can decide whether or not she's had any sexual experience before this brave stab at fellatio, on a bloke who has made it clear he finds her repulsive. Subsequently, she's simply a happy wife and mother to the boy hero, and I suppose one has to be glad he doesn't chuck her over for some cuter specimen. But this is one of the incidents, and not the only one, where a somewhat shallow concern for social issues comes nastily unstuck.

The feel-good factor is more important than serious thought in the culture as well as in the character-building, for it transpires that Rational Capitalist Caldeon is about as much like a repressive régime as Nou Occitan is like mediaeval Europe. Giraut's startling success in getting the Caledon 'aintellects', the silicon civil service, to approve his Occitan Centre, may be put down to the machinations of the baddie, who wishes to use Giraut as an agent provocateur (and who has found a way to hack these unhackable accumulators of precedent). But Aimeric's hated father, the Chairman of the Board of Rationalisation, from whom he fled into exile, turns out to be a most benign patriarch. Other Caledon officials, except for the one bad apple, are equally good-willed. The young rebels have a faith in their state's institutions (which does not turn out to be misplaced) which would be bizarre indeed in the dissidents of a real repressive régime. One almost gets the idea that John Barnes wants to make sure he says there isn't much wrong with Muscular Capitalism (or whatever it's called. I really cannot fathom where the Christianity comes in. *Sell all you have and give it to the poor* would get a pretty blank response, as an idea, from the most desperately disaffected value-adder in this novel.)

Characterisation is often fairly arbitrary: people tend to respond and react as the plot demands. The relationship between Giraut and Aimeric is an exception. Though we see the older man only through Giraut's eyes, the unfolding chronicle is free from inconsistency or crass errors of judgement; and one of the book's redeeming features. As the aging swinger accepts that he can't walk away from the culture that made him, and shoulders the burden of duty—without which he was so lost in feckless Occitan—he gains a gravitas that belongs to no other character. When the young heroes in the Occitan centre still seem to be enjoying a long, engrossing sleepover party, Aimeric is the one who almost makes the whole affair seem grown-up, serious, deadly.

Before I read *A Million Open Doors* I was looking forward to Nou Occitan. I know a little, not a lot, about the original Occitan. I thought it would be good to meet a passionate re-enactment of the original romantics, and I didn't think the creation of the Troubadours' age sounded too far fetched. After all, ethnic groups do behave like this. Look at the Amish (cited by Barnes himself). Look at the staggering feat of cultural preservation between the original great diaspora of the Jews and the return to Israel. I was disappointed to discover that Giraut Leones and his cronies knew as well as I did that they were faking. On practially every page of the first chapters Giraut reminds himself, and us, of the truth: this is totally artificial, we're acting like this because we know we're supposed to, we're wearing fancydress... This does make sense, if *One Million Open Doors* is about the end of the elaborate game of the 'thousand cultures'. But the fictional price is high. It is already difficult to make an economic crisis convincing, when the story is set in an apotheosis of the American Dream. But when we also have strong intimations that *nothing* we see is real, it is dangerous for a novelist to keep reminding us about the safety nets, the circuit breakers, the padding hidden in the theme park scenery. He might ruin the illusion completely.

The culture of Caledon is far more solid than that of Nou Occitan, and seems to have John Barnes's honest approval. Yet it is still make believe. The Caledonians play at the protestant work ethic the way Nou Occitan plays at swordfights, and their attempts at puritan hardship are really pretty pathetic. Nothing can dent the unlimited peace and plenty of the 'settled worlds'. The Council of Humanity AIs have a complete model of their cosmos. There's no guesswork, nothing can go wrong. Even if you die in a neuroducer sword-fight, from heart-failure at too much nervous excitement, your 'psypyx' record will keep you on hold until a new body can be grown. Even if you have transplant problems and that doesn't work out, 'you' merely go into storage until the technological fix arrives... Even at the end of the Caledon story, when everything has been as disastrous as possible, and a few people are actually really dead, it's just a glitch. *Everything's going to be all right.*

The last chapters of *One Million Open Doors* pass in a rush of adrenalin and needless (temporary, of course) tragedy, as most of the rebels decide to go on a camping trip in the middle of the revolution, and suddenly discover some possibly alien archaeological remains. The effect of this long interlude is so unbalancing that it's as if the book is either genuinely unfinished, or demands serious cut and pasting to get things back in order. Or both. But finally, Giraut returns to Nou Occitan (still frankly struggling with his Margaret's awful shortcomings). We meet parent-world Occitan, the suburban family behind the mediaeval scenes: there's a wedding and a promise of more adventures. There is an attempt to rehabilitate the life of Art and Beauty, which collapses, for me, in the thoroughly nasty scene when Giraut thrashes one of his former friends for some extremely Giraut-like vanity, bullying, bad sex and posing around. The self-knowledge part of the growing up, it seems, is far from complete. We'll have to see whether a trip to Compassion-land (or something) works any wonders in the next instalment.

Nou Occitan could be called one of sf's more successful attempts to depict a society devoted to Art, since a successful description of an artists' colony is a story about a bunch of egotistical wankers sitting around stabbing one another in the back. But the conflict between the licentious culture devoted to art, and the repressive one devoted to money, never really gets off the ground, not because the Occitanians are more phoney than any other of the thousand cultures, but because the whole settled world cosmos is devoted to the creation of wealth. The artists are as keen on added value as the utilitarians. As Bieris explains it to the dubious Margaret: Giraut's jovent reputation as a brawler and a versifier has vital importance, because this is the coin in which Nou Occitan fortunes are made. He's making business contacts and establishing dominance ranking. Likewise the dissidents of Caledon are clear that they're taking an idealist stance strictly because their government's being unreasonable. They are eager to get the politics sorted out and settle down to make money out of their avocation, like normal folks. And of course, the Council of Humanity are the most devoted capitalists of all. The sacred market place is rather less worshipped in Christian Capitalist Caledon than by the Council itself: for there's no possibility, no chance, no way, that They will let anything interfere with free market trading. Indeed the *real* conflict, nasty as you like, would arise if any of the 'thousand cultures' tried to say no to the revolution, and refused to let McDonalds move (back) in.

Art happens in *A Million Open Doors*. But, posing apart, art isn't a political creed, and John Barnes doesn't succeed in convincing us otherwise. Perhaps making money is a political creed—it's a point of view. But if so, no one in this novel sees anything wrong with it, and indeed any serious opposition to capitalism would put rather a strain on the fabric of feel-good golden-age sf! As a political essay then, *A Million Open Doors* is shadow boxing. There is no conflict, the big fight is a fake. It's still an entertaining yarn. There are unpleasant lapses, yet the adolescent male hero is often engaging and the bratpack has its moments of genuine emotion and excitement. I don't reproach the book for bearing no resemblance to any forseeable future, or for ignoring the gadgets. Maybe the real future is pretty painful to contemplate, and candid escapism is an honest and cheering response. Or perhaps, quite legitimately, the intensely detailed technology that engaged sf recently no longer looks like the important area of change. Human affairs and social issues are once more in ferment; and *reintegration* is arguably our future's great problem (seen from now), so that's what sf will write about. Over here, it's hard to miss the horrific struggle for the re-integration of greater Europe. Over there in the US the age of the peace dividend makes it harder to ignore the problem of the melting pot that refused to melt. I wish *A Million Open Doors* had something substantial to say about these problems: something more honest and more grown-up. But escapism and feel-good flattery of the dominant ideology, dressed up as social comment, is a depressing spectacle. If this is satire, it's definitely the white-sliced kind. And I don't think the mind police of Rational Capitalism are going to be worried.

16: *Winterlong*: Elizabeth Hand at the End of the World

The ocean wrinkled, darkened to indigo as the image shifted. I saw a long line of blackened crags emerging from the water like knots of charred bone, some of them smoking as though racked by volcanic activity. Another string of letters and numerals appeared—

> LAT 02 10' 5-LONG 114 44E, CONFIG 9743
> PRIOR STATUS: JAWA

> 'Where is this?' I asked with dread.
> 'Jawa' the scholiast murmured.
> I shook my head in disbelief. 'But it's gone. There's nothing there'...

I was eleven. I was spending my customary winter weeks in bed. (My health improved, but I was twenty-five before I felt normal without a partial hibernation.) I had read the first volume of a wonderful adventure. My mother came into the room with new library books—that magical yet somehow threatening apparition—after the long hours alone (for years my favourite story of all time was Ray Bradbury's 'The Emissary'). I saw the dingy olive grey spine of a tall, quarto volume. I can still feel the crushing disappointment: she's brought the same book back again. My God, no. She hadn't. It was Volume Two, *The Two Towers*. Take me away. Carry me away. Leave the meat behind.

In my devouring need for more of the stuff that made me high, I didn't notice I was rushing towards destruction. Other dramas close *in media res*, with a wedding or a funeral. The modern novel may drift off in inconclusion. Once the vital tension is broken a Fantasy series can amble away into soap-opera, as happens in countless Tolkien imitations. A trilogy is a world. This is true of any fiction, not only the overtly fantastic. At the end of the third volume, the world ends. It must.

> 'The Ascendant Autocracy at Vancouver mistakenly believed the tsunami that destroyed their holdings at Araboth was the result of an Emirate attack. On twenty June O.S.C they sent twenty thousand troops to attack the Emirate's city of Tarabulus. Emirate troops retaliated with protonic weapons of intervention directed at Jawa.' The image flickered and changed to a close up, empty

turquoise waters flecked with gold and white beneath the remorseless sun. The glowing letters shifted until they spelled out another message.

LAT 04 11'5—LONG 107 30' CONFIG 9899 PRIOR STATUS: DJAKARTA, JAWA.

It had been the Ascendant's primary base in the Malayu Archipelago, one of the only remaining technopolies in the world.
'It's gone,' I whispered. 'How can it be gone?'

A world ends, a world begins. Despite the token foregrounding of a few hobbits, *The Lord of the Rings* has the point of view of the Men, the coming race. These other charming folk, the elder peoples—hobbits and elves, wizards and ents, dwarfs and goblins—are heading over the hill to dreamland. They're dead meat.When their turn comes will the Men go as quietly? We don't think it looks likely. We imagine a raging close. But we won't be telling that story. Not in real life. Who will?

Winterlong: 'You Must Be Their Mother.'

Imagine a room in a ruined palace, deserted gardens outside, (already one knows about the world beyond: don't ask). You are sick, but not exactly suffering. Mind-wrenching medication (kept in a tiny fridge by your bed) is like sweeties, the long names as familiar and cosy as the names of chocolate bars. Sweeties of all kinds are like medication. You take the tousled luxury of your sick room, your dainty food; a bandeau made from the feathers of a humming-bird, as a matter of course. You know dimly that you are owed these things: because if you could leave this world; if there was still a world outside, what is happening to you would be called pain and terror and corruption.

Winterlong comes in bite sized chunks, beginning with the concentrated excellence of a contained novella, a first person narrative by Wendy Wanders: experimental subject at the Human Engineering Laboratory, HEL; chiefly under the care of Dr Emma Harrow. Wendy is autistic. HEL's medication has blasted a way through the neural blocks and gifted her with language; and somehow turned her into a psychic vampire. A taste of blood, a drop of saliva, gives her access to the emotion flooding in chemical configuration through those vital fluids. Wendy has no access to emotions of her own. She likes these distanced hits the stronger the better, savours the rush of lust; of suicide; of hatred.

Wendy can also kill. She is being used in a supposed therapy programme. Getting wired up to her strange mind/brain can sometimes break another

mind free from despair or nightmare. But some patients wake from the
networking trance and commit suicide. Wendy is not aware that she and
her companions in HEL might be valued for this ability. She perceives the
deaths as crimes for which she can't be punished, part of the indulgence
owed to her: 'I can't be responsible, I'm not responsible.' Through her
uncomprehending reports of conversations with Dr Harrow, a fragmented
picture emerges of a destroyed and crazy world. It transpires that one of
the two remaining military powers is moving in to scavenge HEL's weird
detritus. Dr Emma Harrow kills herself, having imprinted on Wendy a
vision of her brother Aidan's suicide: and the compelling image of a green-
eyed boy, spirit or demon, who tempted Aidan into death.

To describe *Winterlong* in synopsis is unsatisfactory, because it is
important that hard information—'Wendy is rescued from the military
takeover, by the aide Justice, who is in love with her'—emerges after the
fact. Wendy can't tell us. Wendy is white-out overwhelmed by the sight
of a bridge over a river.

> Too much, I wanted to scream, and instinctively crouched and turned
> to strike my forehead against a piling. Even there the world loomed,
> a stream of tiny scarlet mites threading through the flaking green
> paint...

Note: the world is too much. Headbanging is not. To Wendy that terrifying
behaviour is a sensible way to get hold of an endorphin rush, when
someone has forgotten your medication. The patient and her minder enter
the City of Trees, which was Washington DC. It is inhabited by a tribe of
museum curators dedicated to guarding the ancient stores of knowledge,
and a tribe of whores, dedicated to a child's dumb ideas of 'vice' and
'decadent beauty', who provide the curators with sex (curators don't fuck
each other, because they are ugly: a necessary concomitant of power and
knowledge). Outdoors prowl the lazars: tribe members who have been
caught in the viral air-raids, are judged infectious and left to wander,
rotting, until they die. They are mostly children. The virus strikes are a
random crossfire effect. There's a war going on between the Ascendancy
and the Balkhash Commonwealth. But the City is not, or has not been, an
important target. (The Botanists trade in opium. There is no shortage of
morpha tubes, candicaine pipettes. There is no shortage of wine, brandy,
lace, silks, braised pigeons, apples, oatmeal. Somewhere there must be land
unpoisoned or maybe hydroponic farms under growlamps. There must be
warehouses of fancy-dress booty. No one in *Winterlong* cares. It's not that
kind of world.)

Wendy's twin, Raphael Miramar, is among the whores. He tries to barter
his looks for power: he fails, kills and rapes (as it were, for the events

happen in that order) a curator girl; takes flight. In a poisoned forest he meets the green-eyed boy from Wendy's induced memory: who means Death. Wendy, disguised (for no clear reason) as a boy, joins a theatre troupe whose diva is a ladylike, passionate, dedicated thespian of a talking chimpanzee, Miss Scarlet Pan—another tortured experimental subject; and a wonderful creation. Fragments drift into view through the heady nightclub murk. An Ascendant space station has exploded, presumably the Balkhash are responsible. An Ascendant military leader, the Aviator Margalis Tast'annin, has been captured and then released by the genetically-engineered aardmen. He has taken roost in a ruin called the Engulfed Cathedral, for a reign of terror rumoured to be connected with a store of ancient weapons…

Raphael becomes evil and Wendy becomes good, by shifts as arbitrary as Wendy's shift into male disguise. They meet, acting out a transcendent destiny. The evil twin dies, which should be good news. But it all happens in the dark. The green-eyed boy who tells Wendy *You must be their mother* seems to be talking nonsense. The lost children of the City are dead and rotten; or if there are any survivors, Wendy shows no interest in their welfare. She has learned to feel and lost her psychic vampire powers. But she's not responsible. She walks away smiling, headed nowhere.

Aestival Tide: The Green Country

> My concern in *Winterlong* is the relationship between consciousness and reality, and in particular the way in which an artistic medium may be used to explore the interstices between the objective, waking world and those other, more richly textured and deeply shadowed realms that most of us visit only fleetingly…

The author's afterword describes *Winterlong* truthfully: a rich, murky, confused dream, overlaid with a haphazard interference pattern of ordered fiction. The sequel, which bears no resemblance to the sequel outlined in that afterword, is a more conventional article. None of the characters of *Winterlong* reappears except the Aviator in different guise. There's a giant ziggurat of a city on a seashore (the coast of Texas apparently). It belongs to the Ascendants. The Aviators, (pilots of splendid semi-sentient aircraft), are the only link with the HORUS stations from which the Ascendancy on earth is ruled. The city is dying. Its population is reduced to the vice-raddled ruling family and hangers on; their engineered playmates; a few thousand foreign guest-workers (i.e. slaves); ditto an army of regenerated corpses for the rough cleaning. Ominous hints from the Architect Imperator, a chap with the provoking name Sajur Panggang, which means grilled vegetables, inform readers at once that the city is about to collapse. The characters take 350 pages of flouncing about being decadent to reach the same conclusion. Little else happens.

Aestival Tide resembles a big-budget silent movie, perhaps *The Last Days of Pompeii*. It has some of the verve and panache: the hordes of girl-extras in gossamer harem-pants, the sumptuously camp sets. But, like a dull disaster movie, the chief entertainment to be had is in laying bets on which of the speaking parts is down for survival, and in what order the others will succumb to: court murder, insanity, the poisonous rose-scented maw of an artificial monster; petrol attack by revolting radicals; falling masonry; the frenzied throat of the storm called Ucalegon. It isn't hard. The Aviator Imperator Margalis Tast'annin was shot in the head in *Winterlong*, and is now a regenerated-dead human persona built into a metal body. He's clearly through to Book Three. The decadent ruling sisters are not going to make it. The hermaphrodite dream-reader Reive, (who passes for one of the city's living toys but is really the legitimate heir of the ruling family) causes panic by scrying the dream of the Green Country, which means destruction. She'll live. Likewise the boy Hobi; and a sympathetic designer of nasty living puppets, the dwarf Rudyard Planck.

And so it transpires. But it doesn't matter. All of them: the kindly court favourite, the boy-wonder, the Hidden Heir, all except Tast'annin will disappear, into whatever temporary refuges they can find, to await the end of the world. The portent of the Green Country doesn't matter either. It warned of the revolt of the elements, the triumph of Mother Nature over her tormentors. But the storm that kills the city of Araboth is hardly a natural disaster (nothing's natural now): and the green earth will not triumph.

Two events in *Aestival Tide* have a bearing on the trilogy. In the fetid undercroft of the ziggurat, where one treads on real, stinking earth, the Architect Imperator's son Hobi is shown a treasure: NFRTI—a store of human cultural memory in the shape of a woman of glass and metal. He wakens her with a kiss. In a huge tank in the menagerie the Zeuglodon— a monster from earth's past, recreated with the cruel addition of sentience and language—predicts a future in which *his* kind will triumph.

Icarus Descending

Despite her brave words, her girlish voice betrayed her...

Memory has been woken, but to what purpose? The glass woman NFRTI, (an acronym devised to be pronounced Nefertity) is a construct called a Nemosyne, a walking library. Her memory has been filled by a saintly woman named Loretta Riding, in the last days of the civilisation that was recognisably ours. Nefertity is a politically correct repository of the feminine and disregarded kind of human history: folktales, nursery songs, the life stories of women. And much good will it do her, or anyone. In the wicked dying world into which she has woken NFRTI could stand as a symbol of the good: but she has no power. Her value is that she was one of a series. Through her, Tast'annin or others may be able to reach the military Nemosyne: the legendary construct that Tast'annin hoped to find under the City of Trees. It remembers where untold riches of ancient weapons are stock-piled: and it can arm and fire them.

But *Icarus Descending* opens with another story, another first person. I is the voice of Kalamat, an *energumen*. The aristocracy of the geneslaves, energumen are human in form, eight feet tall, (that's about two and a half metres, in Europe) strong in proportion and more than humanly intelligent—or so we're told. Divinely tall and most divinely fair, they come feminine and masculine. As a precaution against revolt each lives only a thousand days. Kalamat and her clone sisters and brothers are servants of the Ascendancy. But all the humans belonging to her station are dead, victims of a plague called *irpex irradians*, which was deliberately introduced by a human sympathiser with the geneslave revolt. The Balkhash Commonwealth, old enemy of the Ascendants, is still a military power on earth, but the slave revolt is rushing from strength to strength. Conflicting messages arrive at the space station. There's a mysterious warning about someone called Icarus, and a summons to earth. An ancient Nemosyne construct named Metatron calls on the energumen to join the rebel slaves, promising that on earth they will be united with their ultimate creator, the genius scientist Luther Burdock.

Kalamat is different from her clone sisters. By some freak she remembers, with the consciousness of the fifteen-year-old girl on whom all the energumens—masculine and feminine—are patterned, her original life. To her Luther Burdock, creator of the first generation of geneslaves, is not a distant mythic divinity but the human father she loves. She distrusts Metatron. Her masculine alter ego, Kalaman, is a pitiless fiend who enjoys the ritual consumption of the living brains of his brothers. He's already been at work destroying humans by the millions so he's happy to be recruited. Kalamat is the one who spots that once they reach earth, the energumen will become cannon-fodder in Metatron's own private war effort. She tries to resist. But she has no power. It appears it makes no difference being superbright, super strong and eight feet high. If you have the soul of a human girl, you're helpless.

Back on earth Margalis Tast'annin, accompanied by the primly protesting, powerless NFRTI, has left the other survivors from Araboth by the road somewhere. He spends a little time writing mental memoirs and thereby filling in the neglected plot, before setting off to hunt for the military Nemosyne, Metatron.

Wendy Wanders, Miss Scarlet Pan and sturdy Jane Alopex—the zoologist curator who was once Scarlet's keeper, and who shot the Aviator—have not been mentioned since *Winterlong*. Wendy's narrative now resumes. They are still walking away from the City of Trees, months behind the rest of the cast. They find refuge in The House of Seven Chimneys, a Nathaniel Hawthorne inn named to invoke previous slave-revolts. Here an aardman—a dog-man, the crudest form of humanoid geneslave—is living as a human with the humans, like a fugitive nigger of long ago. More chunks of plot are filled in: phantasmagoria is shredding up, replaced by more conventional fiction. Wendy and Scarlet do not profit from the change (sturdy Jane was and remains a minor character). Wendy observes Miss Scarlet with the freed aardman, and suddenly sees her as a mere animal in clothes. Raised political consciousness has somehow made the engineered ape less like a person. Wendy meanwhile reverts to a woman's clothes and frets because the cut of her skirt is unflattering. She doesn't have much else to think about. Wendy as a blurred figure of hope and purpose has vanished. She will pass through this last volume as a piece of baggage. The active voice in *Icarus Descending* belongs to the Aviator Imperator Margalis Tast'annin, who at least used to be a Man.

The orgies of *Winterlong* and *Aestival Tide* were oddly chaste confections. The lost children of a botched civilisation tottered in grown-up finery, playing at vice: trying and failing to understand what used to be special about torture and murder. Sex, in the sense of passion or lust, is almost absent in this trilogy. But Elizabeth Hand is a writer who embraces gender difference—whether or not she notices where this embrace is leading her. To be feminine is to be subservient: there's no possiblity of escape. That's the meaning of those frocks and curls. It's a pity for this world that *to be feminine* is also the chief attribute of virtue. Effeminate Raphael became evil when he ceased to be a sex-object. The sisters who ruled the city of *Aestival Tide* were frivolous monsters, unable to handle their power. Despite favouring the female side in naming her 'gynanders', when the writer wants to suggest that a mere hermaphrodite may be a person to reckon with: Reive becomes male.

> For the first time Ceryl noticed how strong (Reive's) jaw was; how her mouth without its carmine pout was in fact thin... Except for the lack of eyebrows and her rounded shoulders, she looked like a young man or a thoughtful boy.

The mad child Wendy Wanders, named by green-eyed Death as mother-to-the-world, has become, in *Icarus Descending*, a woman and a cypher. She has nothing more to do.

Bring on the End of the Universe

The masculine energumen have manipulated human communications to bring about a last spasm of violence. The Ascendancy and the Balkhash Commonwealth have wiped each other out. Scarlet Pan has vanished. Wendy and Jane and Tast'annin and NFRTI are separately brought to the Command Headquarters of the Revolt: which is being masterminded by the satanic Metatron—*eminence noir* behind a succession of brief-lived vat-grown simulacra of the long dead Luther Burdock. Icarus turns out to be a serious-sized asteroid on collision course with earth, a looming catastrophe which was noticed hundreds of years ago and then ignored. The ex-slaves will not inherit the earth. They will escape destruction in a starship ark. Last minute attempts to wrest control of this venture from Metatron fail. In a final hugger-mugger sequence whoever's still breathing of the trilogy's human cast gets bundled aboard. Kalamat dies, reunited with her beloved Daddy. The ship takes flight, flying mother nature's silver seed to a new home… And that's it. But what an ominous seeding.

The Boy in the Tree

> But you know, Margalis, it's no crazier than what they teach us here. Focusing on some inner landscape so we don't see our hands burning to bone in front of us. Focusing on the sound of the Gryphon's engines, so we don't hear the pilot screaming in the other seat… Swearing off the most basic human emotions. Cutting open nursling aardmen to see if they will scream under the knife.

One can construe a planned narrative thread for the *Winterlong* trilogy, rejecting suspicions that characters fall by the wayside by accident rather than design; and that this may be not so much a coherent single work as a three-book contract taking whatever shape came easiest. But why go through such contortions, when the separate images are so much more than any possible whole? Thus in *Icarus Descending* the story of Aidan Harrow is at last completely told. The suicide of Dr Emma Harrow's brother, a sinister supernatural mystery in *Winterlong*, is revealed as a principled act of dissidence. Aidan, as an Aviator cadet and Tast'annin's classmate, read samizdat texts (printed books: they don't have post-literacy media, it's not that sort of world). He saw the slave revolt foretold, and the descent of Icarus. He killed himself as the only rational response to his training, and to the state of things. Does it matter whether or not this Aidan was in place from the start, in the writer's grand design? Not particularly, not to me.

But the green-eyed, beautiful Boy in the Tree who invited Aidan to suicide is still Death in person... real as far as any other person is real, here at the end of all human perception. The emergence of this neuronal ghost, as a shareware infection in the swampy dissolution of human consciousness, is one of the best things in the trilogy. The other best is Wendy's psychic vampirism. Shame she had to lose it so soon: she was never the same.

Let us consider the Boy in the Tree. What has to happen, for *Winterlong* to come true? There is a woman in HEL who remembers the first Ascension: Wendy devours her nightmares, and she kills herself. But with no special longevity, she remembers a world quite like our world; and there are so many other survivals of our culture, it's obvious that this final disintegration is not supposed to be far away from our own time. At the beginning of the end, apparently, a space-capable élite escaped into orbital habitats. Later another 'élite' got out there and replaced them: and what passed for civilisation on earth took refuge in vast ziggurat cities. As *Winterlong* opened, maybe two hundred years from now (in some sense) the final stage had begun. Wars, plagues and Man-made environmental disasters had devastated the earth, the ozone layer was gone. Etc., etc.

Leave out the space stations and the geneslaves, in case we are already too poor. Leave out the asteroid: it isn't necessary. No invention is necessary. By the year 2000, the global population will have risen to about 6.2 billions, at a conservative estimate. By the end of this decade, 60% of the urban population of Asia, including the Pacific Coalition from whence Elizabeth Hand's last world-destroying Empire hails, will be living in squatter camps without access to sewage treatment or clean water. That's already inevitable: and things will get much worse unless something changes. It won't be exactly population pressure that will take us to *Winterlong*, as far as sheer numbers go. But the pressure of so many lives of the kind we live now will provide the wars, the 'viral strikes', the degraded farmland, everything. It needs nothing else. Nothing complicated, nothing weird.

As a feminist who is tired of hearing that the Women Question is trivial, solved, and anyway no way could it possibly be as central as I make out, it gives me bitter pleasure to tell you that the way to halt this cascade of destruction is nothing else but a global improvement in the status of young women. In every situation, throughout the so-called Developing World, where women gain status, self esteem, and control in their lives the birthrate falls, the environment improves. The fewer children live better lives, and the society that rears them cares more about its future. The status of women in human society could well be the difference between life and death. Yes. Think about it, boys and girls. Otherwise, it's your grandchildren, *you will meet them*, who will have to start squeezing through that very nasty bottleneck which now stands dead ahead, which is the gate to the end of our world.

17: *Plague of Angels*: The Fiction of Sheri Tepper

Sheri Tepper is a prolific and energetic writer who has established a capacious niche for herself over the last decade in the area between science fiction and fantasy. The first of her three recent novels, *Sideshow,* is set in a distant future, after the Dispersion of the human race (or perhaps I should say Man, since this—for her own thematic reasons—is the term Tepper prefers) over a large and scattered array of habitable planets. The Dispersion (as has been established in previous Tepper novels) is technologically advanced and *ftl* capable, though cultures within it maybe more or less wilfully 'primitive'. But it was at least partly effected by means of the Arbai Doors, whereby individuals, groups and whole populations have travelled from planet to planet, through time and space. The Arbai, (like the Heechee in Frederick Pohl's *Gateway* sequence; and one could give other examples) are beings who have retired—apparently—from the cosmic scene, leaving behind artefacts of fabulous power. Humans encounter these artefacts and are profoundly changed by them. But Arbai technology doesn't just *seem to be* supernatural. It genuinely *is* the Supernatural, as far as humanity is concerned. The other significant Arbai relic, besides the Doors, is a phenomenon (featured in the previous *Raising the Stones* and also in *Sideshow*) as 'the Arbai device' and also as 'the Hobbs Land Gods'—a kind of paranormal fungus that can infest whole planets and has the effect of bringing the inhabitants' mythologies to life: gods or demons, with all their imagined powers made concrete and effectual.

Sideshow, opens with the birth of miraculous Siamese twins, on earth in the USA in the 1990s. Gender, in the sense of social differences between the sexes, is immediately a major issue. The twins, who rationally must be identical and therefore of the same sex, have their indeterminate sexual organs rebuilt as boy and girl. Society, represented by their parents and the Catholic Church, insists that this be so. Contention is established—between the mother and the father; between a patriarchal establishment and the women who endure its stupidities with helpless, resigned contempt.

Meanwhile, in the city of Tolerance on the post-Dispersion planet Elsewhere, some members of the governing council are becoming alarmed at a planet-wide trend towards extreme nastiness. On Elsewhere the political set up is something like the situation in the thousand settled worlds of John Barnes's *A Million Open Doors*. There is a global government, but different states are allowed to make up their own laws, however brutal or bizarre, and do what they like to their own citizens, so long as they don't disturb their neighbours. Non-interference is the most sacred precept of the planetary culture. But Zasper Ertigon, one of the Enforcers whose job is to protect and maintain Elsewhere's colourful diversity, fears that the scourge of the Hobbs Land Gods, may have reached Elsewhere, with peculiarly unpleasant consequences. And here, as on earth, there is a child—not so strange as the twins but clearly singled out. She is being groomed, it becomes obvious, both by Ertigon and by a more mysterious sponsor, for some remarkable destiny.

When they grow up, the miraculous earthly twins Nela and Bertran find work in a freak show. They are spirited away from this unhappy situation by the Arbai themselves, who are obviously in on the cosmic plot, by means of an Arbai Door, and arrive in the city of Tolerance. Fringe Owldark, Elsewhere's child of destiny, has by this time become a Council Enforcer. She is despatched, with the twins and others, to discover the source of the plague of nastiness—the team disguised as a troupe of travelling entertainers, the 'Sideshow' of the title. Elsewhere's hands-off liberalism is indicted as the adventures that follow uncover more and yet more gaudy and inventive horrors. Still looking for the Hobbs Land Gods, the plot of *Sideshow* homes in on a province whose cultural practices include Female Genital Mutilation and other features of the most distressing forms of misogny known on earth in our present day. Meanwhile only Boarmus, the chief of the Council, knows that the founding elders of Elsewhere are still in some sense alive, and presiding over their great project, the careful preservation of 'human diversity'—or, as some might say, the preservation of every different variety of oppression and cruelty ever invented by Man. The Hobbs Land Gods have fertile material to work with. But even the Arbai themselves are unable to face the awesome forces that Fringe must encounter, in a final, extended confrontation that marks the end of the reign of Man.

A summary of the plot of *Sideshow* gives an air of urgency that's deceptive. Sheri Tepper is an expansive writer. Years go by, filled with episode on episode of free-flowing invention, before the emergency announced in chapter two is addressed—the flow interrupted by an occasional time-out passage where heads are counted and the reader is reminded that there's a crisis going on. It is characteristic of a Tepper novel that one is never sure whether the plot wasn't invented afterwards, and inserted into the ebullient narrative at judicious intervals on Search-and-Replace. This suspicion in no way detracts from the reader's pleasure, but it does cast doubts on the writer's seriousness of purpose. Grave questions are raised in *Sideshow*. Is US Liberalism, the creed of the right-on self-righteous, a mask for cruelty and craven self-interest? Are women, intrinsically and in every way, superior to Man? If we make our Gods in our own image, are they no less truly Divine Beings? But the questions are struggling in a mass of tireless storytelling; and the apocalyptic climax adds nothing to the standard model of sf answers-to-everything.

Plague of Angels, the next novel, returns to earth; and a different scenario from the Arbai stories, though the themes and favourite motifs remain. The setting is a future USA long devastated, depopulated and strangely altered. The existence of technologically advanced and even Utopian societies on the seaboard Edges is a dim rumour to homesteaders in the mountains of Manland. Closer at hand are the cities: squalid, exciting places where adventure can be found; and the bizarre 'archetypal villages' scattered through the wilderness, where fairytale characters play out their roles. Abasio, whose mother went to the city looking for fun and came back mortally sick and pregnant, leaves his grandfather's farm and sets out to seek his fortune. On his way he encounters a female orphan who is being smuggled into an archetypal village; and then, a pair of terrifying cyborgs. He learns that more and more of these strange entities are stalking the land, searching for an 'orphan female child'.

The cyborgs, we discover, are emissaries from the Place of Power, where the descendants of an original technocrat élite are preparing to follow the missing masses of the population, who left earth long ago to colonise the galaxy... just as soon as they can find one vital missing component for their space shuttle. In fact the only person who still believes in this permanently stalled mission to the stars, is 'The Ellel' present head of the chief of the scientist and technician clans. Already bitter and twisted, as a female leader in a Man's world, Ellel is rapidly becoming very peculiar indeed. Her colleagues don't know about the distasteful relationship (à la Norman Bates) she enjoys with her dead father, but they know that the cyborg army she has unearthed has an awesome potential for destruction; and they have uneasy suspicions about the fate of a succession of 'orphan female children' retrieved by the monsters. There's something about a prophecy... When Abasio and *his* female orphan, now named Olly Longaster, meet again, and set off for the Place of Power in search of Olly's secret destiny, they don't know about Ellel. But they know enough of the growing cyborg plague to be aware that stakes are high and a happy ending is unlikely.

Plague of Angels is a fairytale as cheerfully, shamelessly obvious in its present-day derivations as a Christmas pantomime. A narrative that seemed pure fantasy at the outset quickly takes the familiar form of a warning message. The archetypal villages, populated by role-playing

Orphans, Oracles and Heroes, actually form a Gulag Archipelago where politically disruptive elements from the coastal enclaves of civilisation are exiled, stripped of their identities and labelled according to their 'crimes'. The cities of Manland are rats' nests of gang-warfare decay; the refuse left behind by the exodus of the middle classes. Their final depopulation is mediated by IDDS—a sexually transmitted immune deficiency disease (like AIDS, only more science fictional); while the people of Edges show that they're worthy to survive by planting trees and embracing Native American culture. However, one waits in vain for the trolls and griffins that also appear, inhabiting the wilderness between settlements, to be explained-down as maybe runaway animatronics, self-replicating theme park escapes; or for the folklorish talking animals to be given an sf rationale. That old familiar warning moves into a different register. Just as in *Sideshow*, the signs and wonders promised by scripture have arrived: and if they weren't real before, they are now. The four Thrones hidden deep within the Place of Power, which mysteriously appeared at the time of the Great Upheavals, are the genuine theological article: the third order of angels, made manifest on earth in the Last Days of Mankind.

Plague of Angels is less crowded than *Sideshow* and equally engaging, though it has the same feeling of plotting after the fact. It's a story that relies heavily on birthmarks, suddenly discovered long-lost relations, oracular pronouncements, contrived tragedy; and characters who behave as if they are game-pieces, picked up and set down wherever the writer needs them. But this is an episode in which the new world is within reach, though the evil past is making a late attempt to fight back, and the overall effect is joyous. *Shadow's End,* Tepper's latest venture in science-fantasy eschatology, has a bleaker tone. The opening scene is on Dinadh, in a simple patriarchal society where Saulez, the narrator, is about to undergo the ritual ordeal associated with a first pregnancy. Thence we move to Alliance Central, a paved-over high-rise planet that was once called earth. Firstism, the belief that the universe is made for Mankind, is the dominant philosophy of the teeming colonised planets of the Alliance, which are devoid of 'all other life'—beyond a few necessary food species. But recently, several of these vast human populations have simply vanished. An unknown hostile alien power is suspected, for convenience named the 'Ularians'. Members of the Ruling Council believe that Bernesohn Famber, a famous biochemist who disappeared some time ago with his heir the dashing adventurer Leelson Famber, on a distant and uncivilised planet, may have had a clue to the mystery. Lutha Talstaff, his former lover, is despatched to the secretive planet of Dinadh to search for Leelson. She takes with her Famber's child, Leely, who appears to be severely autistic and has been rejected by his father.

On Dinadh, pregnant Saulez suffers her ritual encounter with the exquisite and sacred 'Kachis', who may or may not be the ancient native sentient species of Dinadh: fails the ordeal and becomes a non-person in her community, a 'Shadow'. Another narrative strand follows the point of view of 'Snarkey', a girl sentenced to electronically mediated non-personhood for petty crimes, who is working for the Alliance Council as a notionally invisible servant—another 'Shadow'. In fact she is a survivor of one of the so-called Ularian attacks, and has access to the place where the Ularian mystery is explained. Likewise Saulez, the disregarded, knows what's really going on on Dinadh. By the time the two shadows have been restored to personhood, Lutha Talstaff, the successful and supposedly emancipated Alliance woman, will have recognised how much she and they have in common. The fate of all women is alike, in a Man's cosmos.

Tepper's God is getting meaner. In the other books, innocent and good-willed victims were accidentally caught in the crossfire when God's emissaries arrived, more in sorrow than in anger, to clear up the mess made by Man. This time, the unpleasant patriarchs of Dinadh and the callous world-pavers of Firstism are up against an archangel with a taste for vindictive invention somewhat startling in the lieutenant of a Benign Supreme Being; and the nasty trap that She and Her Superior have set up to catch the wicked, punishes the innocent first and most cruelly. This is, of course, in line with what we observe in nature (where you'll rarely find a wealthy arms dealer stepping on a left-over landmine). In other respects, *Shadow's End* is disappointingly monochrome. The Firstists are blandly and obviously *wrong* in the style of the dullest of sf satire; and the Ularian visitation is a poor, bland sort of emergency compared with the constantly intriguing behaviour of the Hobbs Land Gods. There's a lot to enjoy in *Shadow's End*, nevertheless: weird landscapes, cosy horrors; a 'virus in human form' good against the Wrath of God (maybe). But, quite aside from problems with some clumsy first-person narration, the rich carelessness begins to stale, and trademark motifs grow too familiar. It's the same problem, the same over-extended final confrontation; and the same solution, *deus ex machina* indeed, that is an admission of the same defeat.

In Sheri Tepper's earlier novel (*The Gate to Women's Country*, 1989), she depicted a female-ordered society defined by the fear of men: the men, who must be contained, managed, controlled like a pack of dangerous wild animals. These three books are full of the same fear: the fear and helplessness of women, and gentle men, before the vast juggernaut powers ranged against them. Even the cherubim turn out to be bullies in the end. Thus present reality defines, inescapably, every imaginary future, 'satirical' or otherwise. Sheri Tepper's fictional picture of sexual politics is not complex. For her, women (generally) are simply the goodies; and men (generally) simply the baddies. It's remarkable how tolerant the male audience for genre adventures of this kind seems to be! But perhaps there's an explanation for men's relatively untroubled acceptance of this brand of feminism. Just as the women in *Women's Country* gained control only by stepping into the power vacuum after 'a great devastation brought about by men', so the goodies in the three more recent novels look for no change in their situation short of Divine Intervention. Though the *problem* is always the bad behaviour of men and the powerlessness of women, relations between men and women are seen as unalterable, and by no chance are men or women asked to change their ways. So there's nothing to be frightened of, really, as long as you don't seriously believe in visitations from the Cherubim. In *Shadow's End* the love between Leelson Famber (who has borrowed his CV and his unforgiveable-but-adorable masculine style from Indiana Jones) and Lutha Talstaff does not reduce their differences. It is an irresistible force, to which Lutha, but not Leelson, has to submit. It is her nature to accept and forgive, as it is Leelson's nature to make selfish demands. For Sheri Tepper it appears that these archetypes are independent of physiology, never mind reproductive role. Nela and Bertran, the Siamese twins in *Sideshow*, remain, when separated and rebuilt from scratch, masculine and feminine—he the egotist, she the selfless and spiritual. All the heroines of the Fall of Man—Sualez, Nela, Fringe Owldark and her immortal mentor Jory in *Sideshow*; Olly Longaster in *Plague of Angels*—are victims: willing victims, noble victims, but sacrificial offerings nonetheless.

It would be wrong to push this investigation too far. Sheri Tepper's work is meant to be popular entertainment. But as she continues to call for change on a vast and cosmic scale, while insisting that change is essentially impossible, her stories become less convincing and even less entertaining. One wonders how long the ideal reconstruction at the end of *Plague of Angels* can last, if male and female 'human nature' has stayed the same as it always was. Perhaps it's too much to ask for a different approach to sexual politics, from Sheri Tepper or from other women writers of this gorgeously catastrophic bent. The present defines the future, and the imagination; and Sheri Tepper has a right to draw the world as she sees it. But when the Apocalypse itself starts to get boring, it surely must be time for a radical re-think of *some* kind.

18: The Furies: Suzy Charnas *Beyond the End of the World*

In the 1970s Suzy Charnas produced two books of a trilogy: the first a very bleak condemnation of patriarchy, the second often taken as an uncritical vision of a separatist women's utopia. *Walk to the End of the World* was set in a tiny and starving coastal enclave—the 'Holdfast'—where a wretched remnant of white males struggled to survive, long after 'The Wasting'—a slow catastrophe of environmental degradation that had destroyed global civilisation. The men held white females captive for labour and breeding. All other races, and most animal and plant species, had vanished or been deliberately exterminated. The book placed the blame for 'The Wasting' on the evils of patriarchy, evils which persisted, intensely concentrated, in Holdfast society. Terror, superstition and madness ruled. Drug-induced 'dark-dreaming', random violence and sexual humiliation were the tools of control of the dominant senior males. Dread surrounded all dealings with women, regarded as mindless but dangerous pieces of property. In the course of the novel the institutionalised hatred between the 'seniors' and the younger men who must inevitably supplant them, led to war— a miniature dust-up by old standards, but disastrous in this context. From the collapse emerged three characters, one young woman and two young men, each endowed with a grimly irrelevant will to live, in a dying world.

Walk to the End of the World, showed women treated as domestic animals—pets, draft animals, factory-farm breeders; and finally slaughtered for meat. It was powerful science fiction. But a vision of the future that appeals to the ravening imagination of William Burroughs— who praised the book highly—isn't likely to offer much comfort to female readers. *Motherlines* followed Alldera, the only significant female character in the first book, as she fled, pregnant and desperate, into the wilderness. She was found and rescued by the Riding Women of the Grasslands. These people—whose existence was barely suspected in the Holdfast—were the descendants of a long ago experiment in parthenogenesis. They were able to conceive, using horse semen to trigger the process, (a breeding population of horses had been preserved from 'The Wasting' by this same experiment). They had developed, over generations a complex nomadic culture based on the 'motherlines', the successive generations of clone-daughters of the original experimental subjects. Alldera discovered other escaped slaves from the Holdfast, living alongside the Riding Women but unable to share their freedoms. She gave birth to a daughter, and with her child became accepted by the arrogant and not particularly open-minded Riding Women; but continued to move uneasily between the two communities, unable to give whole-hearted allegiance to either.

Motherlines was a book written from the heart of Seventies feminist experience. That the Riding Women were physically brave, strong and multi-competent: hard-fighting warriors and skilled horsewomen, living in harmony with nature (as much of it as remained) goes without saying. These were favourite romantic images of feminist sf, enduringly popular and still in currency today. One thinks of the all-female Matriarchal Bronze Age tribes recreated by DNA transformations from modern human colonists, on the planet Jeep in Nicola Griffith's *Ammonite;* of Maureen McHugh's cross-dressing women warriors. But in *Motherlines*—as is not always the case with the later fantasies—every detail of the separatists' picturesque lifestyle has political significance. The cumulative effect of this underpinning is a dogmatic, doctrinaire, transliteration of feminist theory. The Riding Women are not only free from male domination, they are free from every convention of male-dominated society. They are a nation of individuals, each genetically related only through the motherline from parent to child; and presenting an ideal of unconstrained selfhood in place of the 'selfless' domestic woman, trammelled by family ties. Taboos limit even the mother-daughter bond, while any other long term sexual or romantic commitment is considered unnatural. Rational self-interest is the whole of the law. Government, in so far as it exists, happens through endless argument. The typical art form of the Riding Women is the 'self-song' which each woman elaborates through her life, telling the hero-tale of her own great deeds: so that where women under patriarchy hold the society together with their folklore and 'old wives' tales', the Riding Women's common cultural heritage is ephemeral, disparate, ready to fly apart.

The Riding Women were an artificial life-form, perhaps without much more bearing on present day reality than other science fictional tribals: cobbled together in the usual way, partly from scraps of reference to historical tribal cultures; partly from the fashionable preoccupations of the time of writing. The ex-slaves, or 'Free fems', were more disturbing. Newly emancipated from an extreme form of slavery, they were damaged and bitter people: sneaky, plotting, petty and spiteful. Alldera was a singular exception. The other refugees from the Holdfast could not be integrated into Riding Women society, and were both physically and psychically incapable of building a society of their own. Being oppressed, Suzy Charnas was keen to tell us, does not make you a nice person. Treated as if they are worthless, people *become* worthless, perhaps irredeemably.

The Furies, the belated third volume of the trilogy, takes up the story where it left off, but almost immediately abandons the aspirational experiment of life with the Riding Women. Alldera has finally succeeded in organising and training the escaped slaves into a fighting force, a project that she had begun with little hope of success in Volume Two. Pursued by a group of Riding Women, who are afraid this incompetent army will achieve nothing except to provoke reprisals from the men, they set off to attack the Holdfast. As they reach the borders they discover a man's corpse hung on a tree. A living man—or rather a gelded 'cutboy', Setteo, once the sex-toy of a senior male—is lurking nearby. In dim memory of Christian myth, it seems he raised this offering believing the sign of the crucified will bring some major change of fortune to the Holdfast. He is quite mad: he hails the women—'Christs', 'Blesseds'—as the answer to his prayers. The Free Fems, at first terrified even by a dead 'master', throw themselves on the rotting corpse and hack it to pieces.

Alldera's plan has been to rescue more fems from slavery, and capture some men to use as studs. This is an urgent problem, since the ex-slaves can't conceive with horse semen, and they are all getting older. But the incident on Corpse Hill shows how little she is able—or willing—to control her followers. Soon a scouting party successfully ambushes a small group of Holdfast men.They are all killed, the idea of capturing breeding stock forgotten. Fedeka, self-appointed religious leader of the fems, and Daya the storyteller, Alldera's current lover, improvise a ritual of mutilation and cannibal feasting around the corpses. Alldera, disapproving but helpless, does not attend the orgy. So the pattern is set. Revenge is placed above hope, the voice of reason is shamed into silence, and the Free Fems have already matched the level of barbarism the men achieved at the final climax of *Walk to the End of the World*.

The first substantial victory comes easily. Superior military technology (the Free Fems have horses) is no respecter of gender. To the amazement of the women, their masters (who are of course weakened by their own recent civil war) seem powerless to resist. Male supremacy tumbles, the first town is taken and sacked. Alldera forgets her queasy doubts and enters without reserve into her followers' merciless joy. Vengeance is meted out on collaborating 'trusties' among the female slaves, the rest of the newly freed are recruited into Alldera's army, and the conquering progress continues. The Free Fems are soon collecting gruesome souvenirs, hacking down unarmed and helpless prisoners, blooding more timid or squeamish recruits in grisly initiations. Tearful and outraged at each fem casualty, appalled by each enemy atrocity, they are as oblivious to the horrors of their own behaviour as any raw male soldiers in the history of war. The dogma of ex-slavedom tells them that they can do no wrong. Male prisoners are taken in relatively large numbers (the whole population of the Holdfast is reported to be a few hundreds), but the idea of using men as studs is repeatedly put aside. Many of Alldera's followers are post-fertile, or believe themselves to be. They are not interested in the future.

The Newly Freed quickly discover that some ex-slaves are more equal than others. One of them, Beyarra-Bey, becomes the pupil of Daya the storyteller, and notes how Daya blatantly falsifies the epic of conquest; how Alldera's unease at her followers' grosser atrocities is excised from the story-song, while the part the 'Newly Freed' have played in the victories is not recorded. Beyarra knows what's expected of an inferior: she keeps quiet. But not all the Newly Freed are so wise. Female slaves, rendered scarce and valuable by the senseless war from which Alldera fled, have been better treated in recent years. The Free Fems remember brutal routine rape, starvation, grinding labour, arbitrary punishment. They resent evidence that the Newly Freed have not suffered the same degree of degradation. Meanwhile, some of the young women are starting to mutter that the men weren't as bad as all that. Fems were gradually bettering their situation without violence: they had a future, which is being stolen from them by this enforced liberation. For these women, especially the young and fertile, being freed by Alldera's army has turned out to be a lot like being liberated by Joe Stalin or—a comparison very much to the point— by Snowball the pig in Orwell's *Animal Farm*. They see stores of food wantonly burned, they see the supply of fertile men dwindling. The cruel and arbitrary rule of Holdfast senior males is being replaced by a régime scarcely less irrational or authoritarian—where hypocrisy barely conceals contempt, and instead of reproduction by institutionalised rape, there'll be no reproduction at all.

Alldera is a true politician. Her sympathy is with the Newly Freed, but her good intentions are at the mercy of the voters' whims. She will not criticise or curb her inner circle. Already, fatally, she sees the crisis in terms of the intrigues and jealousies among her own intimates; which engage her full attention, until she encounters a figure from her own past. Eykar Bek, one of her male companions on the original *Walk to the End of the World* has survived. He has become 'the Librarian', a tolerated eccentric in the diminished male community of the city where Alldera was once enslaved. When he comes secretly to plead with her for the safety of his precious books, sexual attraction between them—bizarrely out of place in the past and equally irrelevant now—is rekindled. They talk together like time travellers remembering another age. But by this point, the usual sanity-preserving mechanisms of war have developed in Alldera's army.

Women were 'fems' to the men, now the Free Fems are calling the men they mutilate and torture 'dirts'. Alldera dare not give Eykar special treatment. After the taking of the city he is penned and put to hard labour with the rest of the men. But overcome by nostalgia and stifled lust for this 'elegant and steely person'—half blind and lame as he is now—she continues to favour him secretly, eventually rescuing him from ill-treatment and taking him into her personal care. But he can do nothing for his fellow men. When he details the Free Fems' war crimes, and begs for mercy, if only for the sake of a human future, Alldera insists that mercy is impossible.

> 'Fems who never dared to speak up to a master must find the courage to strike a man, to wound him, to kill him in battle. People need to do it first in a situation that's safe for them,'… 'I did want something else… But Eykar, who can make a new, whole self without spending the ocean of old poisons first?'

It is hard to tell whether Alldera sees where this reasoning leads and still sincerely believes in what she's saying; or whether—like many a conquering hero—she simply hasn't the courage to risk political suicide. It doesn't matter. She is already, it seems, doomed. The Free Fems, appalled by her relationship with a 'dirt', no longer trust their leader. Daya the storyteller, treacherous and fascinating, has become the centre of a plot to destroy the woman she both worships, and envies to the point of hatred.

Suzy Charnas's view of human nature *in extremis* is stark, searching and merciless as it was in the earlier chronicles of the Holdfast and the Riding Women. It allows for no disinterested virtues, no pure emotions, no sentiment stronger than self-pity; and above all recognises no moral superiority between the sexes. There may have been occasions in human history when a horribly wronged subject race rose in armed struggle and managed to remain forbearing and dignified in victory. I'd be glad to be corrected, but I can't think of an example right now. The Free Fems behave just as real-world history would predict in such a situation. But—relatively speaking—they are no less brutal in their dealings with each other. Alldera—a natural leader not because of her stronger intelligence, but because in spite of it she shares her followers' worst beliefs—rejects the temptation of mercy with a regret that seems little more than squeamishness. Beyarra the beautiful, in a society where faithful love has been extirpated and sex is a currency of status, dispenses her favours cynically: 'If you had to sleep with someone to get what you wanted, it was nice if they had an attractive body…' If the Free Fems ever could have been more sane and human than their masters, it is too late. They have returned to the Holdfast only to demonstrate that they are incurably infected with its poisons. Women under patriarchy become as corrupt and callous as men, and will prove it as soon as ever they get the chance.

Not even the Riding Women, some of whom followed Alldera to turn her back and have stayed to marvel at her success, are excepted from this rule. As inter-generational conflict between the women takes the foreground, and the fate of the new slaves, the 'dirts', slips from view, *The Furies* resembles nothing so much as a reworking of *Walk to the End of the World* with a female cast. There was no hope for Charnas's tiny, crazy remnant of humanity, when the men were in charge. Sixteen years on, with a different party in power, there doesn't seem to be much improvement.

In one of the last scenes in the book, Eykar Bek laughs at himself for imagining that the Free Fems had returned to the Holdfast to forge a new relationship with their old masters: 'What nonsense. The central matter of the femmish conquest was, of course, the relation of the fems to each other, among themselves and to the Wild Women who returned with them...' If the separatist tribal culture in *Motherlines* was an experiment based on Seventies feminist theory, *The Furies* may be regarded as an updated despatch from the same camp: and in this respect the *Animal Farm* fable is full of grim revelations about the state of play in the Women's Movement. There aren't many illusions left. We see how quickly the leaders of the revolution can become a new class of exploiters; how swiftly the reformed institutions of the revolutionary state degenerate; how easily the pursuit of just compensation for the victims of oppression slides into the unprincipled trimming of a vote-hungry politician; how women, just as well as men, can use other women selfishly and cynically. But do these revelations concern 'women', exactly, as a special group and a special case? The savagery of the Free Fems' revenge on their former masters seems to demonstrate that 'women' behave exactly like other human beings. Even the one inescapable difference between the sexes, reproductive function, is reduced to naked economics. Male fertility, to the Free Fems, is a means of production, no different from any other asset reclaimed from their former masters. A pregnancy is property, to be stolen (if you can get away with it) or paid for. If there *are* such things as intrinsically feminine qualities, they do not emerge in the action of this novel.

The absence of male characters was a strength in *Motherlines*. Arguably the absence of any convincing male voice is a strength in *The Furies*. But the character of Eykar Bek, guardian of the relics of civilisation, is an anachronism in this murderous and murdered future. The past he and Alldera visit in their conversations seems rather more like the late twentieth century than anything described in the previous two volumes, and Bek sounds like a wistful New Man, who can't understand why 'the feminists' are still so hostile to him—a million miles away from the 'Eykar Bek' of *Walk*. His sycophantic observation about the women needing to sort things out with women first would be inadequate—and sycophantic—as a rationale for the (relatively!) mild backstabbing squabbles of real world feminism. It sounds a very false note amidst the blood-drenched savagery of these pages. If power is everything and sexual physiology is nothing— a proposition that Charnas demonstrates most convincingly—what's so special about 'women' after all? I wanted somebody to ask that question. I wanted someone to ask, were women not implicated at all in 'The Wasting'? It was male-dominated applied science that made the survival of the Riding Women possible, what are we to make of that irony? These questions cannot be discussed in *The Furies*, because the time for questions is over. But this silence uncouples *The Furies* from the real world, and feminist political purpose, at the very point where fiction and reality should speak most clearly to each other. As things stand, this could be any doomsday scenario about a slave-race on the rampage. Revenge is sweet, but, unfair as it seems, the victorious rebels soon lose the world's sympathy, as the counter-atrocities begin to pile up.

Walk to the End of the World had a compelling thriller plot. *Motherlines* had its colourful, richly detailed exercise in social engineering. The narrative of *The Furies* is more difficult to follow and more harsh than either. It presents, without much distraction from the storytelling, a series of scenes from the death throes of a species. Finally, and significantly, the most reliable observer of these events is neither a man nor a woman but Setteo, the mad 'cutboy'. Through the bloody, oblivious progress of Alldera's army, Setteo, Charnas's impotent Christ-figure, gives a 'crazy' commentary that reveals the true horror of the situation. From his visions of the Cold Country, the dead land which encompasses and interpenetrates the remaining fragments of the living world, he testifies for the White Bears, who represent the murdered ones: 'They grieved constantly but silently for loss of everything that had lived in the Warm World before the Wasting, from leviathan to all the small birds of the air...' Setteo's passages, in writing of great beauty and power, rise from a waste of mean *realpolitik*, to invoke a nemesis, and a scale of sorrow, that makes the grievances between the two factions of the destroyers look petty indeed.

At length we discover, with relief, that *The Furies* can end without a strew of principal characters' bodies all over the stage. The tormented Daya is playing Iago to a General with better survival instincts and more cunning than Othello; and there is even a minimal suggestion that the women will manage to do business with each other, and make use of the men. Their régime will survive, just as the Holdfast men managed to survive somehow, for a while. But the nihilism that made *Walk to the End of the World* so powerful subverts this sort-of happy ending. *The Furies* is an angry book, that ends with a sense that the spending of that 'ocean of old poisons' is a doomed enterprise. It's an ocean that will never be emptied, the cycle of abuse will never be broken. There are no solutions here, the world is still damaged beyond repair: and the White Bears are waiting.

19: *Alien Influences*: Kristine Kathryn Rusch in the Dark

Where do aliens belong? The purist, (or purest) school of sf thought says that aliens are not science fiction because they are not within reach of our extrapolation. The space flight wildly imagined by the scientifiction of the genre's early days was just within the bounds of prediction, and it has duly happened (though so far on a somewhat more modest scale than envisaged). Aliens don't belong in this category. They do not represent a calculable possible development from a known situation. Whether or not they're out there, our own galaxy—in so far as we seem to know it—is such a huge place, interstellar distances so intractable, that in reason we can't *expect* extraterrestrial contact. Whatever you may think of the logic of this argument, both science fiction and fantasy writers continue to describe the unpredictable encounter with more or less of extrapolative rigour, and bear the reproach of the purists with stoicism. But we have to admit, in every case the aliens are not themselves. They are exploited Third Worlders, Evil Empires, unexplored aspects of the human psyche, devils, angels, elves, characters in a historical romance about foreign travel; perhaps they are 'the other'. We cannot write about the real aliens until we've met them. Instead we use their name, and talk about something else.

The aliens in Kristine Kathyrn Rusch's *Alien Influences* have a distinctly nineteenth-century feel. They are native peoples encountered by human colonists in search of raw materials. They smell funny, they look funny, they don't wear proper clothes or live in proper houses. They don't have to be paid when you take their stuff. They are weak and vulnerable and yet also regarded as extremely dangerous. They are perhaps magical but their magic is helpless before the human rush to plunder. In every case they are being decimated: and true to our past though shocking to late twentieth-century sentiment, practically nobody cares.

The title of the novel refers to an instrument (in the legal sense) called the Alien Influences Act, which has recently become law in human space, or at least all of human space that appears in this novel—comprising a disparate collection of space bases, where civilised life happens; and a further group of planet-surface colonies, which are in the process of developing from raw trading stations to permanent communities. The point of the Act seems to be that if it can be proved that a human committed some crime under 'alien influence', the crime must be judged not by human law but by the law of the non-human community, if it can be discovered. It's going to be a difficult law to implement, since no effective communication has yet been established with any of the non-humans encountered; and the general attitude to aliens ranges from indifference to violent hostility, with a little predatory acquisitiveness on the way. But it is characteristic of this novel, which specialises in effective blanks, that we never find out exactly how the Act's supposed to work. The law, in *Alien Influences*, is something to be invoked with care and ceremony *so that it can be ignored*. This is a time and space where jurisprudence, psychology, government, bureaucracy, forensics, are all highly important: but only as empty ritual. The content has vanished.

The story begins on a planet named Bountiful. There's a colony, a single human speck on the edge of a desert. It is devoted to processing and shipping the highly profitable and certified harmless recreation drug known as Salt Juice. Next door to the humans' dome there's an encampment of the now very scarce native people known as the Dancers. Unfortunately for this magical and picturesque remnant tribe, the humans have recently discovered how to process Salt Juice without the help of local skilled labour... The bodies of five human children have been found, successively, each mutilated in accordance with the well-known Dancer puberty rite. A xenopsychologist, Justin Schafer, is called in: a sensitive and troubled individual who is soon sure he's being used in a plot designed to justify a genocidal police action. After a sixth death he divines that the killers are the children of the colony themselves—acting, perhaps quite innocently, under 'alien influence' in the meaning of the Act. He realises too late that his discovery serves the genocidal humans as well as if he'd declared the Dancers themselves responsible, and in trying to save the natives he has betrayed the human children to a terrible fate.

The eight twelve-year-olds involved—John, Beth, Pearl, Dusty, Max, Allen, Skye and Verity—are whisked away to Lina Space Base, to stand trial. They are objects of superstitious dread, and treated with considerable brutality. Dania Zinn and Harper Reeves, attorneys appointed by the base authorities, attempt a humane assessment of their level of responsibility. Like Justin, they suspect a cover-up. But the fear of these children's evil alien powers turns out—it seems—to have some foundation. The assessment process is destroyed by a couple of bizarre incidents, involving the death of one child. The others are shipped off to a high-security prison planet for juveniles, for an indefinite term—where they will be separated, because of the fear of their 'group mind'. The case of the Dancer Eight will never come to trial.

The first part of the book is gruelling reading. The experience of the close-knit group of children torn apart on Lina base is an unremitting record of bureaucratic and institutional viciousness. In the second part, when the story is resumed after a gap of years, the tension is relaxed. We discover that yes, there was a conspiracy. At the time of the Dancer Eight events, government and private interests were united in trying to bury research about Salt Juice, which is actually highly addictive and also has very nasty effects on the personality. Investigation of the children's case couldn't be allowed, because it would have uncovered the truth. The human adults on Bountiful were all junkies. Their children had been sexually and violently abused, emotionally deprived, and kept catastrophically ignorant. They turned to the Dancer puberty ritual in the desperate, sincere belief that it would turn them into adults, so they could legally escape from their hideous homes. They did not realise that human physiology was different. All this is now well-known, at least in the circles in which Bizarre Xenoforensic Cases Of Our Times are discussed. But there has been no reparation. The children have served the sentences that were imposed without trial, and simply been released to vanish into the abyss of human space's underclass. It remains for Justin Schafer, still racked with guilt over the consequences of his detective insight, to redeem himself: and for John, the leader of the Dancer Eight, to trace his friends and rescue their ruined lives.

Are Kristine Rusch's aliens supposed to be fantasy or science fiction? The question is easily resolved. The Dancers' curious physiology—the way they seem to be able to walk on air, the telepathy, the hands which are grasping tools and also genital organs, the sexuality which is, nevertheless, treated as identical to human female and male; the drastic metamorphosis at puberty—all this is described but never *explained*, until at last John is told, by an even more fantastical alien, that what seemed like magic really was magic; and moreover the Dancers' powers really were transferred to the human children. Though other alien species we meet—like the unfortunate seal-like Minarians—seem bound by our physical laws, the Bodeangenie who comes to John's aid is a desert djinn straight from Hollywood, pure Robin Williams only not so loud; and the Dancers are the same kind of unreal. If this wasn't enough, both writer and publisher have placed the book's marketing signals firmly in the 'soft sf' or 'science fantasy' bracket. This is meant to be one of those spaceship fairytales. And as a fantasy thriller *Alien Influences* works well, in spite of at least the usual amount of glitches, hitches and authorial tap-dancing, plus the very evident influence of minimum attention-span tv fiction. Yet this story has elements, irreducible to carelessness or the influence of the small screen, that make it a strange sort of fantasy, and a strange sort of thriller: a genuinely disturbing and disquieting novel, more than the sum of its parts, that achieves its effects in ways which are hard to pin down without close examination.

One aspect of science/fantasy fiction's changing treatment of the alien is the question of relativism: briefly, *of course, we look just as weird to them.* In *Alien Influences* relativism does not apply. We are not weird. We are not aliens, we can't be because aliens means *not human.* Admittedly the novel is to some extent a fix-up, which makes for an uneven narrative. The hard line on aliens as deviants comes in the 'decadent space hotel' chapter, where a brothel client's tentacles and watery habitat are conflated with a willingness to buy the sexual services of an unconsenting minor, as equally evil and disgusting. The same crude prejudice is not found elsewhere. But though non-humans may be benign, they may be magical, they may be cute, it is telling that the only alien who talks and behaves like *person* is a magical sprite wearing a human body as his favoured disguise. In the codes of science fiction and fantasy, the rejection of relativism signals a return to the past, when the treatment of extraterrestrials naïvely reflected a real-world view of *foreigners* as smelly, ugly, poorly dressed, stupid, probably not even able to speak English. Or else just plain bad guys. But in *Alien Influences* there is no such simple regression. This is not an account of first contact encounters with novel lifeforms, the instinctive recoil from the unfamiliar; nor of the inevitable distaste for competitors in the struggle for *lebensraum.* Its treatment of the alien, the other, is a record of people who have tried to understand and failed, who have done their best and been defeated by the uncaring mass of majority opinion, or by their own personal flaws. It is almost a counsel of despair.

Alien Influences is in some ways reminiscent of Carolyn Cherryh's claustrophobic epics of bad government in the deep future. It's an extended courtroom drama (that never gets to court) where single personalities loom large while a sweeping backdrop is dismissed to a minor role. But in Cherryh, a writer of the modern era, there is a scale between the individual and the vast theatre. Here there is none. There is no big ideological split, no greater loyalty that may be invoked, no State in any form that either commands respect or provokes rebellion. The ominously named Provisional Government of Rusch's human space is a military junta (I confidently assume) that seized power by force and intends to keep it, occasionally pretending to offer to rectify the irregular situation—an offer no one in their right mind will take seriously. Citizenship is irrelevant. Elements of *Star Trek* plotting and costume may be found in Rusch's scenario, but there's no trace of the comforting presence of Starfleet Command. There is no web of political and social infrastructure to unite human diaspora, nothing to hold people together, nothing between soul and soul except the lightless void.

When Justin Schafer is called to Bountiful as an expert witness, everything seems normal. This is a fictional murder investigation, with the usual elements plus a science-fantasy décor—the children's mutilated bodies, the cold storage drawers in the morgue, the photos (hologram movies) of the victims in life; co-operation or hostility from the witnesses; hints at a conspiracy. But the illusion of twentieth-century normality soon begins to break down. Justin does not examine the evidence. He experiences his own psychological state; his psychic pain cut and lit by the physical pain of exposure to Bountiful's fierce sun. His recent humiliation in another alien influences case is far more real to him than anything outside himself. That's not too strange. Fictional detectives all have their quirks. Then, it becomes clear that the evidence that he is offered is not evidence. There has been no investigation. We are shown all the usual signs of forensic science. We watch walk-round hologram movies of the children at play, and of the discovered bodies: but science itself is absent. Nobody has asked questions, nobody has taken measurements. When Justin arrives at the conclusion that the children are doing the killing, it's by a leap of empathy backed by one slight observation. The children themselves, until that leap, seem a normal, affectionate bunch of kids, locked in their own small world as children tend to be. The only excuse for believing them even physically capable of the crimes is some fairytale about a super-sharp yet primitive Dancer knife, somehow able to perform with surgical accuracy on human anatomy, in the hands of a child. Eventually, there will be an explanation for the way things happened on Bountiful. It will be confirmed that the non-existent investigation was ruthlessly managed by government and private greed, and that the impossible crimes really did have the help of magic. The explanation is inadequate. However self-obsessed the psychologist was, it is hardly fair to tell us he spent a period of several days with an entire population of psychotic crack addicts, and interrogated their abused children at length, without noting anything off in anyone's behaviour or appearance. But all thriller writers cheat, and this cheating works to powerful effect. Concentrating on emotion and on immediate experience, dismissing any wider view, Rusch creates a compelling mystery that grips not by suspense, but through bewilderment: *Why doesn't anybody notice that what's going on here doesn't make sense?* In the later part of the book, panic-inducing confusion clears, as the action moves into a straightforward quest-adventure and the plot retreats into fairytale. But the sense that there is no centre, no truth, nothing to depend on, is never dispelled—so that the fairytale ending, ironically, is the means by which common sense sneaks into the story at last. In the face of Kristine Rusch's universal dark, flight into a dreamland of Disney genies and happy wish-fulfilment amounts to a rational response.

Alien Influences, as it turns out, isn't really about aliens—which is no surprise. It is very much about alienation, on every scale. Bad things have always happened to aliens in science fiction. In modern sf, which has had to accommodate in turn (with more or less of individual authorial resistance) the civil rights movement, feminism, and the vaguer concept of 'ethnic diversity', plenty of helpless aborigines have suffered *in spite of* the efforts enlightened humans. In Rusch the whole liberal-intellectual apparatus that created those 'enlightened' views is no longer functional. Arguably, in some sense individual virtue wins out: but only by magic. The situation for what we call humane values, fair dealing without magic, is desperate.

In this anarchy the most banal devices of science fantasy take on bleak and sinister meaning. There are no maps of the time-space envelope, vast as it must be, that contains these free-floating bases and habitable planets. Every star is simply called the sun. The action takes place in a simultaneous present, where the paradoxes of interstellar distance have vanished. Characters communicate and travel through the unimaginable void in some way that achieves the same effect as telephones and plane flights between US cities, and never run into any of the difficulties that rack the brains of pure sf writers. It's as if *the universe,* the huge awesome object that we, in our time, worship with such scientific devotion, has ceased to exist. The novel is structured the way they'll teach you to do sf in the most pedestrian creative writing class. Partly a fix-up of previously published stories, it is built from a series of single viewpoint passages clipped together like prefabricated units. But here the sealed units seem to echo the theme of utter alienation. What is John, the leader of the Dancer Eight, doing, while Anita the corrupt art dealer is having her screen time? Nothing. He is sitting in his box, staring ahead of him alone in the dark, waiting to be switched on again.

As always when dealing with genre fiction, it is difficult to say how much of a writer's effect is a deliberate sytle, how much the reader's *objet trouvé* and how much just a case knowing what the market will bear. Every equation (so they told Stephen Hawking, about *A Brief History of Time*) is going to halve your sales figures. People don't want science in their science fantasy, and they quickly tire of social and political detail (arguably, the people in this sense don't want *science fiction* at all). For some time now, but especially since literary academics in the 1980s discovered William Gibson's *Neuromancer*, there has been a kind of slow rush to discover sf as the literature of post-modernism. I have read and heard plenty of solemn papers discussing the portents. I don't want to make the mistake of attributing to a skilled and entertaining commercial writer a purpose, and a pretension, for which she has absolutely no responsibility. But however it came about, in showing the space faring future as a new dark age, Rusch both exposes her present and achieves an arresting kind of realism of prediction. It is easy in our small world for the mass mind to be interested in aliens, when they are offered as tasty morsels of media-fodder; or for the literati, to whom 'they' present an engrossing metaphor for the human condition. But *out there*, somewhere in the future of our unstoppable expansion (if it does prove unstoppable), the chances are they'll just be in the way. It is easy for us to believe that our cosmology, our worries about the curvature of space-time, puzzles about what happens to identical twins if one goes off on a starship, will be just as absorbing when interstellar travel is a commonplace. *Out there*, who is going to remember these ancient, long solved problems? *Alien Influences* is fantasy by all the usual standards. Yet its picture of life after science—where the experiment has collapsed and the goal of progress has vanished, but the structures are still expanding and the gadgets still buzzing away—convinces (I think) as a post-modern science fiction should, on the same terms as sf has always functioned: because it's a future I can believe in from exactly here and now.

20: No Man's Land: Feminised Landscapes in the Utopian Fiction of Ursula Le Guin

South

The sound of the word South is the sound of softness and plenty. South is the preferred aspect for an Emperor's palace in traditional Chinese geomancy. South is the direction in which people of the northern temperate zone turn, when they want to imagine relaxation, warmth, repose. We head south, like the birds in winter, to escape from hardship. The South is a garden world where there is no conflict between nature and culture; where sweet fruits drop from the bough; where food plants grow and domestic animals give their service as if of their own goodwill, without any need for the violence and coercion of the plough that cuts open the earth, the goad that drives the cattle. Feminised utopias, whether or not imagined by women, are full of the warm south. Tolkien's entwives—though their ideal land is criticised by their creator, who prefers a masculine wilderness[1]—are the guardians of a garden world. In the eighteenth-century idyll *Paul et Virginie*,[2] a work that profoundly influenced George Sand and the whole pastoral Utopian tradition, a Caribbean island is the paradise in which the children of nature live without sin, nurtured at the bosom of their mother earth. The South is a place where dominating masculine attitudes to the world and to other people (nature red in tooth and claw: you have to be cruel to be kind) are proved unnecessary, and soft feminine values—gentleness, affection, tenderness—can thrive.

Feminised and feminist utopias of the twentieth century have this same character. The best known of early twentieth-century feminist utopias, Charlotte Perkins Gilman's *Herland*,[3] describes a country in the South (somewhere in Central America, to be more precise) where men have been unknown for two thousand years. Though Gilman's authoritarian and élitist Utopia has its distasteful side for modern readers, the female-only culture *presents itself* as a commonalty from which violence and coercion have been banished. *Herland* is a garden world, where compassionate farming and the gentle but intensive education of children are perceived as the most important activities of public and private life. In the period[4] when Ursula Le Guin was producing her most important and most influential Utopian writing so far, examples of the feminised pastorale abound. Joan Slonczewski *A Door Into Ocean*, Vonda McIntyre's *Dreamsnake*,

Marge Piercy's *Woman on the Edge of Time*, imagine feminist or feminised cultures where advanced scientific techniques are handled with authority and confidence by the female utopians. Sally Gearhart's *The Wanderground* gave feminised spirituality and communion with the (female) earth the status of magical power. Suzy Charnas's Riding Women, in *Motherlines*, are more like guerrilla survivalists than farmers. But they too have a communion with the earth, with their animals: a non-coercive relationship and affinity with nature. Even Joanna Russ, the great polemicist, dreamed of *Whileaway*, her high-tech supported all-female colony (or alternative earth) as a world of the south, a serene garden paradise.

Ursula Le Guin's most purely Utopian narrative, *Always Coming Home*,[5] inhabits this gentle land. It describes the culture of the Kesh, a people who 'might be going to have lived'[6] in California, at some time in our future. The Kesh are pastoralists, hunter-gatherers, gardeners. Their society does not exclude men. Instead some masculine activities—making war, hunting, promiscuous sex—are restricted to special enclaves or special licensed reversals: feast days when men are allowed to behave badly for a few hours, just as a treat. Other traditional masculine preserves—intellectual and spiritual authority—have simply been hijacked; they belong to women now. Advanced technology, another male-gendered preserve, is no longer a human concern. It is pursued by intelligent machines, for their own purposes. The world of the Kesh is not literally a 'No man's land', like *Herland* or *Whileaway*. Nor is it an exclusive club like Sally Gearhart's *Wanderground*, or like the Mattapoisett farming commune of Marge Piercy's *Woman on the Edge of Time*, which a few men may enter because they have proved that they are not going to behave badly. But it is a world which is ruled by no man: in which *no man* can construct himself as master of any aspect of the universe, without being perceived and treated as a psychopath.[7]

Always Coming Home is exhaustive and practical as a gardening manual. With some cunning it disguises the softness, the wish-fulfilment of its inner landscape, by giving the Kesh a fairly harsh, though beautiful and rewarding natural environment. The future California in its pages is imagined so thoroughly, from zoning regulations to trade relations, and with such sparing use of magic, that it brings paradise very close to real world Utopian thinking and practice. Small is beautiful. Consume less. Grow your own food, make your own power by sustainable means. Put a big share of your resources into childcare. Recycle everything. Show your wealth by giving gifts. Enjoy and celebrate your domestic life, abandon arid intellectual and technological aspirations... It might be looked on as the farthermost development of the feminised ideal world that has ever yet been attempted. Certainly the appearance of this compendium in

1985—with its anthology of Kesh poetry, richly decorated text, its glossaries—dictionaries; even a companion tape of 'Kesh' music played on 'Kesh' instruments—seems to have marked the end of something: the end of one Southern voyage of exploration. Nothing quite like *Always Coming Home* has been produced since. Feminised worlds and enclaves where everybody eats their greens and practises non-violence still thrive in the genre of science fiction and fantasy. But they are less significant, no more than an option among others for self-congratulation or comforting escapism.

Always Coming Home is a classic Utopia: not so much a novel as a collection of descriptive writings. The framing narrative, the life-story of a young woman whose father is a member of a recidivist, militarist, male-dominated tribe, the Condors, provides the only plot logically available to Utopian fiction: a challenge from the world outside paradise, that allows us to compare and contrast the ideal system with the bad old ways. The time, insisting on the need for practical, immediate Utopian change, is close enough to our present for the Kesh to feel the lasting ill-effects of male-dominated twentieth-century excess. But the palimpsest of cultural reportage, from character-portraits to recipes, includes a running commentary in the voice of 'Little Bear Woman'—that is, Ursula—expressing doubts about the whole project. Utopia, as Le Guin herself told us in the earlier story, 'The Ones who Walk Away from Omelas',[8] is an idyll that we may imagine, but we are not allowed to enjoy. In 'The Ones Who Walk Away' the existence of an ideal society mysteriously depends on the sufferings of a starved and filthy child kept sobbing in a dungeon. The gloriously happy and perfect young people of Omelas are each taken to see this child, as an initiation into adulthood. Most of them are able to accept the bargain. Some of them (only a few, we are told) are not. To immerse yourself in Utopian thinking is to refuse to engage with the real, suffering world. There's something smug about the exercise. Isn't the society where 'everybody' is good, simply a society described from the point of view of those who stand to benefit most?[9] The essential conformism of Utopia would shock many of us, in any other context.

In another major novel, Ursula Le Guin imagines a different Utopia, and one which avoids most of these strictures. In *The Dispossessed*[10] an explicitly *unnatural* society, a community of anarchists, has left the splendidly fertile but wordly world and society of the planet Urras, to set up an Utopian colony on the inhospitable surface of Urras's moon. Anarres is far from being a rich, soft, paradise. It is a barren semi-desert where existence is a painful struggle. Yet relaxation, warmth and repose beyond the hopes of non-Utopian mortals are found in comradeship, and in the moral certainties of a political code. *The Dispossessed* is complex and subtle in its treatment of the anarchists and their worldly neighbours; and the dilemma of a man of genius, torn between freedom and responsibility. To discuss the novel as a whole is beyond the scope of this paper. But the division of labour between the Utopian husband and wife, Shevek the physicist and his wife Takver, is striking. Shevek is a genius, and therefore a law unto himself. The political Utopia can't hold him, nor can the worldly world. Takver is not a genius, therefore she is left behind to keep house and raise the children, in conditions of considerable hardship. She accepts her lot with serene self-confidence and plenty of political rationale. She is not a victim. She is an ordinary, willing foot-soldier of the Good State. It's just her luck to have fallen permanently in love with an extraordinary person. But it is rather difficult for a feminist to read *The Dispossessed* without noticing Takver—without noticing that Ursula Le Guin's Utopia offers the main female character nothing that she couldn't have any day of the week, as a compliant woman, in the normal working of any society in our familiar, non-Utopian old world. Homelife, her children, her garden: a low-status job that doesn't interfere with her childcare; sometimes a little spare time for her art.[11]

In *Always Coming Home*, a woman's traditional domestic sphere is glorified. In *The Dispossessed*, Takver's confinement in the domestic sphere is something that Utopia doesn't regard as a problem. Most men of Anarres, arguably, share most of her fate. In another, less substantial novel, *The Word for World is Forest*,[12] the feminised landscape itself becomes a character, and women are mainly absent. In this story the south is another planet: a Garden of Eden world cloaked in soft, secret mysterious forests and inhabited by a gentle people—the Athsheans—who spend much of their lives in a magical, subconscious dreamtime continuum. In Athshean society (we are told) the males have the spiritual authority, the females have civil and political power: sex roles are immovable but have parity of esteem. But the Athshean protagonist is male. Explicitly (his wife has been killed in a brutal rape) and implicitly (his whole planet is being raped by capitalist exploiters from earth), his heroic task is to defend the womanhood of his world, the suffering, helpless female landscape. *The Word for World is Forest* is Le Guin's direct, impulsive reaction to several concerns: the war in Vietnam, the recalcitrance of the nuclear weapons lobby; the wholesale destruction of the natural environments of *this* world. And of course, the Athsheans are finally goaded beyond endurance. The little, soft-spoken modest jungle people get organised (digging tiger pits, vanishing into mazes of tunnels) and conduct a swiftly successful guerrilla campaign against the stupid, loud, ugly, militarist, male-supremacist American invaders. (Nominally the *human* invaders, but the cultural identity of these villains is never in doubt.) In her Foreword to the 1977

UK edition, Ursula Le Guin declares that she regards *The Word for World is Forest* as a failure, and blames herself for 'succumbing to the lure of the pulpit'. In fact I find the book a cheerfully cathartic fable. Agreed, it would be simplistic to read this as real-world commentary. But Captain Davidson, chief white male, is a splendidly horrible baddie—and why shouldn't the reasonable people be simplistic about their ideas once in a while? Everybody else does it. Why shouldn't there be counter-cultural pantomimes, with villains for us to hiss and heroes to be cheered?

The south is a beautiful country. But the problem for feminists, in the feminine Utopia—the problem recognised in the unease expressed by 'Little Bear Woman' in *Always Coming Home*—is twofold. One aspect is historical. The anger expressed so directly in *The Word for World is Forest* is equally present in *Always Coming Home*. It is hard not to feel angry, when contemplating the plight of the beautiful, bountiful earth at the end of the twentieth century. But when the world without men, or the world in which 'male nature' is treated with contempt, is described as a paradise to which we can escape, then women, explicitly and implicitly, find themselves denying responsibility for everything that has happened until now. To declare oneself incompetent is an uncomfortable position for a feminist. And if women have no share in the blame for what has gone wrong, if their part has been to represent wholly ineffectual goodwill, then what guarantee do we have that a feminine régime can change anything?

The other aspect is conceptual. The feminised landscape of Utopia— loving and giving, unselfish and uncomplaining as a compliant woman (like Takver in *The Dispossessed*) —is a dangerous construction. In accepting this model feminist writers embrace an age-old tradition, in which 'woman' and landscape are one.[13] This is a seductive idea. Much of feminist thought is bound up in a love of the earth and—more broadly—in a fearless accept-ance of continuum, not separation: a rejection of paranoid boundaries between humans and other systems. But it has disquieting implications. To put it succinctly: gardens do not write books. Landscapes, however beautiful, do not get up and read out critical papers at conferences. They may *act upon us* passively and gently, if we are receptive. They do not act.

Shortly before I was asked to write this paper I had discovered, or re-discovered, another Ursula Le Guin story about women in a landscape, discussed in a study of Utopian fiction by women called *Worlds of Difference*.[14] The story is called 'Sur',[15] that is 'South'. It describes an imaginary feat of antarctic exploration performed by a group of South American women in 1910. It reveals that these women secretly, shunning all publicity, reached the southern geographic pole before Amundsen and his party (but concealed the fact ever afterwards, for fear of upsetting the poor gentlemen). An excellent essay by Naomi Jacobs,[16] 'The Frozen Landscape', presents this story of extreme hardship in a violently inhospitable landscape, as feminist Utopian fiction. For the rest of this paper, I plan to examine in detail what grounds there might be for such a proposition.

The Ice Barrier

We travel south, from the temperate north, into warmth and comfort. But if we continue the journey, eventually there is a change. The first well-to-do Scottish settlers in New Zealand built their houses and gardens *facing south*. Naturally: what other direction would they choose, for warmth and shelter? It took a while before anybody noticed what was wrong. If we progress beyond daydreaming, penetrating deep into the hinterland of Utopia, we find that the Good State is not easy or soft or passive. It is a hard place to live, and a hard state for human beings to maintain. A journey through the soft south and onwards, leads us to the ice.

The Kesh suffer only because of the sins of the past; and from minor recurrences of male-militarist sickness. The anarchist colony of *The Dispossessed* has the problems of real-world twentieth-century political Utopias. The fluid, individualist anarchy of the founder, Odo has fossilised into a fixed creed called *Odonism*, imposed by bullying social pressure if not by force. Kibbutz-communism has hardened into a centralised economy run by self-serving bureaucrats. The famines and droughts that plague the Anarres colony,[17] the unforgiving harshness of the terrain, reflect the unremitting difficulty of Utopian life in a complex human society, a society where people still *act*, still have aims and schemes that go beyond the timeless cycles of the Kesh. Women in such a society; women trying to live such a life in any society, have a more difficult time than men. They have to satisfy the demands of the ideal, and also the demands of their traditional role. They must become both the earth and the plough. This is the experience of any woman who attempts to combine 'natural' womanhood with a life of ideas.

Science fiction is supposed to be inimical to women readers. But there are many women who started reading science fiction as girls, precisely *because* there are so few women in the stories. Since Mary Shelley, female writers and readers of speculative fiction have enjoyed the freedom of stories in which womanhood is marginal or absent; and Ursula Le Guin belongs, or belonged, to this tradition. Perhaps the wholesale denigration of supposedly male activities in *Always Coming Home* can be read partly as a deliberate correction of the absence or marginalisation of female interests in her earlier work. *The Left Hand of Darkness*, Ursula Le Guin's justly renowned and most famously 'feminist' novel, is an Utopian fiction that tackles directly the problem of female presence in the male-supremacist story of scientific romance. The Gethen, inhabitants of a planet called 'Winter', are a variant of the human species in which individuals remain neuter most of the time, becoming sexual for short periods in a regular hormonal cycle. Each individual may become either male or female for his[18] period of 'kemmer', depending on the timing of the hormonal changes (individuals who become pregnant remain female for the pregnancy and some time after). Any Gethenian may become pregnant, or father a child: many have had both experiences. Thus for the Gethen the conflict between (female) nature and the life of the mind should not exist.[19] And yet, unfortunately or significantly, this is not the effect in the narrative. Let me say again what has been said before: there are no women in this ground-breaking study of sexual roles in sf. The single woman's voice is that of the outgoing planetary observer, who frankly washes her hands of the whole affair: and indeed the whole novel confirms rather than disputes the proposition that female characters have no place in a scientific romance. Our viewpoint is that of a male ambassador from earth. He has arrived alone, unarmed: his mission is to convince the Gethen that other inhabited worlds exist, and gather them into the human fold. He is, from the Gethenian point of view, constantly 'in kemmer'—sexually aroused as a male. A Gethenian coming into the sexual period in his company is bio-chemically compelled to become female (if there are any homosexually oriented Gethenians, they aren't discussed). Since Genly Ai, the ambassador, has the typical reactions of a more-or-less decent but conventional human male, a Gethenian who 'becomes a woman' like this suffers a fairly catastrophic loss of face.[20] But Genly's friend Estraven, who provides the Gethenian side of the story, has nothing disparaging to say about Genly's permanent maleness—in which he finds a lot to admire.[21] The project is assimilation: but the burden of proof (in spite of the ambassador's deliberately modest and suppliant approach) is with the female. Can Genly accept the semi-female Gethenians, the 'men' who are also women?

Winter is not as harsh as Anarres. It has its seasons of richness. But it is cold: much of the land is cold desert and tundra. Finally, Genly Ai and the Gethenian, Estraven, have to cross the icy wilderness together. This journey, a pure feat of will and endurance in defiance of inimical natural forces, brings them together. But still, Estraven's female sexuality is explicitly rejected by the both the adventurers. The female character (here I paraphrase Joanna Russ) may write the scientific romance, may appear in it as a neuter person. Her predicament may be discussed. But she may not take part in the adventure as a woman.

To become a woman is to *lose face*, to lose persona; to give up the role of the protagonist. This loss, accepted with humility by the whole human society of the Kesh in *Always Coming Home*, is the blank ice that lies at the end of the southern journey. But to go into the ice and survive represents the pursuit of personhood. This is the struggle and dilemma that Genly Ai, the male voice of this feminist novel, calls 'the heart of my life'.

No Man's Land

The Story 'Sur'

The story called 'Sur', subtitled 'A summary report of the Yelcho expedition to the Antarctic, 1909,1910' is simply constructed and easily summarised. The unnamed narrator describes how she became fascinated by tales of Antarctic exploration. Finally she and her friends, a company of South American gentlewomen of several nationalities, set off together, financed by a munificent benefactor (again unnamed) in the steamer *Yelcho*. They are landed at Orca bay on the shore of the Ross Sea. They build a camp by digging sleeping cubicles in the ice; and a party sets out to cross the Ice Barrier and reach the south geographical pole. The Pole party returns triumphant, to find that their youngest comrade, Theresa, is heavily pregnant. Having been kept ignorant of the facts of life she was not aware of her condition when she set out. The baby is safely born, they are taken off by the *Yelcho* and return home. Later, news of the Amundsen Expedition and the tragedy of the Scott party reaches South America; and they know they have been the first at the Pole. But they have concealed the trip under various explanations, and no one ever knows what they have done. This report, the story 'Sur', is a keepsake the narrator plans to tuck away in the attic, with her daughter's christening dress and her son's first rattle.

'Sur' is a fine story. The feminisation of a masculine legend is both funny and very moving. Of course it goes without saying that the women have extraordinary powers of endurance, immense reserves of womanly common sense, and prove equal to the most horrendous conditions. 'Sur' is even more fun to read if you happen to be familiar with Antarctic exploration lore. Some mysterious items called 'finneskos', casually mentioned as part of the attic trove in which the story will be buried, are the Norwegian reindeer hide boots (with the fur outside) that were used by all the Antarctic explorers of that day. The *Yelcho* was the steamer lent by the Chilean government to Sir Ernest Shackleton to rescue his stranded crewmates, after his party's epic journey to fetch help, in a tiny open boat, when the *Endurance* had been broken up by pack ice in the expedition of 1914.[22] It was the Northern Party of Scott's 1911 expedition, who were not involved in the doomed polar attempt, who dug the ice-burrows in which they spent the antarctic winter and survived. The Adelie penguins affectionately described by the narrator are regarded, touchingly, as *people*, and their kindly, intelligent manners recounted minutely, in several of the male explorers' reports.[23] The agony of the Ice Barrier journey—the blizzards, crevasses, lost goggles, the cocoa and spirits eked out in terror of starvation; the psychological horror of the Ice 'good God, this is an awful place…'—all these details are taken from the real-world records.

But we are also reminded, continually, that these are women. Our narrator says, on the difficulty of putting the expedition together: 'Of those few who shared our folly, still fewer were able, when it came to the point, to leave their daily duties and commit themselves to a voyage of at least six months… An ailing parent, an anxious husband beset by business cares, a child at home with only ignorant or incompetent servants to look after it: these are not responsibilities lightly to be set aside. And those who wished to evade such claims were not the companions we wanted in hard work, risk and privation.' Elsewhere we are assured that the Expedition had only notional 'officers', and all decisions were taken in common. The narrator's claim that she and her companions were all 'by birth and upbringing, unequivocally and irrevocably crew' is at first sight curious, given their obvious social status. But they are women. They are not free agents, they have never been free agents. They are the property of their families, or their husbands' families: and this stolen journey can't change that situation.[24]

'Sur' may be read superficially as celebration of female power, a glorious role-reversal. Here is a group of women taking on a male adventure: doing something completely pointless and insanely difficult, out of that naked, Faustian desire to extend human boundaries which only men are supposed to feel. And they succeed. They do it *better* than the men, because unlike male explorers they haven't abandoned family responsibilities to take this trip, and they don't dominate or coerce each other. But all the wealth of convincing detail and emotional appeal should not distract us from the fact that these Argentinian, Peruvian, and Chilean ladies *didn't do it*. Amundsen, Shackleton and Scott did. This is not a story of achievement. It is a story of longing, longing for the forbidden. And a story of mourning, mourning for those lives, long over now, of women whose hunger for adventure, whose Faustian desire to go a little farther, to find out what lies beyond, was stifled through endless years of home duties, childcare, husband-cosseting. The narrator's repeated denial of any desire for fame or renown cannot be taken at face value. She tells us that this report is going to be hidden away in an attic. But of course that isn't what happened. This report appeared in the *New Yorker*. The purpose of the story 'Sur' is exactly the opposite of what the narrator declares it to be, it is precisely a *claim to fame*. It is a claim to the forbidden territory of achievement, endeavour, exploration.

The Female Choice Hypothesis

There is a theory current in the science of human sexual behaviour, that says all forms of human creativity—art, music, science, adventure—have their origin in the male need to attract the female. Like a male bower-bird a man tries to have something a little extra, so that the females will choose him as a mate for their pragmatic female reasons: a man who can afford to waste time that could be spent on hunting food must have good genes. This is why men do the extending of the boundaries, exploring, making *more*: more wealth, more art and thought, more territory, and why women do everything else, everything rooted and real. Women perfect and enjoy what they have, they do not explore the unknown. This is the view reflected in *The Dispossessed*; and in *Always Coming Home*—which takes the extreme view that the Faustian desire is always destructive, always leads to madness and desolation. But there is more to be said about the female choice hypothesis. For of course women are genetically descended from men *and* women, and vice-versa. We are not dealing with two separate species here. A woman who chooses an artist as her mate—maybe for pragmatic reasons, maybe even for a *stupid* reason, maybe she likes the pictures and she reckons she can hunt for two if he's going to spend his life painting—runs the shocking risk of having artistic daughters, and pragmatic sons.

The story 'Sur' reclaims a woman's inheritance from the father. It opens wounds, not only in its stifled longing for adventure, but in the way it invokes the desperate plight of all those millions of girl-children who are and have been denied their rights, who are not considered part of their father's family. 'Sur' is not strictly an Utopian story, because it does not present another world, better than this one. Instead it offers the Ice: a blank, an empty place on the map. Laying claim to No Man's Land, Ursula Le Guin's explorers are claiming to be the daughters of men. Inventing No Man's Land, which means to create more mind, means going into the Ice and leaving the soft south behind. Exploring No Man's Land means accepting that to be a woman, with all a woman's earth-grounded and gentle values, who is also a *person*, a protagonist, is to attempt something new, unknown, difficult. And this is where the journey south, through Ursula Le Guin's fiction, ends: and begins.

Notes

Chapter 1: Getting Rid of the Brand Names

1. Samuel Delany, *The Jewel Hinged Jaw* (New York: Berkley, 1977).
2. William Gibson, interview in *Interzone*, 13, Summer 1985.
3. Lucius Shepard, *Green Eyes* (New York: Ace, 1984), p.3.
4. C.S.Lewis, *The Silver Chair* (London: Geoffrey Bles, 1953). The reference is to the Puffin edition, 1965, p.153.

Chapter 5: Fools: The Neuroscience of Cyberspace

1. Donald Michie, 'On Machine Intelligence' (Edinburgh, 1974), p.156, quoted in Margaret Boden, *Artificial Intelligence and Natural Man*, (Hassocks: Harvester Press, 1977), p.4.
2. William Gibson, *Neuromancer* (New York: Ace, 1984), p.67. All subsequent references are to the Victor Gollancz edition, (London, 1984).
3. In fact, a platinum and cloisonné *head*, ibid, p.207. Who says sf writers have no sense of humour?
4. Thus a famous hypothesis from fiction, that self is memory, appears to be on a sound experimental footing. For Proust's account of the toast incident, real-world original of the madeleine incident in *À la recherche du temps perdu*, see the collection of essays and letters *Contre Sainte Beuve*, translated and edited in English by John Sturrock (London: Penguin, 1994), pp.53–4. I was sorry that Edelman didn't mention Marcel Proust, along with Descartes, Aristotle, Freud, in his catalogue of spiritual ancestors. But though there are surely neuro-scientists who read storybooks, perhaps there are few who perceive the shared territory, or expect to find their science in a novel.
5. Melissa Scott, *Dreamships* (New York: Tor, 1992). The fate of the AI entity Manfred is a sad case of legal discrimination. Accused of murder, his defence is that he thought humans were indefinitely replicable and immortal as he is himself. He didn't know you could kill a human by electrocuting the biological machine that was running the program. So he's innocent. But his misunderstanding is taken to mean 'he' doesn't understand personhood, therefore doesn't qualify as a person, and can be wiped, without trial, as a dangerously faulty program. Poor Manfred!
6. C.J Cherryh, *Cyteen* (New York: Warner, 1988). And other novels in the 'Merchanter Universe' series. C.J. Cherryh's azi are vat-grown humans—an unlikely development for us, since we are not short of the commodity in question. But science now strongly suggests that if an artificial/biological mind could be created, in any form, what you'd get would be a human being, neither more nor less. Could such a machine be useful to us? Maybe we'll have to build them, and then lobotomise them.
7. See (for instance) an interview with William Gibson in *New Musical Express*, 30 October 1993.

8. Pat Cadigan, *Mindplayers* (New York: Bantam,1987).

9. Pat Cadigan, *Synners* (New York: Bantam, 1991), p.355.

10. See the descriptions of various 'neurotic programs' and their interactions with (sometimes) unwary humans, in Margaret Boden, *Artificial Intelligence and Natural Man*, pp.21–63.

11. Pat Cadigan, *Fools* (New York: Bantam, 1994), p.242.

12. See Melissa Scott's *Trouble and Her Friends*, (New York: Tor, 1994); and Neal Stephenson's *Snow Crash* (New York: Bantam, 1992).

13. Pat Cadigan, *Synners*, pp.347–60.

14. Claims for these technologies may be doubted (*post hoc, ergo propter hoc?*). If the neurons are firing in certain areas, after the wet toast is nibbled, you can't be sure that what you are watching is the subject 'revisiting his childhood'. He may be secretly thinking of something different, that he'd rather not discuss with you.

15. Donna Haraway, 'A Manifesto for Cyborgs' in *Simians, Cyborgs and Women* (London: Free Association Books, 1991).

16. Bruce Sterling, in *Mirrorshades: The Cyberpunk Anthology* (London: Paladin,1986).

17. Kevin Kelly, *Out Of Control* (Reading, Massachusetts: Addison-Wesley, 1994). The quotation is from the opening chapter 'The Born And The Made'.

Chapter 6: Trouble (Living In The Machine)

1. Lisa Mason, *Arachne* (New York: William Morrow, 1990).

2. William Gibson, *Neuromancer*, p.12.

3. Lisa Mason, *Arachne* (New York: William Morrow, 1990), p.35.

4. Melissa Scott, *Trouble And Her Friends (*New York: Tor, 1994), p.133.

Chapter 8: Aliens in the Fourth Dimension

1. Saucer shaped flying machines: Hypersonic flying saucers driven by microwaves are at present the goal of serious researchers in the US (reported in *New Scientist*, 2017, 17 February 1996). MRI imaging of brain activity, involving something oddly similar to those old sciffy hairdryers, is already reality.

2. Valmiki, writing in the third century BC, Christian chronology.

3. Mungo Park, travelling in Africa in the eighteenth century was staggered by the size of the cities he found, comparing urban conditions very favourably with those in Britain (Mungo Park, *Travels In The Interior of Africa*, 1799).

4. Although Octavia Butler's trilogy '*Xenogenesis*' develops a 'slavery' narrative of alien invasion of great complexity.

5. Pleasingly, for me, a quotation from a *Porgy and Bess* lyric (George Gershwin and Dubose Heyward, 1935) intended to be sung by a black American who finds refuge from cultural domination in this defiant thought.

6. Annie Coombes, *Re-inventing Africa* (London and New Haven: Yale University Press, 1994).

7. Joanna Russ in *The Female Man* (New York: Bantam, 1975) makes a similar observation about idyllic separatism.

Chapter 20: No Man's Land:
Feminised Landscapes in the Utopian Fiction of Ursula Le Guin

1. See J.R.R. Tolkien, *The Lord Of The Rings* (London: George Allen & Unwin, omnibus edition, 1968), p.497.

2. Bernadin de Saint Pierre, 1737–1834, *Paul et Virginie* (Paris: Bookking International,1993). The revolutionary statesman and novelist's idea of heroic feminine virtue is reactionary to the point of absurdity. But Virginie *is* the hero of this Utopian fiction, informing it with her innocent vision of a gentler, better world.

3. Charlotte Perkins Gilman, *Herland*, 1915 (New York: Pantheon, 1979).

4. Notionally, from 1969 to 1985, between the publication of *The Left Hand of Darkness* and *Always Coming Home:* but any dates must be approximate.

5. Ursula Le Guin, *Always Coming Home* (New York: Harper and Row, 1985).

6. *Always Coming Home*, Ursula Le Guin's introduction.

7. *Always Coming Home* includes, in its framing narrative and in individual portraits of unhappy men of this kind, explicit descriptions of male 'delusions' of mastery, military, intellectual, emotional, mystic, as all of them literally insane.

8. Ursula Le Guin, 'The Ones Who Walk Away From Omelas' first published in *New Dimensions*, 3, 1973; collected in *The Winds Twelve Quarters*, (London: Victor Gollancz, 1975).

9. As 'Little Bear Woman' ruefully points out (*Always Coming Home*, p.147), to create the beautiful, uncrowded world of the Kesh, she had to massacre millions and millions of innocent human beings: and the massacre continues. Kesh infant mortality is high enough (because of diseases caused by old-days pollution lingering in the environment) that over-population is never likely to be a problem.

10. Ursula Le Guin, *The Dispossessed* (New York: Harper Row, 1974).

11. Odo, the founder of the anarchist political movement, was a woman, but she appears in *The Dispossessed* only as a statue in a public garden. Shevek has a revered teacher, also a woman, but she dies disappointed and thwarted by the (apparently otherwise male) Anarres scientific establishment—like any number of our own great female scientists.

12. Ursula Le Guin, *The Word For World Is Forest* (New York: Berkley,1976).

13. *The Dispossessed*: Shevek's sense of the woman buried in Urarasti artefacts is first mentioned on his space trip from the moon to the planet, and reiterated throughout: on Anarres women have—in theory—been freed from this incarceration, they are no longer 'part of the landscape'.

14. Naomi Jacobs 'The Frozen Landscape', in Jane L. Donawerth and Carol A. Kolmerton, eds, *Worlds of Difference* (Liverpool: Liverpool University Press, 1994).

15. 'Sur' was first published in the *New Yorker*, February 1982; subsequently collected in *The Compass Rose* (New York: Harper and Row, 1982).

16. Associate Professor of English at the University of Maine.

17. But the great famine on Anarres is still an Utopian feature, in which extreme privation can be glorified by human compassion and communist ideals. In the real world, famine in the rigid Political Utopia is an unmitigated disaster. See accounts of the Chinese famines of the post-war decades, that led directly to the inhuman excesses of the Cultural Revolution.

18. Notoriously the male pronoun is used for Gethenians throughout, on the grounds that it is less specific, more general than the female. Invented gender-neutral pronouns have not been particularly successful with any readers. But *The Left Hand of Darkness* would have been a very different book, if the Gethenians had been called 'she'. For one thing it would certainly have been much less popular with the science fiction audience.

19. The implications are summarised by a female observer from another planet: 'consider: anyone can turn his hand to anything. This sounds very simple but the psychological effects are incalcuable. The fact that everyone... is liable to be "tied down to childbearing" implies that no one is quite so thoroughly "tied down"... Therefore nobody here is quite so free as a free male elsewhere...' From 'The Question of Sex', Ursula Le Guin, *The Left Hand of Darkness* (London: Granada, 1973), pp.66–70.

20. See Genly's deeply embarrassed response when his friend Estraven 'becomes a woman' in the Ice Barrier episode. And this is not only true of human/Gethenian relationships. See the occasion when a political opponent tries to corrupt Estraven by deliberately 'becoming a woman' in his company, *The Left Hand of Darkness*, p.108.

21. Estreven on Genly: 'There is a frailty about him. He is all unprotected, exposed, vulnerable, even to his sexual organ...: but he is strong, unbelievably strong...', *The Left Hand of Darkness*, p.155.

22. Ernest Shackleton, the man who looked after his crewmates 'as tenderly as if he was a woman' should always be honoured by all 'female' (by conviction) explorers for his staggering, and successful, determination to get everyone home alive from this disaster.

23. See Herbert Ponting (Scott's Photographer) on the Adelie, Herbert G. Ponting, *The Great White South* (London: Duckworth, 1921), pp.227–60, 'The Real Inhabitants'.

24. The narrator's afterword is a sad roll-call of wasted lives, telling how difficult it was for the sledge-mates ever to meet; how there were no more adventures. It reminded me of the similar roll-call that ends every record of the real-world antarctic explorers of those years. Many of the young men who survived the Ice unscathed would be dead within the decade: victims of a catastrophic outbreak of male-dominated militarism.

Bibliography

Asimov, Issac, *The Gods Themselves* (London: Granada, 1972)

Atwood, Margaret *The Handmaid's Tale* (London: Cape, 1986)

Barnes, John, *A Million Open Doors* (New York: Tor, 1992; London: Orion, 1993)

Belsey, Catherine, *Critical Practice* (London: Methuen, 1980)

Benford, Gregory, *Timescape*, (New York: Simon & Schuster, 1980)

Boden, Margaret, *Artificial Intelligence and Natural Man* (Hassocks: Harvester Press, 1977)

Bradley, Marion Zimmer, *The Ruins of Isis* (Norfolk, Virginia: Donning/Starblaze, 1978; London: Arrow, 1980)

Brin, David, *Glory Season* (New York: Bantam,1993)

Butler, Octavia, *Mind of my Mind* (New York: Doubleday, 1976; London, Sidgwick & Jackson, 1978)

Cadigan, Pat, *Mindplayers* (New York: Bantam, 1987)
Synners (New York: Bantam, 1991)
Fools (New York: Bantam, 1992)

Charnas, Suzy McKee,*Walk to the End of the World* (New York: Ballantine, 1974)
Motherlines (New York: Berkley, 1978)
The Furies (New York: Tor, 1994)

Cherryh, C.J.,*The Chronicles of Morgaine* (London: Methuen, 1985; USA: *The Gates of Ivrel*, 1976; *Well Of Shiuan*,1978; *Fires of Azeroth*, 1979)
Serpent's Reach (New York: Daw, 1980)
Downbelow Station (New York: Daw, 1981)
Cyteen (New York: Warner, 1988)

Datlow, Ellen, ed., *Alien Sex* (New York: Dutton, 1990)

Delaney, Samuel, *The Jewel-Hinged Jaw: Notes on the Language of Science Fiction* (New York: Berkley, 1977)

Delillo, Don, *White Noise* (London: Viking Penguin, 1984)

Donawerth, Jane L., and Kolmerten, Carol A. eds, *Utopian and Science Fiction by Women* (Liverpool: Liverpool University Press, 1994; Syracuse: Syracuse University Press, 1994)

Edelman, Gerald, *Bright Air, Brilliant Fire: On The Matter Of The Mind* (New York: HarperCollins, 1992)

Gibson, William, *Neuromancer* (New York: Ace, 1984; London: Victor Gollancz, 1984)
Virtual Light (New York: Bantam, 1993; London: Viking Penguin, 1993)

Gilman, Charlotte Perkins, *Herland*, serialised in the *Forerunner* 1915 (New York: Pantheon, 1979)

Hand, Elizabeth,*Winterlong* (New York: Bantam, 1990)
Aestival Tide (New York: Bantam, 1992)
Icarus Descending (New York: Bantam, 1993)

Herbert, Frank, *Dune* (London: Victor Gollancz, 1966)

Haraway, Donna J., *Simians, Cyborgs, and Women* (London: Free Association Books, 1991)

Jones, Gwyneth, *Divine Endurance* (London: George Allen & Unwin, 1984)

Escape Plans (London: George Allen & Unwin, 1986)
White Queen (London: Gollancz, 1991)
North Wind (London: Gollancz, 1994)
Phoenix Café (London: Gollancz, 1997)
Kelly, Kevin, *Out of Control* (New York: Addison Wesley, 1994)
Lefanu, Sarah, *In the Chinks of the World Machine* (London: Women's Press, 1988)
Le Guin, Ursula K., *A Wizard of Earthsea* (New York: Parnassus, 1968)
The Tombs of Atuan (New York: Atheneum, 1971)
The Farthest Shore (New York: Atheneum, 1972)
The Left Hand of Darkness (New York: Ace, 1969)
The Dispossessed (New York: Harper & Row, 1974; London: Gollancz, 1974)
The Word for World is Forest (New York: Berkley, 1976)
Always Coming Home (New York: Harper & Row, 1985)
'Sur: A Summary Report of the Yelcho Expedition to the Antarctic, 1909–1910', *New Yorker*, February 1982
Lewis, C.S., *The Lion, the Witch and the Wardrobe* (London: Geoffery Bles, 1950)
Prince Caspian (London: Geoffery Bles, 1951)
The Voyage of the Dawn Treader (London: Geoffery Bles, 1952)
The Silver Chair (London: Geoffery Bles, 1953)
The Horse and his Boy (London: Geoffery Bles, 1954)
The Magician's Nephew (London, Geoffery Bles, 1955)
The Last Battle (London, Geoffery Bles, 1956)
MacDonald, George, *Phantastes* and *Lilith*, first published 1858, 1895 (London: Victor Gollancz, 1962; 1971)
McIntyre, Vonda, *Dreamsnake* (New York: Houghton Mifflin, 1978)
Niven, Larry, *Ringworld* (New York: Simon & Schuster, 1970)
Piercy, Marge, *Woman on the Edge of Time* (New York: Knopf, 1976)
Ponting, Herbert, *The Great White South* (London: Duckworth, 1921)
Pournelle, Larry, (with Larry Niven) *The Mote in God's Eye* (New York: Simon & Schuster, 1974)
Rusch, Kristine Kathryn, *Alien Influences* (London: Orion, 1994)
Russ, Joanna, 'When It Changed', *Again, Dangerous Visions,* ed. Harlan Ellison (New York: Doubleday, 1972); collected in *The Zanzibar Cat*
The Female Man (New York: Bantam, 1975; London: Star, 1977)
The Two of Them (New York: Berkley, 1978; London: The Women's Press, 1986)
Scott, Melissa, *Dreamships* (New York: Tor, 1992)
Trouble and her Friends (New York: Tor, 1994)
Shepard, Lucius, *Green Eyes* (New York: Ace, 1994)
Short, R.V., and Balaban, E., eds, *The Differences between the Sexes* (Cambridge: Cambridge University Press, 1994)
Stephenson, Neal, *Snow Crash* (New York: Bantam, 1992)
Tepper, Sheri, *Raising the Stones* (New York: Doubleday, 1990)
Sideshow (New York: Bantam, 1992)
Plague of Angels (London: HarperCollins, 1994)
Shadow's End (London: HarperCollins, 1994)
Tolkien, J.R.R., *The Hobbit* (London: George Allen & Unwin, 1937)
The Lord of the Rings (London: George, Allen & Unwin, 1954, 1954, 1955)
Wittig, Monique, *Les Guérillères* (Paris: Les Éditions de Minuit, 1969) Tr. David Le Vay (London: Peter Owen, 1974)

Acknowledgements

The Essays

'Deconstructing the Starships' was originally a speech given at the June 1988 presentation of the Arthur C. Clarke Award, at the Institute of Contemporary Arts. 'Getting Rid of the Brand Names' was first published in *The World and I* (New York: The Washington Times Corporation) in October 1987, as part of a feature called 'Science Fiction and Reality'. 'The Lady and the Scientists' appeared in *Strange Plasma*, 3, (Cambridge Massachusetts: The Edgewood Press) ed., Steve Pasechnik. 'Dreamer 1' and 'Dreamer 2' were commissioned by British Telecom Information Technology Systems Division in 1988. 'My Crazy Uncles' was originally a paper read at a meeting of the C.S. Lewis Society in June 1994; subsequently published in the *New York Review of Science Fiction*, 87, November 1995. 'Fools' was originally a paper read at a conference held at the University of Teesside in April 1995, and subsequently published in *The Governance of Cyberspace*, ed. Brian Loader (London: Routledge, 1997). 'Trouble' was originally a paper read at a postgraduate conference called *Looking at the Future*, held at the University of Sussex, May 1994. 'The Brains of Female Hyena Twins' was originally a paper read at the second annual conference of the Academic Fantastic Fiction Network, at Reading University in December 1994, subsequently published in the collected papers of that conference, *Strange Attractors*, ed. Mark Bould; and in *Foundation*, 63, pp.86–93. 'Aliens in the Fourth Dimension' was originally a paper read at a conference on Speaking Science Fiction, held at the University of Liverpool in July 1996.

The Reviews

In the Chinks of the World Machine: Sarah Lefanu, *Foundation*, 42; *Consider Her Ways:* C.J.Cherryh, *Foundation* , 49; *Alien Sex*: Ellen Datlow, *The New York Review of Science Fiction*, 27; *Snow Crash:* Neal Stephenson, *The New York Review of Science Fiction*, 48; *Glory Season*, David Brin, *SFEye*, 12; *Virtual Light:* William Gibson, *Foundation*, 60; *A Million Open Doors:* John Barnes, *Foundation*, 59; *Winterlong*: Elizabeth Hand, *SFEye*, 13; *Plague of Angels:* Sheri Tepper, *Foundation*, 63; *The Furies:* Suzy Charnas, *The New York Review of Science Fiction*, 68; *Alien Influences*, Kristine Kathryn Rusch, *Foundation*, 65; *Feminised Landscapes* (Ursula Le Guin), was originally a paper read at a conference held at the University of London, March 1996.

Index

Aldiss, Brian, 146

Aleutians, 109–19

aliens, 10, 15, 19, 25, 35, 80, 108, 109–19; in the anthology *Alien Sex* 142–44: 161; in Kristine Kathryn Rusch's *Alien Influences* 192–98

Amis, Martin, 3

Amundsen, Roald, 203, 206, 207

artificial intelligence, development of, with reference to cyberspace fiction 77–87; 151, 210

Asimov, Issac, 17, 18, 136

Atwood, Margaret, 3, 4, 6, 31

Baker, Scott, 143

Ballard, James, 25

Balzac, Honoré de, 6

Barnes, John, reviewed, 161–66; 179

Barthes, Roland, 5

Baynes, Pauline, 63, 65, 73

Bear, Greg, 18, 31, 201, 203

Belsey, Catherine, 5

Benford, Gregory, 17, 18, 125

Benson, Robert Hugh, 67

Bester, Alfred, 12

biological determinacy, 30

bisexuality, 124

Boolean algebra, 146

Bradbury, Ray, 168

Bradley, Marion Zimmer, 12, 124, 129

Brin, David, reviewed 153–55

Browning, Elizabeth Barrett, 142

Brunner, John, 25

Bryant, Ed, 143

Burroughs, William, 142, 184

Butler, Octavia, 22, 28

Cadigan, Pat, 34, 84–89, 93, 98, 143, 210

Carr Jayge, 124

Carter, Angela, 124

chaos theory, 32

characterisation, (its problems for the sf novelist), 5, 17, 28, 128, 157, 164

Charnas, Suzy McGee, 26, 31, 124, 127, 128, 154; reviewed, 184–91; 200

Cherryh, Carolyn J., 26, 28, reviewed, 131–39; 140, 195, 210

Christianity, 29, 46, 63–73, 145, 162, 164, 186

clones (human), 6; Carolyn Cherryh's 'azi' 83n, 131–39; David Brin's semi-parthenogenetic separatists, 153; Elizabeth Hand's 'geneslaves' 173; 210

Clute, John, 129

co-education, 27

Cold War, the, 6

colonialism, 35, 89, 109, 119, 125, 146, 162, 166, 181, 193, 200, 201, 204

computers, 20, 25, 37, 38, 47, 49, 52, 59, 77–88, 91–97, 150, 151, 155, 157, 162

consciousness, 7, 32, Gerald Edelman's theory of 80–83; evolution of compared with development of the Internet 84–89 and 85–98; and language 118–19; political, raised, 128–30, 151, 'relationship between consciousness and reality' in the fiction of Elizabeth Hand, 171–76,

constructed worlds, as the language-game of science fiction, 9–15; in Children's Literature, 60–65, in cyberspace, 94–95

criticism, literary, 4, 6, 15, 80, 111, 123, 129, 131, 140, 152, 157

cybernetics, 6, 78, 151

cyberpunk, 33, 80, 84, motifs of, 85; 88, fear of the body, 92–94; 98, 146, 151, 152, 156–58, 160

cyberspace, 16, neuroscience of, 77–90; fiction, in revolt against the physical body, 91–98; 146, 158, 210

'dark matter', theory, 31

Darwin, Charles, 82

sexual difference, 105; critical
advantage, 113, 115; 133, 151, 162,
165, 166, 178, 186, 200
telepathy, 117, 194
television, (and video, as leisure
technology) 37–59; 71, 73, a
species of cyberspace, 83, 94; 108,
111, 115, 136, 156, 160, 194
Tepper, Sheri, 154, 155, 161,
reviewed, 178–83
testosterone, 33, 34, 106, 107
Theroux, Paul, 3, 4
Third World, 16, 149, 159, 192
time travel, 6, 116, 126
Tiptree, James Jnr (Alice Sheldon),
21, 28, 123, 124, 126, 144, 159
Tolkien, J.R.R, 11, 12, 15, 60–73, 199,
see also Middle Earth
Tolstoy, Leo, 9
Turing, Alan, 78, Turing Test, 79
Turing police, 77, 80, 86; Turing
Machine, 95
Turner, George, 24, 158
Tuttle, Lisa, 144

utopia, 23, 24, 34, 88, 110, 125, 153,
154, 180, 184, 199–208

Varley, John, 27
veiled women, 29
Vines, Gail, 101, 104
violence, 27, 30, 36, 46, 67, 96, 99,
100, 104, 148, 151, 157, 162, 174,
184, 187, 193, 199
virtual reality, 84, 85, 98, 146, 147,
148, 157, 161 see also cyberspace

Weaver, Sigourney, 24
White Queen, 107, 112, 118
Wilber, Rick, 143
Wilhelm, Kate, 17, 132
Williams, Charles, 67, 73,
Willis, Connie, 142, 143, 145
Wittig, Monique, 31

Zelazny, Roger, 12, 161
Zoline, Pamela, 26, 27